INTERVENTION
and REVOLUTION

The United States in the Third World

INTERVENTION
and REVOLUTION

The United States in the Third World

Revised and Updated

by RICHARD J. BARNET

A MERIDIAN BOOK

NEW AMERICAN LIBRARY

TIMES MIRROR

NEW YORK AND SCARBOROUGH, ONTARIO

Library of Congress Catalog Card Number: 68-23846

Originally published in hardcover by The New American Library, Inc.

The revised edition originally appeared in paperback as a Mentor Book.

MERIDIAN TRADEMARK REG. U.S. PAT. OFF. AND FOREIGN COUNTRIES
REGISTERED TRADEMARK—MARCA REGISTRADA
HECHO EN FORGE VILLAGE, MASS., U.S.A.

SIGNET, SIGNET CLASSICS, MENTOR, PLUME, MERIDIAN AND NAL
BOOKS are published in the United States by
The New American Library, Inc.,
1633 Broadway, New York, New York 10019, in Canada by The New
American Library of Canada Limited, 81 Mack Avenue, Scarborough,
Ontario M1L 1M8

FIRST MERIDIAN PRINTING (Revised Edition), NOVEMBER, 1980

1   2   3   4   5   6   7   8   9

PRINTED IN THE UNITED STATES OF AMERICA

For JULIE, BETH,
and MIKE

Acknowledgments

I AM INDEBTED to many persons who have read all or part of this book in manuscript, especially my associates on the American Society of International Law Panel on Civil War and my colleagues at the Institute for Policy Studies. Neither group of critics can of course be held responsible for any views or interpretations which I have advanced. I also wish to thank officials of the Department of Defense, the Agency for International Development, and other government agencies for their helpfulness in supplying statistics and data. Special mention must be made of the assistance given me by Marvin Holloway and David Morris, former students at the Institute, as well as by Sally Nash, Diane Latham, and Barbara Johnson in helping to prepare the manuscript for press. The debt to my dear wife cannot be adequately expressed.

Contents

Part
ONE

CHAPTER **1**

Guardian at the Gates

One

THE COLD WAR arose over the fate of Central Europe, but it has been fought almost everywhere else. For over twenty years the principal battle station between East and West has been tense but still. In the middle of Europe spies meet in cafés and pursue one another in back alleys. Individuals are occasionally shot or kidnapped in Berlin. The waves of diplomatic crises over Germany and Berlin are not easily forgotten. But despite the billions appropriated on both sides of the line to maintain their huge permanent armies, the mammoth stocks of nuclear weapons of all shapes and sizes strewn about the continent, and the central importance of Europe as the chessboard of the Cold War, there has been less violence on that continent in the last generation than in any other twenty-year period in modern history.

Elsewhere the picture of the contemporary world looks different. Since World War II the continents of Asia, Africa, and South America have been continually swept with violence. There have been a few old-fashioned wars between states where armies cross frontiers in strength to enforce demands against another government. In their border disputes India and Pakistan have behaved much like their European teachers. Israel and Egypt too have used political violence according to the conventional pattern and fought the sort of war which the nuclear powers now no longer dare to fight.

Most of the political violence that has inflamed human society since 1945, however, has been of a special character. Its source has not been conflict *between* states, but conflict *within* societies. The wars of our time have not been primarily fights for territory, raw materials, colonies, or the preservation of the king's honor, although all of these have at some point been involved. Essentially, contemporary wars have been fights for the rights of various political groups within the former colonial appendages of Europe to take political power and to exercise it on their own terms. According to Secretary of Defense Robert McNamara there have occurred in the last decade over "149 serious internal insurgencies."[1] These have been colonial wars against a European power or wars against a domestic ruling class or elite. In each case they are fought for a local political purpose. They are struggles of new states to decide what they shall be and, most importantly, who will run them. They take the form of civil wars but they are really revolutions.

One consequence of the easing of verbal taboos in our time is that words that used to be whispered in alleys have been incorporated into the daily chatter of polite society. Once domesticated, they lose their power along with their magic. "Revolution" is one of these words. Senators, lecturers before ladies' groups, and the mass-circulation magazines all talk about the "revolutions" of our time—the revolution of rising expectations, the development revolution, the technological revolution, and on television, even the revolution in breakfast cereals and hair creams. We have succeeded in assimilating an awesome word into our everyday vocabulary but not into our understanding.

It is not altogether surprising that revolution has been a difficult phenomenon for Americans to grasp. Unlike the Cold War itself, in whose shadow the decolonization of Asia, Africa, and Latin America has been carried out, the internal violence of the Third World* falls outside the

---

* "Third World," a term originated by the French (*Tiers Monde*), refers to what remains of the planet after subtracting the developed world of North America, Western Europe, and the Soviet Union. It is roughly equivalent to what used to be called the underdeveloped world, or in official U.S. parlance "L. D. C.'s" (Less Developed Countries). Even though Europe is not usually thought of as part of the Third World, I have extended the term to include Greece

traditional framework of European Great Power politics. The Soviet-American confrontation can be seen as the latest and most formidable of the great national rivalries that have marked the modern nation-state system, a contest for power, economic advantage, and prestige, fought largely by unarmed bureaucracies rather than the armies they control, because for the first time in history both sides are too well armed. Revolutionary violence in the Third World, on the other hand, arises over quite different issues and is not subject to the same restraints. The principal issue is not national security but making a nation. Unlike the leaders of developed nations, the enemies which revolutionary leaders see are not at the gate but already inside. Their country is occupied either by a foreign colonial power or by local landlords, generals, or self-serving politicians. As they see it, the issue is liberation. The goal is a radical redistribution of political and economic power to overcome centuries of political oppression and crushing poverty. The means is seizure of political power.

In many of the decolonized countries of Africa and Asia leaders have come to power with revolutionary programs but have failed to dislodge the old ruling classes. Revolutions have regularly been aborted, suppressed, and more than once perverted by revolutionary politicians themselves. But the revolutionary idea—that radical change is necessary, that it is inevitable, and that it can come only by seizing the machinery of the state—has steadily grown. In the early years of the postwar period the primary revolutionary goal was national independence. Increasingly, revolutionaries of the Third World have come to believe that "neoimperialism"—economic exploitation by the developed nations in collaboration with a local privileged class—is as suffocating as the old-fashioned colonial administration. True, revolutionary governments, as in Algeria and Indonesia, have become more conservative as the early leaders of the independence wars have been replaced. Several revolutionary regimes have been turned out by military coups, as Nkrumah was in Ghana.

Throughout the hills and jungles of the Third World,

---

because its economic and social situation during its civil war was much closer to that of the underdeveloped countries of Africa, Asia, and Latin America, than to its more developed European neighbors.

however, the efforts of revolutionary movements to take power by violence have grown in the years since the war. In the past few years revolutionaries have carried on guerrilla operations in Angola, Ethiopia, Venezuela, Peru, Bolivia, the Congo, Thailand, Mozambique, and Cameroon, among other places. Most of these have been small operations involving perhaps no more than 200 or 300 guerrillas. (One of the largest efforts, the attempt of the Patriotic Front of Thailand to seize the northeast province, involves no more than 1,600 guerrillas.) Many of these revolutionary movements have found inspiration in the writings of Fidel Castro, Ernesto "Che" Guevara, and Mao Tse-tung, for these are revolutionaries who have had successes and they purport to offer a strategy of victory for a small armed political movement. But Guevara's assertion that "a nucleus of thirty to fifty men . . . is sufficient to initiate an armed struggle in any country of the Americas," has not so far been borne out. As revolutionary movements have increased in size and daring, government efforts to suppress the movements have increased much faster. In Guatemala, Bolivia, Venezuela, and elsewhere, counterinsurgency campaigns have for the moment apparently broken the backs of tiny guerrilla movements. But the brutality of counterinsurgency operations also has the effect of turning reformers into revolutionaries for another round. The counterinsurgency campaign in Guatemala in a few months in 1966–67, according to *The Economist*'s correspondent, "is believed to have claimed more lives than all the insurgent activity of the past five years." Since the "clean-up" of a guerrilla zone necessarily involves killing the innocent, the process alienates the population from the government and creates revolutionary sentiment. The wave of revolutions that Castro predicted and tried to set in motion has not yet happened. But in a world facing famine, accelerating social dislocation, massive technological intrusions into remote areas, and intensifying ideological conflict, it is unrealistic to think that revolutionary activity will subside in the closing years of the century.[2]

Weak though contemporary revolutionary movements are, compared with the power of the state they are seeking to seize, their proliferation is a spectacular development which has decisively changed the character of world politics. A generation ago the lands of the Third World were politically inert, objects of international bargaining, and patient servicers of the international economy. What happened there could normally be decided in European chancelleries or, in the case of Latin America, in Washington. Now, through violence the revolutionaries are demanding and receiving attention. They have demonstrated that the basic assumption of stability on which traditional peasant societies have rested is no longer valid. They have served notice on the comfortable that at least some of the poor peasants who make up the Third World are slowly coming to believe that they may actually have the power to change the wretchedness of their lives and that they must use it.[3] A Conference of Three Continents held in Havana in 1966 to discuss revolution and to coordinate resistance activities was attended by eighty-two separate delegations from Asia, Africa, and Latin America. While the communist governments and some neutralist governments sent delegations, the majority was made up of organized opposition parties or guerrilla bands dedicated to some sort of Marxist strategy for revolutionary change but not under the discipline or control of either Moscow or Peking.[4] In most cases they are far more radical in outlook, far more prone to use violence than the communist parties under the domination of the Soviet Union. Most of these insurgent movements are preparing for or are actually engaged in armed struggle against their governments, although their present numbers are small and their positions weak. For the most part they accept a Leninist or Marxist analysis of world politics and social change and they seek the solidarity and support of the established communist parties and governments. Some have received money, arms, and advice from Cuba, Russia, or China. But the indigenous revolutionary refuses to give allegiance to any brand of orthodoxy, be it Russian, Chinese, or Cuban. Whatever his personal psychological motivations may be, his overriding concern is to change brutal conditions in his own land. Increasingly in recent years, at the Havana meetings and subsequent gatherings, one revolutionary leader after another has declared that armed struggle is the only path to radical social change. Counterinsurgency campaigns have grown more sophisticated and more formidable. It is becoming clearer to revolutionaries that armed struggle can succeed only when the old regime is unusually vulnerable. Despite the success of official terrorism and the failure of insurgent terrorism, revolutionary consciousness is growing throughout the Third World.

Revolutionary movements grow in the soil of exploitation and injustice. The concept of colonialism is a total reproach to Western civilization and its professed ideals, for its essence is to treat man exactly as every prophet and moral philosopher from Christ to Kant warned us not to treat him—as a means, not an end. Whatever ancillary benefits colonists may have received from foreign masters, the economic well-being of the home country, not the health of the colony, defined the relationship. But the moral depravity of the colonialist does not mean that revolution is pure heroism or that its leaders are saints. Revolution is ugly and violent. It devours its children and innocent people along with it. The revolutionary always starts from a position of weakness, and he resorts to terrorism, the weapon of the weak—the derailed train, the bomb in the officers' club, or the cut throat of the colonialist collaborator (real or suspected). The revolutionary, even when he is fired by a righteous cause, often marks his success by reverting to the political type he supplants. He becomes a political intriguer, a persecutor of critics, a lover of luxury, or an addict of personal adulation.

A recurring tragedy of the past two hundred years is the betrayal of revolution, often by the men who made it. The historic aim of revolution, as Hannah Arendt has pointed out, is freedom, the opportunity to participate in the political process.[5] Yet the Russian Revolution, which was fought in the name of freedom, degenerated into the bloody despotism of Stalin. China, Yugoslavia, the radical African regimes, Cuba, and North Vietnam have all promised far more freedom than they have delivered. The revolutionary regimes have largely eliminated starvation, spread education, and made dramatic progress toward industrialization. But, as Barrington Moore puts it:

> . . . communists cannot claim that the mass of the population has shouldered a lesser share of the burden of suffering under their form of industrialization than they did under the preceding forms of capitalism. . . . there is no evidence that the mass of the population anywhere has wanted an industrial society, and plenty of evidence that they did not. At bottom all forms of industrialization so far have been revolutions from above, the work of a ruthless minority.[6]

Two

The United States government has seized upon the moral ambiguity of revolution to justify a global campaign to contain it, to channel it into acceptable paths, or to crush it. In 1938 President Roosevelt had to summon all his political powers to block the Ludlow Resolution for a constitutional amendment forbidding the President to send troops overseas without a national referendum. Less than ten years after its narrow defeat, his successor secured broad congressional support for use of American military power to put down violent revolution abroad. "We cannot allow changes in the *status quo*," the President declared, "by such methods as coercion, or by such subterfuges as political infiltration,"[7] making clear that it didn't matter whether revolutionaries were natives of the country they wished to change or not. Since violence is the engine of political change over most of the globe, President Truman committed the United States to a prodigious task.

The context of the Truman Doctrine made it perfectly clear that its target was not all "violence" or all "coercion" or all "changes in the status quo," but only those having something to do with "communism." The justification for treating communist revolutions as a unique political phenomenon rested partly on the premise that they were manipulated by the Soviet Union and partly on the dogma that the coming of communism to a society meant the end of its political evolution. It was assumed that once the "iron curtain" descended upon a country, history stopped. It was lost forever, trapped in an ideological straitjacket. In the twenty years since the war, we have seen the fallacy of this latter assumption. Romania, Hungary, and the Soviet Union itself have undergone profound political and social change. They are still communist regimes, but their character has evolved in many important ways, far more radically, certainly, than many right-wing dictatorships that have come to power by military coup but are exempt from the Truman Doctrine.

The word "communist" has been applied so liberally and so loosely to revolutionary or radical regimes that any government risks being so characterized if it adopts one or more of the following policies which the State Department finds distasteful: nationalization of private industry, particularly foreign-owned corporations, radical land reform, autarchic trade policies, acceptance of Soviet or Chinese aid, insistence upon following an anti-American or non-aligned foreign policy, among others. Thus, the American ambassador to Cuba at the time of the brief Grau San Martín government in 1933 found it to be "communistic." In 1937 Cordell Hull privately spoke of the Mexican government, which was nationalizing U.S.-owned oil properties, as "these communists down there," but made no public charge. Since the Second World War, however, the term "communist" has been used to justify U.S. intervention against a variety of regimes with widely differing ideologies and relationships with the Soviet Union, including Arevalo's Guatemala, Mossadeq's Iran, Goulart's Brazil, Sukarno's Indonesia, Caamano's Dominican revolutionary junta, as well as insurgent movements in Latin America, Africa, and Southeast Asia.

Indeed, from the Truman Doctrine on, the suppression of insurgent movements has remained a principal goal of U.S. foreign policy. It has been the prime target of the U.S. foreign-assistance program, most of the funds for which have gone for civic-action teams, pacification programs, support for local police, and, above all, military aid to the local army.[8] Such expenditures are designed to strengthen the hand of the recognized government to put down the challenge of revolution. Economic aid is extended to Third World countries not only to buy their support on foreign-policy issues but also to lubricate the process of "gradualism" and strengthen the forces of "stability."[9] In other words, U.S. policy is to support governments that promise to revolutionize their societies from above, although, as the continued support of military dictators and reactionary regimes demonstrates, this is scarcely a requirement. U.S. officials, some as advisers to local police, others as Green Berets attached to local armies, are presently assisting governments to put down insurgent movements in Guatemala, Thailand, and elsewhere in Latin America and Africa.[10]

Counterinsurgency continues to be the major preoccupation of U.S. military planners.[11] They have mounted large programs to train local armies in counterguerrilla tactics, but these have been unequal to the task. Consequently, during the postwar period, on the average of once every eighteen months, U.S. military forces or covert paramilitary forces have intervened in strength in Asia, Africa, and Latin America to prevent an insurgent group from seizing power or to subvert a revolutionary government.

Until the Vietnam War was perceived to be a failure, U.S. intervention steadily increased throughout the postwar period. In 1965 an American expeditionary force was sent to Vietnam and Marine divisions landed in the Dominican Republic to prevent insurgents from taking power. Such major commitments demanded a clearer articulation of U.S. policy. "Revolution in any country is a matter for that country to deal with," President Johnson declared as he ordered the Marines to Santo Domingo. "It becomes a matter for hemispheric action only when the object is the establishment of a communist dictatorship."[12] The Johnson Doctrine merely stated more explicitly and honestly an American policy that had in fact persisted since the end of World War II: The United States will oppose where it can or where it dares the establishment of new communist or communist-leaning governments, whether they come into being through foreign invasion, domestic revolution, or election. Insurgent movements with radical programs, Marxist rhetoric, communist connections of any kind, or an anti-American bias are simply assumed to be the product of conspiracy by the "forces of international communism." The presence of a communist element—even the possibility of subsequent communist takeover—justifies U.S. intervention. As President Johnson put it at the time of the Dominican crisis, "the old distinction between civil war and international war has lost much of its meaning."[13] Faced with the unprecedented phenomenon of revolutionary violence erupting in pockets scattered across three continents, U.S. officials have attempted to squeeze it into a familiar framework with a set of ready explanations and old solutions. The framework is Great Power aggression, which, as World War II demonstrated, could be launched on a global scale and carried out by the subtle techniques of the fifth column. The tested remedy is the application of overwhelming military force. When it became clear that the costs of the counterinsurgency war in Vietnam exceeded all possible gain to the United States, the interventionist strategy was overhauled. The Johnson Doctrine was discreetly replaced by the Nixon Doctrine, to which we shall return in the last chapter.

Three

This book then is an historical survey of U.S. intervention in revolutionary warfare in the Third World since World War II. It attempts to trace the development of the American commitment to oppose internal violence and radical political change in such places as Greece, Lebanon, Vietnam, the Dominican Republic, Guatemala, British Guiana, Iran, and the Congo.

The biographies of these commitments can tell us something of the purpose and meaning of what four Presidents have called the "American Responsibility" to keep the peace. "We did not choose to be the guardians at the gate,"[14] President Johnson once stated in a display of the anguish of power. One of the purposes of this book is to inquire how it happened that America has become what President Kennedy called "the watchman on the walls of world freedom."[15]

Why a great nation embarks on a campaign to bring order to other societies is not a simple question. Historical analysis offers a set of standard explanations: the restless energy of the powerful, diversion of attention from unsolved domestic problems, insecurity at home, passion for spreading civilization, idealistic commitment to a world order, the quest for markets and raw materials, and, simply, a lust for conquest. As for postwar America, three principal theories have been advanced to explain her assumption of responsibility for opposing revolution in the Third World.

There is the official ideology, which holds that the United States, having come to manhood, was tapped by history for a global mission of peacemaking and reform.

"History and our own achievements have thrust upon us the principal responsibility for the protection of freedom on earth,"[16] President Johnson declared at a Lincoln Day dinner in 1965, a trace of sadness mixed with pride in his voice. "For the next ten or twenty years," his predecessor observed three years earlier, "the burden will be placed completely on our country for the preservation of freedom."[17] The world community, at least those members of it with decent motives, look to the United States to lead the world and to keep order. For there is no one else. The power of the United States permits it to transcend the petty conflicts that obsess most of its neighbors on the planet. "It is a very old dream," President Johnson told his countrymen in April, 1965, "but we have the power and now the opportunity to make that dream come true."[18] The dream is Perfect Peace, a world in which "disputes are settled by law and reason." The United States, uniquely blessed with surpassing riches and an exceptional history, stands above the international system, not within it. Alone among nations, she stands ready to be the bearer of the Law.

A few years ago the secretary of defense called in a group of foreign-newspaper correspondents to a special briefing at which he explained at great length that the United States is not and cannot be "the policeman of the world." Ruffled by criticism of the mushrooming commitments the United States has taken in the name of "peacekeeping," Secretary of State Rusk also used to make a point of inserting in his speeches a stock denial that America plays or seeks the gendarme's role. But the official objections to the epithets of the critics have more to do with public relations than substance. For a variety of reasons the image of the neighborhood policeman is more tarnished than it was a generation ago. In the age of big-city riots, police review boards, and the police state, the neutrality and responsibility of police are no longer taken for granted.

But the police idea is strongly entrenched in official ideology. It is merely expressed in other words, like "guardian" or "watchman," or, as in the Congo and Dominican operations, "rescuer of women and children."[19] The world looks to Washington for protection against the insurgent band as well as the foreign invader. The American Responsibility is to provide it, whatever the cost, wherever it can. Intervention, with all its paraphernalia—

the aid missions, the CIA operations, the roaming fleets bristling with nuclear weapons, the Green Berets, the pacification teams, and ultimately the expeditionary forces —is the inevitable consequence of greatness. It is the burden and the glory of the Republic.[20]

Critics of American foreign policy tend to doubt the necessity or the wisdom of this self-appointed mission. Some with a sense of history are well aware that the United States is not the first powerful nation to explain the great role it has claimed for itself in terms of burden and sacrifice. For Cicero too the fledgling empire of the first century B.C. was a "guardianship," a domain over which the Roman people, whether by force or persuasion, could enforce the law of Rome and secure justice for primitive peoples. The British Empire was the "White Man's Burden," imposed by the stern hand of History. "Empire is congenial enough to the Englishman's temperament," George Unwin wrote during World War I, "but it is repugnant to his political conscience. In order that he may be reconciled to it, it must seem to be imposed upon him by necessity, as a duty. Fate and metaphysical aid must seem to have crowned him."[21] In every century, powerful nations have reluctantly "come of age," playing out their imperial destiny by carrying on a *mission civilatrice* on the land of some weaker neighbor.

Yet many critics cling to the view that like everything else about America, her imperialism is exceptional. It springs from the purest motives. Senator J. William Fulbright, for example, while totally hostile to the policy, stresses American idealism as the furious energy which has prompted the United States to stand guard around the world against revolutions.[22] Such critics do not doubt the sincerity, only the wisdom, of official statements such as Under Secretary Ball's remark that the United States has "a role of world responsibility divorced from territorial or narrow national interests."[23] America's leaders may be guilty of the "arrogance of power," a bit quixotic in attempting to remake the world in our own image, naïve in thinking that a new liberal order can be ushered in so quickly, but they do not act from the base motives of the older empires. "Unlike Rome, we have not exploited our empire. On the contrary, our empire has exploited us, making enormous drains on our resources and our energies,"[24] concludes Ronald Steel in his analysis of what he calls "the accidental empire."

Generations of British schoolboys have been delighted by Sir John Seeley's famous phrase that England conquered half the world in a fit of absence of mind. Such a self-image set them apart from the gross plunderers of the past. The Victorian imperialists were decent, civilized men who stumbled into a global domain. Indeed, as a historian of the time, G. P. Gooch, pointed out, taking over backward nations such as India did not increase England's power, only her responsibilities.[25] Like these British critics, most of the small group of U.S. commentators who criticize the American empire at all see it as a consequence of bumbling, misguided benevolence, and "the politics of inadvertence."[26]

For all the pride Americans have in Yankee shrewdness at home, there is a folklore tradition that the United States is continually duped abroad. Wily European statesmen from Clemenceau to Stalin have lured our Presidents beyond our shores and tricked them into underwriting their empires. Where the United States finds itself involved in a foreign adventure, it is because she has nobly, if foolishly, agreed to pull someone else's chestnuts out of the fire. If she has managed to turn burdens into opportunities and responsibilities into assets, this has been a happy accident. But quixotic idealism that requires the spending of billions to maintain overseas armies and to finance corrupt regimes is a luxury, these critics assert, when U.S. cities are falling apart and the money could be spent so much better here.

Americans who reluctantly find they must criticize the U.S. crusade against revolution are naturally attracted by this national self-portrait of a well-meaning bumbler. It is consistent with one stream running through our history, a strong anti-imperialist tradition. But it is only a partial vision. Even America is not lucky enough to find herself with the mightiest military force and the greatest aggregate of wealth in history through aimless altruism alone.

Other critics of U.S. policy toward insurgent movements look for more familiar and more sinister motives. Drawing on the theories of Hilferding, Hobson, and Lenin of fifty years ago, they ascribe the development of America's self-proclaimed guardianship not to exceptional idealism but to economic imperialism. They see America not as a bumbler but as a country that has adroitly used its power and good fortune to consume sixty percent of the world's raw materials each year, to manipulate the global

money market, and to control much of world trade.
Those who hold these views include not only official
communist propagandists, orthodox Marxist critics, a few
remaining American populists of the tradition of Robert
La Follette and Charles Beard, but also most politicians of
the Third World, not only the revolutionaries in the hills
but also many of the presidents, premiers, and generals in
the palaces.[28]

"With only one-fifteenth of the world's population and
about the same proportion of the world's area and natural
resources," the Advertising Council of America, Inc., has
observed in its brochure *The Miracle of America*, "the
United States—has more than half the world's telephone,
telegraph, and radio networks—more than three quarters
of the world's automobiles—almost half the world's radios—and consumes more than half the world's copper and
rubber, two-thirds of the silk, a quarter of the coal, and
nearly two-thirds of the crude oil."[29]

These figures cause the Advertising Council to glow
with pride and self-congratulation, but for critics they
offer a sinister explanation of America's global role.
America, like Britain before her, they say, is now the
great defender of the Status Quo. She has committed
herself against revolution and radical change in the underdeveloped world because independent governments would
destroy the world economic and political system, which
assures the United States its disproportionate share of
economic and political power. Such critics point to the
widening disparity in income levels between the United
States and the rest of the world: In 1965 the individual
income level in the United States was 3,500 dollars, 650
dollars in Greece, 718 dollars in Argentina, 123 dollars in
Thailand, 97 dollars in Pakistan, and 65 dollars in Mali.[30]
They note the fantastic climb in direct private U.S. foreign investment—from 7.2 billion dollars in 1946 to more
than 70 billion dollars in 1971.[31] They cite the swift and
powerful attacks the United States has mounted against
governments like Castro's Cuba, Arbenz' Guatemala, and
Mossadeq's Iran which threaten to nationalize American
companies or to radically revise the terms of trade and
investment They conclude that America's preeminent
wealth depends upon keeping things in the underdeveloped
world much as they are, allowing change and modernization to proceed only in a controlled, orderly, and non-
threatening way. President Johnson's occasional remarks

that the poor nations envy us our wealth and would like to take it away from us[82] confirm their view that there is considerable method in what appears to be America's foreign-policy madness.

The United States supports right-wing dictatorships in Latin America, Southeast Asia, and the Middle East, they argue, not because it is confused but because these are the rulers who have tied their personal political destiny to the fortunes of the American corporations in their countries. The Batistas, Castelo Brancos, Tsaldareses, Somozas, Kys, and a parade of other reactionary potentates who have been feted at the White House permit or encourage American corporations to exploit their countries under highly favorable terms. The Castros, Mossadeqs, Arbenzes, Tarucs, Bosches, and other revolutionary or nationalist leaders have radically different political constituencies and interests. For them creating "a good investment climate" for the United States and developing their own country are fundamentally conflicting goals.[88] Therefore, the United States has a strong economic interest in keeping such men from coming to power or arranging for their removal if they do.

This view of reality is an updated version of the traditional model of economic imperialism. Government protects the foreign investment of its businessmen through military intervention and political control. There is a strong element of truth to it, enough to satisfy America's enemies and some of her friends that it is an adequate explanation of U.S. policy toward the former colonial world. But just as "inadvertence" or misplaced idealism is not sufficient to explain a highly consistent policy of opposing revolution, neither is "the pursuit of profits" nor the search for stable markets and raw material sources. No doubt U.S. investments abroad have been an important factor in strengthening American commitments to oppose radical movements in the underdeveloped world. It is true that U.S. military and political activity in the Third World has expanded as foreign investment has increased. Foreign sales by U.S. companies based abroad increased five times in the years 1950 to 1964. Profits from foreign investment, particularly in extractive industries, are unusually high.[84] It is true also that with respect to vital raw materials America is a have-not nation. As early as 1952, the President's Materials Policy Commission discovered that while at the turn of the century U.S. industry extrac-

ted from the American earth fifteen percent more raw
materials than it could use, there was now an annual
deficit of ten percent, and the prognosis was for greater
shortages of vital materials. American businessmen from
time to time unwittingly testify for the Marxist critics. In
1965, for example, the vice-president for Far Eastern
operations of the Chase Manhattan Bank spoke of the
commercial significance of the U.S. commitment to Vietnam:

> In the past, foreign investors have been somewhat
> wary of the over-all political prospect for the region.
> I must say though that the U.S. actions in Vietnam
> this year—which have demonstrated that the U.S. will
> give effective protection to the free nations of the
> region—have considerably reassured both Asian and
> Western investors. In fact, I see some reason for hope
> that the same sort of economic growth may take place
> in the free economics of Asia that took place in
> Europe after the Truman Doctrine. . . . The same
> thing took place in Japan after the U.S. intervention
> in Korea removed investor doubts.[35]

There is also considerable evidence that U.S. business has
heavily influenced the character of the U.S. foreign-aid
program in the Third World and that large corporations
wield considerable influence on the direction of foreign
policy through lobbying, political contributions, and "lending" key personnel for the national-security bureaucracy.

Yet when all the evidence is marshaled, something is
missing. To argue, as Lenin did, that the interventionist
drive of the nation-state is attributable primarily to the
basic needs of capitalism to export capital and to gain
access to markets and raw materials is to ignore remarkably similar patterns of behavior in noncapitalist states.
The drive to project power and influence, the will to
dominate, and the frenetic search for security are characteristic of the large industrialized state, whatever its
economic system. It is not hard to find instances where the
machinery of government in the United States is used to
promote and protect private investment. The activities of
the State Department, the CIA, and the Pentagon in the
Guatemalan invasion of 1954, the Bay of Pigs episode of
1961, and the Dominican intervention of 1965 are plausible cases where the protection or recovery of economic

interests was an important consideration. But the intervention in Vietnam cannot be explained in these terms; there was virtually no American investment there to protect. Indeed, by 1968 the prosecution of the war aroused increasing opposition in the business community because of its unfavorable economic effects.

Classic theories of economic imperialism, which view the state as an agent of the most powerful domestic economic interests, underestimate the independent role of the national-security bureaucracy which in the United States has taken on a life and movement of its own. It has the money and power at its disposal to develop within very broad limits its own conception of the national interest. To a great extent interventionist policy is the result of the development of the technology of intervention. Thus, for example, once counterinsurgency forces or spy ships are available the bureaucracy quickly finds that their use is essential. The principal justification is the drive for security which is so open-ended a concept that it permits the accumulation and projection of military power and political influence to become ends in themselves. The urge to achieve stability and control over the world environment by taming and cooling independent political forces in other countries is probably inherent in the hierarchical character of the foreign-policy bureaucracy.

Behind the bureaucratic compulsion to control as much of the world political environment as possible there lies a host of real human fears and drives that are not adequately dealt with in traditional models of economic imperialism: the fear of attack, the fear of losing influence and respect, the fear of falling from the pinnacle of power, the urge to make other societies conform to a preconceived design, and the rationalized faith that the national interest and the welfare of mankind coincide. Even where the efforts to dominate appear to run counter to rational economic interests, the will to dominate persists. To argue that these fears and drives are ultimately rooted in economic relations may or may not be true, but if economic causation is defined so broadly, it does not seem to be a sufficiently incisive tool for either explaining or predicting the interventionist behavior of the modern state. In short, while the ideology of official altruism that four administrations have offered as the explanation of America's role in the postwar world required us to believe that our government is different from all others and,

indeed, from all other human institutions, neither the
politics of inadvertence nor the traditional analyses of the
politics of capitalism provide an adequate alternative.

In *The Roots of War* I have attempted to develop a
theory as to the internal dynamics behind America's
choice to commit so much of its energy and resources to
the suppression of insurgent movements. In this book we
are concerned, primarily, with what United States officials
did, how they explained their actions to each other and to
the public, and, ultimately, what the results of these actions have been. I have sketched the three hypotheses
concerning the motivation and the dynamics of this crucial drive in American foreign policy to suggest the range
of intellectual frameworks within which it is possible to
think about intervention and revolution. As I have suggested, none of them is adequate, although all are part of
the conventional idiom of political debate. If we wish to
understand the mainsprings of American foreign policy, or
of any nation, for that matter, we must start by looking
deep into domestic society. The world view of a nation's
leaders is a product of the institutions of their civilization.[36]

NOTES—CHAPTER ONE

1. Robert S. McNamara, Address to the American Society
of Newspaper Editors, Montreal, Canada, May 8, 1966.

2. For an account of recent U.S. efforts at counterinsurgency in Latin America, see Norman Gall, "The Legacy of
Che Guevara," in *Commentary*, December 1967, pp. 21–44.
The quote from Guevara is on p. 37; *The Economist's* assessment of counterguerrilla operations in Guatemala is quoted
on p. 42.

3. For a typical Third World view by a former African
leader, see Kwame Nkrumah, *Neo-Imperialism: The Last Stage
of Imperialism* (New York, 1966).

4. For a sympathetic account of the conference, see Albert
Paul Lentin, *La Lutte Tricontinentale: Impérialisme et Révolution après la Conférence de La Havane* (Paris, 1966), especially
ch. II.

5. See Hannah Arendt, *On Revolution* (New York, 1963).

6. Barrington Moore, *Social Origins of Dictatorship and
Democracy* (Boston, 1966), p. 506.

7. Harry S. Truman, Address before a Joint Session of Congress, March 12, 1947.

8. It is true that military aid, which in 1956 represented
about 70 percent of the foreign-assistance budget, has de-

clined in recent years relative to total aid expenditures. However, if we analyze aid for the years 1950–1967, exclusive of Marshall Plan assistance to Europe, AID officials have confirmed to me that military assistance, defense support, and related expenditures for keeping internal order represent a substantial majority of the total assistance budget for these years. Precise figures are difficult to calculate since some military assistance figures (India and Pakistan, for example) are classified. Others, such as the Export-Import Bank, are described as being for nonmilitary purposes, but are in fact used to finance military purchases. See Agency for International Development, Special Report Prepared for the House Foreign Affairs Committee: *U.S. Overseas Loans and Grants, July 1, 1945–June 30, 1966* (Washington, D.C., 1967).

The Agency for International Development has prepared the following chart, at my request, in which column I represents total economic and military aid; column II, quasi-military aid; and column III represents remaining economic aid that is neither military nor for "supporting assistance" (police, counterinsurgency programs, etc.). The chart shows that from 1953–67 economic aid has been $16,092 million out of a total of $62,238 million.

(millions of dollars)

	TOTAL ECONOMIC AND MILITARY	TOTAL LESS MILITARY	TOTAL LESS MILITARY AND SUPPORTING ASSISTANCE*
1953–57	24,449	9,142	1,312
1958	4,024	1,620	580
1959	4,076	1,916	993
1960	3,711	1,866	974
1961	3,478	2,012	1,242
1962	4,035	2,508	2,076
1963	4,178	2,297	1,889
1964	3,659	2,136	1,802
1965	3,339	2,026	1,602
1966	3,727	2,543	1,854
1967**	3,562	2,459	1,768

* Data shown for FY 1962–67 are Supporting Assistance. Data prior to FY 1962 cover Defense Support and Special Assistance.

** Preliminary data.

9. The emphasis of official explanations of the aid program before Congress has changed somewhat over the years. In 1950, Secretary of State Acheson argued for aid to underdeveloped areas "as Measure of National Security." In presenting the legislation he said:

This legislation that is before you, this "Act for International Development," has the same broad purpose. In a very real sense, it is a security measure. And as a security measure, it is an essential arm of our foreign policy. For our military and economic security is vitally dependent on the economic security of other peoples.

But our foreign policy is not based on security alone. We have never been satisfied merely to resist a threat—of communism or any other "ism." Our policy is broader than this. It is essentially constructive. It is based on the assumption that, in the world today, our own welfare is closely related to that of other peoples. We can participate in this kind of a program because it serves both the interest of other peoples and our own interest as well.

Economic development will bring us certain practical material benefits. It will open up new sources of materials and goods we need, and new markets for the products of our farms and factories. Our friends in Europe, who depend far more than we do on foreign goods and markets, will benefit in similar ways. The volume of world trade will inevitably expand.

And finally, the peoples of the underdeveloped areas will begin to see new opportunities for a better life, and they will associate those opportunities in their minds with the helping hand of the American people. Even more important, they will associate economic progress with an approach to the problems of daily life that preserves and enlarges the initiative, dignity, and freedom of the individual. (*Department of State Bulletin*, April 10, 1950, pp. 552–555.)

In 1967 the administrator of AID, William Gaud, defined the purpose of the aid program in these words:

At the same time the proposal mirrors AID's belief that agriculture, health and education are the dominant challenges in development; that development succeeds best in those countries that give scope to the dynamic forces of private initiative; that policies must minimize the effect of assistance programs on the U.S. balance of payments deficit in the interest of stability of the dollar; and that AID owes American citizens efficient administration of the programs their taxes support.

On the other hand, the fiscal 1968 program reflects evolution, constructive change, and the search for better ways of making American assistance work:

It identifies increased agricultural production—the War on Hunger—as the highest development priority, links it to vigorous action in the related field of population, and implements recent administrative changes for more efficiently coordinating these urgent programs. . . .

It sets forth a significant shift in aid for Africa, with increased emphasis on using multilateral and regional arrangements and a reduction in the number of bilateral programs. . . . (Agency for International Development, *Proposed Foreign Aid Program, FY 1968*, Washington, D.C., 1967.)

10. For official admissions that U.S. "civic-action" teams have been operating in Guatemala and Honduras and reports that Green Berets are in Guatemala, see Gall, "Legacy of Che Guevara," p. 41.

11. In 1971 the United States, despite the Vietnam withdrawals, still had 803,901 soldiers in 110 countries, according to a Pentagon public affairs spokesman.

12. Statement of Lyndon B. Johnson, May 2, 1965, quoted in Ronald Steel, *Pax Americana* (New York, 1967), p. 232.

13. Lyndon B. Johnson, Address at Baylor University, May 28, 1965.

14. Statement of Lyndon B. Johnson, July 28, 1965.

15. Statement of John F. Kennedy, quoted in Steel, *Pax Americana*, p. 3.

16. Address of Lyndon B. Johnson, February 12, 1965, quoted in *The New York Times*, February 13, 1965.

17. Statement of John F. Kennedy, August 28, 1962, quoted in *The New York Times*, August 29, 1962.

18. Lyndon B. Johnson, Address at Johns Hopkins University, April 7, 1965. For authoritative statements by individuals who have played a role in shaping postwar U.S. foreign policy on the definition of the American Responsibility, see: John F. Kennedy, *The Burden and the Glory* (New York, 1964); W. W. Rostow, *The United States in the World Arena: An Essay in Recent History* (New York, 1960); McGeorge Bundy, ed., *The Pattern of Responsibility* (Boston, 1951); Dean Acheson, *Power and Diplomacy* (Cambridge, Mass., 1958); Dean Rusk, *The Winds of Freedom* (Boston, 1961).

19. See chapters 8 and 10 of this book.

20. The following are typical articulations of the ideology of the American Responsibility:

   a) In a system such as the contemporary one, there is no substitute for constant and alert manipulation and adjustment of concrete interests by interacting states. The United States in particular must so act, as the primary global power, alone or in conjunction with the other imperial state or states as they develop the will and capacity to cooperate in the interest of minimum world order. (George Liska, *Imperial America: The International Politics of Primacy*, Baltimore, 1967, p. 46).

   b) In the 19th Century and until the First World War England was the world's policeman. At tremendous cost the British fleet was kept to a strength larger than all the other navies in the world combined. In those happy days sea power was equivalent to world power. From the time of the Monroe Doctrine on we have been protected by the British fleet. But in the First World War we discovered that sea power was not what it once was. America had to be sworn in as deputy world policeman and go to the rescue of the chief. In fact, the necessity of assuming the role of world policeman had descended on us, but we were completely unaware of it. (Thurman Arnold, "The Growth of Awareness: Our Nation's Law and Law Among Nations," in *The International Lawyer*, July 1967, p. 540.)

c) See also Herbert Dinerstein, *Intervention Against Communism* (Baltimore, 1967).

21. George Unwin, quoted in Harold Laswell, *World Politics and Personal Insecurity* (Glencoe, Ill., 1965), p. 90.

22. For Senator Fulbright's views, see his *The Arrogance of Power* (New York, 1967).

23. George Ball, "The Dangers of Nostalgia," in *Department of State Bulletin*, April 12, 1965, pp. 535–536. Mr. Ball thought this role was "something new and unique in world history."

24. Steel, *Pax Americana*, p. 17.

25. Gooch's analysis of the British Empire is discussed in Laswell, *World Politics*, p. 89.

26. See Arthur Schlesinger, Jr., *The Bitter Heritage* (New York, 1967).

27. In his message to Congress on conservation in 1962, President Kennedy observed, "During the last thirty years this nation has consumed more minerals than all the peoples of the world had previously used." John F. Kennedy, quoted in James F. McDivitt, *Minerals and Men* (Baltimore, 1965), p. 4.

28. See, for example, the 1924 platform of the Progressive party, Charles A. Beard, *The Idea of the National Interest* (rev. ed.: Chicago, 1966). See also numerous statements of Nasser, Nkrumah, Sukarno, and Latin American politicians, for example, Kwame Nkrumah, *Neo-Imperialism*.

29. Francis Xavier Sutton, *et al.*, *The American Business Creed* (Cambridge, Mass., 1956), pp. 19–20.

30. These figures are found in Agency for International Development, *Proposed Foreign Aid Program, FY 1968*, Table III. All such figures are, of course, highly approximate.

31. For figures on U.S. overseas investments, see William Beard, "The American Stake Abroad," Appendix to Beard, *The Idea of National Interest*, pp. 441–445. Of course, most of the increase in foreign investment is attributable to investment in the developed countries of Western Europe.

32. President Johnson made such remarks on several occa-

sions during a tour of Vietnam in 1967; for example, see *The New York Times,* November 2, 1966.

33. For an insight into a nationalist noncommunist's bitter perception of U.S. objectives in Latin America, see Juan Arevalo, *The Shark and the Sardines* (New York, 1961).

34. See Beard, "The American Stake Abroad," pp. 441–445.

35. Quoted in Harry Magdoff, "Economic Aspects of U.S. Imperialism," in *Monthly Review,* November 1966, p. 13.

36. For a discussion of the relationship of U.S. political institutions and ideology see my *The Roots of War* (Atheneum, 1972). See also Karl Mannheim, *Ideology and Utopia* (New York, 1959). For discussion of these questions with respect to the Soviet Union, see Zbigniew Brzezinski, *Ideology and Power in Soviet Politics* (New York, 1962).

CHAPTER 2

Two Worlds in Collision: The National-Security Manager and the Revolutionary

One

THE CONTINUING AMERICAN CONFLICT with revolutionary movements arises from a fundamental clash of perspective on modern political history between those officials in the State Department, Pentagon, CIA, and the White House who manage U.S. foreign relations—the National-Security Managers—and the Revolutionaries, who guide insurgent movements.* The conflict is fed by

* In probing the ideological conflict between the National-Security Manager and the Revolutionary, we shall be talking about each as if he represented an ideal type. Reality, of course, is less obliging. One can find in the State Department and in the White House sharp disagreements on questions of national security, counterinsurgency, and the proper "posture" of the United States towards the Third World. One need only look at the polemics from the communist world on revolution, relations with the capitalist world, and various strategies for change to recognize that revolutionaries dedicated to radical social change through a radical redistribution of political power do not all agree with one another. Nevertheless, a reading of a great number of memoirs, congressional testimony, and analytical writings by National-Security Managers reveals that to a remarkable degree they share common assumptions about the nature of politics and a common view of the world and how to change it. The same can be said about contemporary Revolutionaries.

two fundamentally incompatible visions of world order.

In the postwar period much has been made of the "ideological conflict" between communism and capitalism.[1] That is what the Cold War is supposed to be about. But in fact many basic perspectives of Soviet and American leaders have always been remarkably similar. To be sure, they have had bitter conflicts over their relative power positions. The United States wanted a role in Eastern Europe that Russia refused to give her. Russia wanted a role in Western Europe and the Middle East which the United States has successfully resisted. They fought to a stalemate in Germany. The two powers have had quite different ideas about how to run their internal societies, but they have shared the same general view of the proper role of a Great Power in the modern world.

They competed for power and influence in the Third World. Each put great stress on its military might. Each invested more in the symbols of prestige, like the space race, than in projects that might change the face of the earth. Each developed military, paramilitary, and diplomatic bureaucracies that were mirror images of the other. Neither was interested in exporting its system to other countries so much as using its system as an ideology around which to rally supporters and clients. The United States was as anxious to create a truly *independent* capitalist economy in the poor countries of Asia, Africa, and Latin America as Russia was to establish *independent* communist regimes there. Indeed, the United States has usually not favored the accumulation of *local* capital and the Soviets have frequently opposed *local* revolutionaries.[2] Khrushchev proclaimed that the Soviet aspiration was to "overtake and surpass the United States" in building the affluent society. Today the Soviet government continues to hold up the American Way of Life, the abundant consumer economy, as the goal of Russian communism. Both powers have found that they can coexist comfortably and compete for power and influence without attempting to convert the other. This is an *ideological* conflict like the one between Ford and General Motors!

Between the National-Security Managers and the Revolutionary, however, there is a real ideological clash. While both use a common rhetoric at times—the speeches of Dean Rusk and Fidel Castro alike make repeated reference to "self-determination," "revolution," "freedom," etc.—the American bureaucrat and the revolution-

ary politician start with radically different pictures of
world politics and a set of directly conflicting interests.
They differ fundamentally even in the way they characterize the issues which divide them.[3]

This clash of perspectives is dictated by radical differences in their education, theoretical and practical, and in
their personal relationships to politics. The typical National-Security Manager during the last twenty years was
trained in law, engineering, or banking. He entered government service in the war. Captivated by a chance to be
a participant in great events, he stayed on or, more often,
returned from time to time. If he has any firsthand knowledge at all of the Third World, it is likely to stem from a
mining venture or the sugar business; or, perhaps, from
wartime service in the oss.*

From his vantage point in the national-security bureaucracy, the National-Security Manager sees revolution in
the underdeveloped world as a problem in the management of violence. Coming to power in the midst of World
War II, he formed his view of international politics from
his experience in the struggle with Hitler. The primary
problem is aggression. The principal cause of aggression is
weakness and instability. Unless aggressors are systemati-
cally opposed by "situations of strength," they will strike
at their weaker neighbors. Nations act in accordance with
Newtonian laws, rushing to fill up "power vacuums" wherever they find them.[4] "Everything that happens in this
world affects us," President Johnson told the troops in
Vietnam in 1966, "because pretty soon it gets on our
doorstep."[5] Stripped of the intellectual counterpoint of the
foreign-policy expert, the President voiced the most basic
and primitive fears of the National-Security Manager.
"There are 3 billion people in the world and we have only
200 million of them. We are outnumbered 15 to 1. If
might did make right, they would sweep over the United
States and take what we have. We have what they want."[6]

No one is more aware than the man with the authority
to launch the nuclear missiles that the United States has a

---

* The observations on the careers, education, and background of the
National-Security Managers is based on a study I have completed of
the four hundred individuals who have held the top managerial
positions relating to national security (down to and including assistant secretary) from 1945 to 1967 in the Departments of State,
Defense, Army, Navy, and Air Force, the Central Intelligence
Agency, the Atomic Energy Commission, and the White House.

commanding position in military and economic power. Since 1945 this country, not content with being *primus inter pares* among the nations, has sought not the delicate balance of power but a position of commanding superiority in weapons technology, in the regulation of the international economy, and in the manipulation of the internal politics of other countries. For the National-Security Manager the acquisition of power is both a necessity and an end in itself. The world is too dangerous and present advantages too tenuous to permit a pause in the relentless drive for more power. He accepts the creed which General Douglas MacArthur used to voice, "There is no security; there is only opportunity." Few events in the world can be ignored. No matter how remote a coup, a guerrilla struggle, an arms shipment, or a friendly visit from one foreign leader to another may be, when viewed from the seventh floor of the State Department it must be recorded as either a national asset or a liability.

The world is full of enemies, but the most powerful is International Communism. Most National-Security Managers have not shared Dulles' conviction that communism is the incarnation of the Antichrist, a creed so dangerous to moral health that one must refuse to shake hands with their diplomatic spokesmen to avoid contamination.[7] To the less passionate ideologues of the Cold War, communism is not a disease but an "organizational weapon." John F. Kennedy expressed the sophisticated view of the world struggle in a speech on disarmament two years before he entered the White House: the national-security problem for the United States arises from "a vicious circle of two great powers contending with each other for sway over the destiny of man." It is a struggle "compounded by the new dynamics of an expansive world Communism, armed with revolutionary doctrines of class warfare and modern methods of subversion and terror."[8] The master planners of the Kremlin and Peking, once in concert and now in rivalry, continually survey the globe, probing for weak spots to which they can rush agitators, guns, or rubles for a cheap victory.

Communist intervention in the turmoil of revolution, decolonization, and civil strife threatens the security of the United States, for if the communists succeed in their bid "for sway over the destiny of man," the United States —as the National-Security Manager sees it—will be reduced to a vestigial enclave. Each revolutionary success, therefore, is seen as a Russian victory and an American defeat. This conviction is reason enough to mount a global campaign of containment, for National Security is its own justification.

But the National-Security Manager is also convinced that he has right as well as necessity on his side. Communist intervention is illegitimate because the communist is by definition a foreign agent. Ho Chi Minh's independence movement, Ambassador William C. Bullitt explained in 1947, was designed to "add another finger to the hand that Stalin is closing around China."[9] Mao Tse-tung too was a Russian agent, according to Dean Rusk in a speech made two years after the Chinese Revolution, when he was in charge of Far East operations for the State Department. Mao's regime was "a colonial Russian government—a Slavic Manchukuo on a large scale—it is not the government of China. It does not pass the first test. It is not Chinese."[10] The National-Security Manager has convinced himself that no people ever voluntarily choose communism, a system founded on a set of economic myths and made to work at all only by the systematic use of terror. Perhaps most of the protectorates of the Free World are not so free, the National-Security Manager concedes in the intimate atmosphere of a Task Force or a "backgrounder," but they are better off than if they had gone communist. And so are we.

Two

Since the dawn of the sixties the National-Security Managers have taken it as an article of faith that the Third World is both the locus and the prize of the Cold War. "Today's struggle does not lie here," President Kennedy told Paul-Henri Spaak on a visit to Europe in the last year of his life, "but rather in Asia, Latin America and Africa."[11] The less-developed lands, John J. McCloy wrote in 1960, "promise to be the principal battleground in which the forces of freedom and communism compete—

a battleground in which the future shape of society may finally be tested and determined."[12] The vision of Armageddon that had sustained the arms race of the fifties, the Nuclear War over Europe, had receded in the wake of a decade of tacit understandings between cautious adversaries and judicious crisis management on both sides of the Elbe. The prospect of the new Armageddon was more frightening, for its terrain was unfamiliar and its weapons unconventional. The clients to be assisted were volatile. They behaved brutally at home and ungratefully toward their benefactors. Yet the decolonizing world, known in the National-Security Manager's vernacular of the fifties as The Gray Areas, had become the major battleground.[13]

For the National-Security bureaucrat, the Cold War conferred a manageable unity upon the landmass of Asia, Africa, and Latin America, with its two-thirds of the world's population, its staggering set of economic and social problems, and its confusing mosaic of race, culture, and politics. For all their differences, the politicians of the Third World shared a common role in the Great Power struggle, and whatever identity such "local" politicians were accorded in the State Department and the White House rested on that role.

The National-Security Manager still tends to look at the "Underdeveloped World" as a vast Gray Area in international politics. No part of it is of intrinsic interest, unless, of course, it supplies some vital commodity. Otherwise it can capture the official attention in Washington only if it symbolizes some struggle which transcends the minor turmoil of native politics. To the man of the West, Paris and Berlin are important places in their own right, for they symbolize his own historical heritage. But Danang, Santo Domingo, and Kinshasa penetrate his consciousness, if at all, only as battlefields, and then only if the fight is about something sufficiently important. He has almost no knowledge about such places, their people, or their politics, and little personal commitment to them. They represent either sources of strength, strategic or economic, or points of vulnerability. "Vietnam is not the issue," National-Security Managers have frequently confided to critics who question whether systematic bombardment is the best way to secure freedom for the Vietnamese people; "it is the testing ground for the Communist strategy of Wars of National Liberation. If they win here, they will strike elsewhere. If they lose, they will not be so ready to start another."

The National-Security Manager is a global thinker. In themselves, local problems of other countries are not worthy of his attention; it is the transcendent importance of local revolutionary struggles that warrants intervention. Interference in purely domestic matters is still unjustified as a matter of law and sound policy. Unfortunately, he hastens to add, the line between domestic and foreign matters has blurred. When political factions struggle with one another in far-off places, their conflict is an expression of a single world-wide struggle. The real contestants remain the same. Only the battlefield shifts. The battle, which takes the form of a series of guerrilla wars, is not about Vietnam or Greece or the Dominican Republic any more than World War II was about Iwo Jima or Sicily. Wherever men struggle for power, one can always find International Communism, the ubiquitous political scavenger, ready to use genuine local grievances as ammunition in a global holy war. Global strategy, more than local conditions, dictates the site of the next engagement between International Communism and the Free World.

At this point let us try to look more closely at the mental set of the National-Security Manager as it bears on the U.S. commitment against revolution. The ultimate bureaucratic dream is the perfect freedom of unlimited power. It is the ability to push a button, make a phone call, dispatch a cable, and know that the world will conform to your vision. The capacity to control, or, as he might put it, to have options, is a much clearer objective for the professional statesman than the purposes to which he would put such power. The guiding stars of the working bureaucrat are not cosmic goals. One can find a few expressions of an official eschatology in flowery speeches on National Purpose, or in the negotiated generalities of the Basic National-Security Policy papers representing the collective wisdom of the foreign-policy bureaucracy. Usually, however, the National-Security Manager prides himself on avoiding theological and "nonpragmatic" speculation. He has faith in his intuitive grasp of the art of *ad hoc* politics. Yet, in developing official policy on U.S. intervention, he is not quite so free as he thinks. Just as he casts his adversary, the Revolutionary—Castro, Mao, Ho— in the inevitable role of foreign agent, so he has picked out a well-worn part for himself. It is the role of the imperial peacekeeper.

Three

The National-Security Manager is of course outraged by any such suggestion. To note that America follows in the footsteps of other great powers offends against a basic tenet of his faith: America is exceptional. The nation which sprang from a unique political philosophy at a unique historical moment, singularly blessed by geography, climate, and the inventive energy of her people, never needed to fall prey to the temptations of the European empires, and never did.

The more historically minded of the National-Security Managers are quick to point out that the acquisitions of the imperialist spree of the McKinley era, such as Cuba and Hawaii, have been either abandoned or incorporated as full participants in the American Union. (Even the imperial settlement of the continental United States does not fit the nineteenth-century pattern. The push to the Pacific was an act of conquest. The Indians were pacified, not civilized; killed or resettled, not exploited.) As late as the mid-forties, he reminds us, the State Department openly sided with independence movements in India, Indochina, and Indonesia and gave support to a radical revolutionary party in China. General MacArthur, the hero of the American Right, used his imperial powers in occupied Japan to sponsor a controlled social revolution in which the landed nobility and the military who had run the country lost their power along with their land. Even in Latin America, where economic penetration under the slogan of "manifest destiny" ran deepest, the United States avoided falling into the colonialist mold. Unlike France or England, the United States did not seek to impose a civilization on those she dominated. Indeed, the countries that most successfully have assimilated the American idiom along with the supermarket and the superhighway are not the backward protectorates where the U.S. military bases dominated the economy, but the developed countries

of Western Europe, which, though respectful, if not subservient, in their foreign policies, are not colonies.

The leaders of independence movements at the end of
World War II helped to reinforce the National-Security
Manager's self-image as an anti-imperialist. Ho Chi Minh
borrowed the words of the Declaration of Independence
to embellish the constitution of the Democratic Republic
of Vietnam and like many other revolutionary politicians
regularly invoked the name of George Washington. Wen-
dell Willkie reported a seemingly inexhaustible "reservoir
of good will" for America among the nationalist leaders of
the world.

The National-Security Manager thus feels that both the
tradition and practice of American foreign policy set it
apart from the classic imperialist model. There is, to be
sure, an American military presence on every continent,
but it is designed neither to acquire territory, to service
the U.S. economy, nor to impose an American Way of
Life on others. Its sole purposes are, he maintains, to
assure the security of the United States and, where possible, to support those who will work for free societies.

To the National-Security Manager, peering out from
the seventh floor of the State Department, the Pentagon
War Room, or the Situation Room in the White House,
the world looks something like a seething caldron. The
eruption of violence makes him acutely uncomfortable,
for it threatens a status quo which, if left undisturbed,
promises to bring a steady appreciation of America's
preeminent wealth and power. Attracted by Litvinov's
prewar rhetoric about the "indivisibility" of peace, with its
anxiety-producing vision of the strong losing their power
by refusing to help the weak, the Managers have come to
feel that when the bell tolls for some corrupt but orderly
government in a far-off land, it is indeed tolling for them.
Whether the psychological roots of this anxiety are the
rich man's guilt in the face of starvation or the terror of
the comfortable in the midst of chronic desperation, the
national-security bureaucrats have taken the early Leninist
dogma that rebellion is contagious and made it an existential fear. Far too sophisticated to accept the "domino
theory" in literal terms, the National-Security Manager
feels that unless the forces of radical change unleashed by
two world wars and the breakup of old empires is held in
check, the United States cannot maintain its present
preeminent economic and political position.

Four

There must be law and order in the world. Violence cannot be tolerated. With these two propositions the National-Security Manager completes a familiar circuit. The powerful have always invoked the law to protect their power and property, and they have usually insisted on the right to help enforce that law themselves. The Pax Romana and Pax Britannica were primarily arrangements to protect Roman and British interests by creating a system of law and order in which those interests could thrive and by supplying the necessary military power to defend the system. Indeed, the word *"imperium"* itself in Roman times referred to the territory under the jurisdiction of the law of Rome. As a by-product, some other nations derived a measure of security. But that was hardly the primary purpose. The benefits flowing to the "world community" of their day were most unevenly distributed. Some peoples did well under imperial protection. Others were crushed. Since he feels no real responsibility to the world community or to any higher power on earth, because there is none, the imperial peacekeeper necessarily applies and enforces the law in a self-serving way. The higher community which American statesmen purport to serve is largely their own creation. In the early postwar days it was a subservient United Nations. Today it is a self-defined Free World.

The National-Security Manager assumes that U.S. interests and those of the rest of humanity coincide. Governments and political movements which contest this idea have ulterior and illegitimate motives. Far from a simple cynic who mouths idealistic rhetoric to mask economic plundering, the Manager sincerely believes that in opposing Third World revolutions the United States is both pursuing its self-interest and promoting the ultimate welfare of the world community. The fight against insurgent movements is rationalized into a continuing crusade for a decent world, the latest episode in the battle to make the world safe for democracy. What gives plausibility to this characterization is that modern insurgent movements, so U.S. leaders have argued, can be lumped with the Kaiser's invasion of Belgium and Hitler's aggression against Europe, for they are all *violent* challenges to the status quo. If, as the National-Security Managers see it, the inevitable involvement of international communism is the key factor that makes U.S. intervention against revolutions ultimately necessary for national survival, the use of violence by the insurgents is the key factor that makes it legally justifiable and morally right.

Like everyone else, the National-Security Manager looks at the issue of violence from a highly personal perspective. He is selective in the violence he notices and inconsistent in the moral judgments he makes about it. On November 23, 1946, for example, at the very moment when the State Department was preparing a major U.S. intervention against Greek "terrorists," a French naval squadron turned its guns on the civilian population of Haiphong and killed more than six thousand in an afternoon. The United States did not protest, much less intervene. Violence in behalf of the established order is judged by one set of criteria, insurgent violence by another. When established institutions kill through their police or their armies, it is regrettable but, by hypothesis, necessary. When the weak rise up and kill, their violence threatens order everywhere. Sympathetic as U.S. bureaucrats were with the objectives of the Hungarian freedom fighters in 1956, they breathed a sigh of relief when they were disarmed.

The National-Security Manager is aware that violence in other countries has political causes, but he sees no other immediate way to handle it than suppression. Reform, modernization, greater political and social justice are all necessary, he knows, to assure stable regimes where the status quo will not be overturned by force. But how can you begin this process unless the snipers and assassins are first rounded up? Once the wretched of the earth and the cynical politicians who manipulate their misery for their own ends are made to see that violence will not work, they may come to cooperate in finding less dangerous ways to political change.

In the long run, political passions will be cooled by the slow process of opening up new doors of opportunity—a revolution from the top. In the short run, those who are impatient with this prolonged prospect will be taught patience by the army or the police.

One reason why the National-Security Manager has such difficulty in coming to grips with the problem of political violence abroad is that, like most Americans, he has not confronted the issue in his own country. Until the wave of Negro riots struck American cities in the midsixties, he pictured his country as a tranquil island in a sea of violence. Because of its tradition of law and order, the United States was uniquely successful in avoiding the coups, rebellions, assassinations, and executions that plagued the rest of the world. The most perceptive foreign observers celebrated our good fortune. Writing in 1888, James Bryce noted that the poor "have had nothing to fight for, no grounds for disliking the well to do, no complaints to make against them."[14] Violence never played a role in American politics, according to tradition, because the system worked so well. Every few years the doors of opportunity have swung open to admit the lowest, the poorest, or the most recent arrivals to the national consensus.

There is enough validity to the national myth of equal opportunity that those who have risen to the top of American society are quite prepared to accept it. In such a well-regulated society, violence is not a phenomenon of politics, but of crime. Those who resort to it are unwilling to play a competitive game open to all but are trying to wreck the game and impose their own rules. The few attempts to practice the politics of violence in America have failed. The Wobblies, the KKK, the Confederacy, and the Whiskey Rebellion were all suppressed. The National-Security Manager cannot see why younger societies now undergoing economic and political development should not also suppress violent challenges from their own populations. And, in the name of order, the United States should help.

Behind the myth of unique tranquillity lies one of the most violent countries in the world. The United States has engaged in eight major wars and over one hundred minor ones in its brief history, including one of the bloodiest civil wars in history. In the one hundred years since that war, we have assassinated our Presidents regularly at twenty-year intervals, missing only Harding and Franklin Roosevelt who died in office. (Roosevelt and Truman were both targets of assassination attempts.) The murder rate is among the highest in the world. Other crimes against persons have reached staggering proportions. The United States spends far more on instruments of violence and on a class of specialists in violence than any other country. The stern-faced generals on pedestals in our parks; the aimless brutality of the animated cartoons; the endless flow of grenades, rockets, and burp guns to amuse the children; and the bloody fairy tales of television are random illustrations of the same point. The nation is held in horrified fascination by violence and those who practice it.

Frightened at the real violence in our midst, we Americans try to deny it by immersing ourselves in the fantasy of violence. Unlike the real world of violence, the violence of the fairy tale is either morally neutral or morally ambiguous. It can be without purpose and without consequence, like a firecracker exploding inside Donald Duck's tailfeathers. Or it can be a detective, cowboy, or other symbol of virtuous authority gunning down some depraved villain. In the fantasy world violence is thus either a harmless game or a just punishment. In the real world it is a necessary instrument to protect the public order in the hands of those with a right to use it. In the hands of those without such right it is the manifestation of a social sickness.[15] The National-Security Manager does not grasp or will not admit that there are societies—some, it now appears, even in our own country—where the channels of "peaceful change" have totally broken down or never existed. He professes to understand the causal connection between misery and violence but he cannot accept the legitimacy of the guerrilla, no matter how just his grievance. For the sake of world order he must be suppressed until safer paths to economic development and political justice can be found. As we shall see, the Revolutionary thinks of political violence in quite different terms. The gulf between the American bureaucrat and the radical Third World politician on this issue is a direct reflection of their fundamentally different visions of the process of political change.

The National-Security Manager builds his model of political and economic development for the "less-developed nations," as he tactfully calls them, from his own picture of American political development. Too sophisticated to think that the American system of government or economy is the answer to the problems of the

Third World or that, even if it were, it could be simply re-created in present societies, he nonetheless sees the process of change in American terms and believes that American techniques offer the only real hope. Projecting his own conception of the dynamics of American life, he concludes that change is primarily a technical rather than a political problem, one that calls for a slow turn of the wheel rather than a sudden jerk. Under the American System man has gone far to transcend political conflict. The "consensus society," a national myth long before President Johnson made it a political slogan, consists of more open channels of opportunities than have ever been available before in human society. As he sees it, old class conflicts and animosities that have torn apart other societies play no role in the land of the Melting Pot. That there is great inequality in American society is clear, but the faith in equal opportunity is a source of personal contentment and national pride for all but a small minority that is very poor and nonwhite.

According to his vision of social change in America, the United States has escaped class conflict because of its economic system, which makes it possible for each man to contribute to the general welfare by looking after his own. The government, he knows, plays a larger role than we care to advertise. But its function is to prime the pump and to stimulate the general growth of the economy, not to make a radical redistribution of political and economic power. The economy continues to grow because the system has learned how to harness technology.[16]

Looking at the underdeveloped world, the National-Security Manager assumes that what W. W. Rostow calls a "high-mass-consumption" society is the real ultimate goal of newly decolonized societies and a proper one. The best way to achieve the "takeoff" that can bring a modest version of the affluent society to poor nations is through technological innovation and the education of an entrepreneurial class that can supply the energy for change. The economic system that stimulates entrepreneurship is private enterprise. Therefore, the developing nations' "greatest need," as Chester Bowles has put it, is "private investment to aid the free sectors of their economies."[17]

Capital for the public sector of infant economies is likely to be wasted. It cannot be absorbed because the entrepreneurial classes who could invest it profitably do not yet exist. Corruption, waste, inefficiency, and political in-fighting all guarantee that grants of capital to new governments to be used to build planned economies would end up in Swiss bank accounts. The process of development is slow, but the attempt to speed it up through nationalization, confiscation, or other radical remedies would lead to the disasters of Stalinism. The National-Security Manager takes some comfort from the thought that the military of the Third World, the class that has most directly and handsomely benefited from U.S. aid around the world, are also the most promising entrepreneurs. In Latin America and parts of the Middle East the military have been "modernizing" influences. Furnished with U.S. training and equipment, they are the first in their societies to apply technology to public problems. They are now equipped for "civic action." The Department of Defense explains it this way: "As the interdependence of civil and military matters is increasingly recognized, the social and economic welfare of the people can no longer be considered a non-military concern."[18]

Five

There is hardly an assumption in this picture of change that the Revolutionary accepts.[19] To him the military represent not a force for "nation-building" but a praetorian guard for the most reactionary elements of his society. For every company of soldiers sent out to build a bridge or repair a hospital there are, he is sure, five or more roaming the countryside looking for political unreliables or hounding the forces of dissent and reform in the city.

In place of the optimistic assumption of gradual economic growth put forward by the National-Security Managers and their experts on "modernization," he sees the harsh reality of peasant life. After ten or fifteen years of U.S. military and economic aid and technical assistance his country is still essentially a one-crop country with an average per-capita income under two hundred dollars, a place where starvation and disease, despite a few local relief and health programs, continue to rise. Like most politicians of the Third World, he accepts the analysis of Raul Prebisch and most other non-American development economists that the gap between the poor nations and the rich is widening, not closing. He has seen country after country in Africa and Latin America fall before military coups. He notes that the professional, entrepreneurial classes on which the United States puts such faith carve out comfortable niches for themselves in the status quo rather than dedicate themselves to technological change. (In the early 1950's Brazilian universities turned out ten lawyers for every student of agriculture.[20]) Private enterprise, as he sees it, finances extractive industries in which both the riches of the earth and the profits they produce wind up in someone else's country. In short, instead of the grim but improving picture of the Third World that hangs in the office of the National-Security Manager, the Revolutionary sees only accelerating misery.

He has some figures to support what he sees with his eyes. The World Conferencee on Trade and Development which met in Geneva in March, 1964, revealed that the share of the underdeveloped countries in world exports declined from almost one-third in 1950 to slightly more than one-fifth in 1962.[21] At the same time, the prices of such primary products as coffee, cocoa, and tin, on which the economies of the underdeveloped world depend, have fallen drastically. Between 1959 and 1961 the price of coffee beans fell almost one-third. In 1965 Ghana could get only 371 dollars for a ton of cocoa. In 1954 the world price was 1,698 dollars.

According to the United Nations Secretariat, these trends mean that the annual gap between what the underdeveloped countries require merely to feed their expanding populations and what they can expect to earn from selling their products on the world market will steadily increase.[22] To the Revolutionary the statistics of starvation are a cry for radical change.

The Revolutionary is a man who is passionately concerned with the degradation of his people and who believes that he understands its cause. For the National-Security Manager underdevelopment is a fact of the natural order. There are lucky nations and unlucky ones, energetic creative peoples, and peoples whom history has passed by. Stifling the Calvinist impulse to call wealth virtue, the American bureaucrat is convinced that the misery of the underdeveloped world is no one's fault except possibly its own. Perhaps they were exploited in the past by imperialist nations, but they received a little civilization in return. If they would work harder, spend the money they do get on the people rather than on bribes and showy buildings, try to keep appointments, and not make irresponsible statements, they would get along better.

To the Revolutionary the growing poverty and desperation of his people is not a natural calamity but the direct consequence of continuing human exploitation—external and internal. The rich nations are getting richer at the expense of the poor, not because history decrees it, but because the developed countries, particularly the United States, have the political power to impose terms upon the underdeveloped world which are profitable for the rich and impoverishing for the poor.[23]

The Revolutionary is convinced that the very policies on which the United States banks its hopes of development actually destroy the possibilities of progress. He accuses the United States of using its foreign-aid funds to sponsor a small entrepreneurial elite who are able to pay for U.S.-manufactured imports, when, if it really wanted to encourage independent economies, it would finance local manufacturing facilities. (The trend is toward increased U.S. investment in factories, but local ownership is minimal.) The Revolutionary believes that his country is assigned a more or less permanent role in the world economy as the poor farmer and miner. Since the price of raw commodities can to a great extent be controlled by the powerful nations, this policy too ensures continued political dependence, with very little prospect of economic self-sufficiency.[24] He is convinced that these policies are deliberate attempts to continue a pattern of exploitation. That the world's greatest capitalist nation should turn out to be the most imperialist merely confirms his deepest ideological prejudices. The performance of the United States at the World Conference on Trade and Development when it voted—often alone among seventy-seven countries—against such propositions as "noninterference in the internal affairs of other countries," "the sovereign right freely to trade with other countries," and "to dispose of its natural resources in the interest of the economic development and well-being of its own people" provided additional evidence.[25] The United States, he is convinced, has economic and political interests that are adverse to the political and economic independence of his country.

The Revolutionry ascribes the plight of his country not only to foreign enemies, of which the greatest is the United States, but also to local enemies, the handful of landowners who maintain a subsistence economy for the peasants and resist land reform, the businessmen who bank their profits abroad and block any increased political power or earning power for the worker, and the military. Every revolutionary movement spreads the myth that the removal of a man or a class is all that stands in the way of progress and justice. But the local targets are plausible enough. In Brazil about five percent of the population owns ninety-five percent of the cultivable land. In every other country in Latin America over fifty percent of the productive land is still in the hands of the top four percent of the population.[26] The landowners resist land reform and are prepared to defend with the army and the police a land-tenure system surviving from the days of colonial land grants. Rebellious peasants, who have agitated for reform or have "squatted" on land, have, depending upon the character of the particular regime, been ignored, harassed, imprisoned, tortured, or murdered. "Each country is being occupied by its own army," the leader of the exiled Liberal party of Colombia declared in 1955. The Alliance for Progress, as President Kennedy put it, was to make the continent "a crucible of revolutionary ideas" and to "reverse the fatal policy of economic colonization, humiliation, and exploitation"[27] which led to the Castro revolution. But the owners of the *latifundia* have shown themselves unwilling to give up their immense economic advantages voluntarily. Land-reform legislation has been adopted in several Latin-American countries, but where it has been implemented at all, it has not begun to touch the problem. Since only five percent of Latin America's land surface is actually cultivated, and all but a small fraction of the population depend on the land for survival—in Brazil forty million out of the seventy million population are outside the cash economy[28]—in the Revolutionary's eyes the situation is clear. The physical survival of the poorest peasants demands a direct confrontation with the latifundists and the governments they control.

The concept of a revolution from above strikes him as a device for continuing the status quo, for in practice the burdens fall once again on the lowest classes. To accumulate capital necessary for an economic "takeoff," the government must be able to tax. But the landlord classes have been highly successful in resisting taxes in Asia, Africa, and Latin America. About three percent of the population pays taxes in Latin America and about one percent in Asia and Africa.[29] So widespread is the refusal to pay that taxation produces only between five and ten percent of the Gross National Product in the Third World.[30] As alternative sources of revenue, governments resort to indirect taxation and austerity programs, which depend upon wage freezes. The success of the rich in avoiding taxes goes a long way to explain why, in Brazil, for example, sixty-three percent of the income for 1957 went to seventeen percent of the population.[31]

Thus the word "stability," which to the National-Security Manager evokes the image of a well-run town or a happy family, falls on the Revolutionary's ears like a death sentence. He is convinced that trying to work within the present political framework is hopeless, for the landowners and the generals who serve them will never voluntarily relax their grip on the scarce resources and undeveloped riches of their country.

Six

The Revolutionary who becomes a guerrilla is a man who believes that all other avenues of political change are closed or the process of change is so controlled and slow as to be meaningless. Luis Taruc, the Philippine Huk leader, began a full-scale challenge of the government after he and other communists were denied the seats in parliament to which they had been legally elected.[32] The Greek communists and members of the South Vietnamese National Liberation Front began terrorist activities when the constituted governments declared them ineligible to participate in the political process and hunted them down as outlaws.[33] This is not to say that a revolutionary movement will not pursue a legal political struggle and a guerrilla war at the same time, if it can; but that violence, for the weak, is a weapon of last resort.

There is a strain in the revolutionary tradition that glorifies violence. In the nineteenth century some of the more romantic anarchists cherished the myth that a well-placed bomb could sweep away the tyrant and open the way to Utopia. In our day, Frantz Fanon, the West Indian psychiatrist who became an Algerian rebel, has struggled to shape an ideology of revolutionary violence. Acknowledging the fact that violence brings suffering to those who practice it, he declares that "decolonization is always a violent phenomenon." It is necessary for the Revolutionary, no matter how idealistic or civilized he is, to become a bomb-thrower and a sniper merely to defend himself against the state whose enemy he has become. The ruling elites will not give up their power and privilege without a fight.[34]

But beyond these traditional explanations for the role of violence in revolution, Fanon offers another. The "wretched of the earth" cannot develop the sense of identity, self-esteem, and political consciousness necessary to challenge the established order without the therapeutic effect of violence. When an intimidated native discovers that the White Man dies when he is shot, he senses within himself a new power. Just as in the American West, the gun becomes "the great equalizer." Once having committed a violent act against the state, the rebel develops the confidence and the anger to repeat it. During the civil war following the Bolshevik Revolution, Lenin noted that those who served in the army became the most militant. Similarly, today the existential condition of becoming an outlaw with a price on his head turns a man into a political radical. A man may start fighting because of a local grievance. He may demand land. He may have been cheated by the authorities. Or he may become a guerrilla because of the vision of achieving national independence from a foreign nation. The commitment to violence, once made, binds him closer to the community of rebels, for he has burned the bridges back to his old life. The only emotional, political, and often financial support now open to him comes from his co-conspirators. Sharing moments of high danger for a great cause creates the intense feelings of camaraderie that warriors have always celebrated. Some professional revolutionaries, therefore, consciously use violence as a technique for whipping up their supporters and increasing their number.

But the Revolutionary uses violence primarily as a political weapon against his enemy, the state, and he uses the particular technique of violence out of necessity. He is not strong enough in the beginning to engage the armies of the state in open battle, nor does he have the political strength to execute a quick coup d'état, the most common and successful form of political violence. As Peter Paret and John Shy have pointed out in the *Marine Corps Gazette*, "Seldom if ever has anyone deliberately chosen a guerrilla strategy when other choices existed. If sufficient military strength is available, conventional organization and tactics produce a decision more quickly; if the goal is political, strength makes possible a coup d'etat instead of a costly, protracted civil war."[35]

The Revolutionary thus begins by using terrorism to make a political point. Harold Laswell has called political assassination "propaganda of the deed." He quotes the letter received by Lord Kimberly, the viceroy of Dublin. "My Lord, we intend to kill you at the corner of Kildare Street; but we would like you to know there is nothing personal in it."[36] In the Huk rebellion, Taruc would arrange for a prominent citizen of a town to be murdered and his body displayed in the main street with a tag, "He resisted the Huks."[37] The Vietcong assassinations in Vietnam, at least until the arrival of the American expeditionary force, were directed against the symbols of the state—teachers, village chiefs, and health officials. In many cases there *was* something personal behind it. The NFL often pinned a note to the shirt of a murdered official listing his crimes. It attempted to explain every killing.[38]

Terror is sometimes used by guerrilla movements to encourage the cooperation of the surrounding population. In the official ideology of the National-Security Manager, this is a convenient explanation for the civilian support which guerrilla armies must have to survive. It disposes of the problem. Thus, according to Robert McNamara, guerrilla movements are gaining "for very simple reasons known as guns, bombs, fighters, and threats."[39] But, as men who have been through a guerrilla war testify, terror has very definite limitations as a political instrument. Che Guevara, the theorist of the Cuban Revolution and adviser to many insurgent movements in Latin America, noted that terrorism "is a negative weapon which produces in no way the desired effects, which can turn a people against a given revolutionary movement. ..."[40] Actual enemies, particularly those who have defected, must be "justly punished," but supporters can be recruited only if they want to fight. An army that fights only out of fear of its own leaders cannot carry out a revolution.

For the Revolutionary, the ultimate and most important use of violence is to disrupt the power of the state, then to smash it. Mao Tse-tung and the more recent theorists of revolution insist that the revolutionary forces must eventually become an army capable of seizing the apparatus of the state. While the orthodox Marxist revolutionaries, including Mao, taught that the revolutionary army was an instrument of the political party, younger revolutionaries including Castro and Regis Debray now argue that the revolutionary army itself, the men who are daily risking their lives, is the nucleus of the revolutionary movement. "Who will make the revolution in Latin America?" Fidel Castro asks. "The people, the revolutionaries, with or without the party."[41] For the modern generation of revolutionaries, violence has assumed the central role.

Fanon's encounters with patients who have committed acts of violence suggest that for the individual revolutionary, violence creates personal moral problems. At the ideological level, however, the Revolutionary disposes of the problem with the same psychological devices which the National-Security Manager uses to defend to himself and others his own use of violence. First, the violence is provoked. If the revolutionaries throw the first bomb, it must be understood as a reaction to the continuing institutionalized violence of the state. The authorities use the police and the army every day to keep the dispossessed peasant below the level of subsistence. His children starve. His crop is stolen. He is the victim of arbitrary arrest. Second, the people and not the authorities temporarily in control of the state have the legitimate claim to use violence. The state has forfeited it by becoming the private preserve of a small class. The National Front, the revolutionary coalition, represents popular aspirations, and the closest thing to a consensus in the society. Thus the revolutionaries lay claim to the basis of legitimacy for the use of political violence, which the state has lost through corruption or tyrannical behavior. If the revolutionaries look like bandits to the men in the palace, the high-living generals and politicians look like thieves and murderers to the men in the hills. Finally, the Revolutionary justifies violence with the familiar argument of expediency. It is a necessary means to a good end. Once the oppressors have been dislodged from power and the enemies of the revolution liquidated, then a good society free of terror and violence can come into being. If the state does not wither away, at least state repression will. In the end, liberation will mean that many violent deaths will have been avoided. Just as the National-Security Manager justifies the use of napalm, antipersonnel bombs, and crop destroyers as the necessary preparation for a peaceful society, so the Revolutionary shares the same guilt-assuaging illusion. Violence can be controlled. Once the objectives for which the killing is done are achieved, the killing will stop.

NOTES—CHAPTER TWO

1. During the history of the Cold War, the ideological struggle has been variously characterized in official rhetoric as a fight between "freedom" and "totalitarianism," between a "world of diversity" and a "world of coercion," and as an "irreconcilable clash of two systems." While these convictions have fired statesmen to greater struggle, they have not been the basis of policy. The Soviet Union and the United States have few basic disagreements, for example, as to what present Egyptian society should look like. They disagree primarily as to which of them should be the dominant foreign influence there, and such policies as each recommends to the Egyptians are designed, to a large extent, to enhance its own role. The revolutionary, on the other hand, has very definite ideas about what his society should *not* look like, even if he has few concrete ideas as to how to achieve the changes he would like to see. (See David Apter, *The Politics of Modernization,* Chicago, 1965.) Unlike either of the Great Powers, the revolutionary's primary interest is in changing a society. Where his vision of his society clashes with the American vision there is conflict.

2. U.S. policy on making capital available to underdeveloped countries has remained essentially as recommended in the *Report to the President on Foreign Economic Policy,* commonly known as the *Gordon Gray Report:* "In contrast to the large-scale grants required to assist in the recovery and rearmament of Europe, the size of grant aid needed to support development is limited." (*Report to the President on Foreign Economic Policy,* Washington, D.C., 1950, pp. 66–67.) The definition of "limited" has become increasingly stringent as loans have replaced grants. (See David A. Baldwin, *Foreign Aid and American Foreign Policy,* New York, 1966.) Between 1946 and 1965 grants for economic development totaled $1.8 billion out of a

total program of economic aid, i.e., unmilitary, of $69 billion. (See "AID Summary Report," quoted in Baldwin, *Foreign Aid*, p. 31.)

3. The terms "revolution," "civil war," and "insurgency" are not precise. A civil war can involve any two or more contending factions in a society. A revolution, as the term is used in this book, refers to an organized effort of a group to overthrow the established order with a view to bringing about a radical change in the economic or social system. Most of the revolutions described in this book were organized by peasant leaders or by middle-class leaders, including military officers, for the benefit of classes hitherto excluded from participation in the political process. Such revolutions should also be distinguished from coups d'état, which are designed to change personnel holding leadership positions without basically changing the political or economic system.

4. For a description of official thinking on "balance of power" and "power vacuums," see McGeorge Bundy, ed., *The Pattern of Responsibility* (Boston, 1951). An interpretation of the Cold War informed by the "balance of power" view of the world can be found in Louis Halle, *The Cold War as History* (New York, 1967). Mr. Halle was a member of the Policy Planning Staff during the Truman administration.

5. *The New York Times*, November 2, 1966.

6. *Ibid.*

7. At the Geneva Conference in 1954, Under Secretary of State Walter B. Smith squeezed Chou En-lai's elbow upon greeting him as a substitute for the proscribed handshake.

8. John F. Kennedy, *The Strategy of Peace* (New York, 1961), p. 52.

9. William C. Bullitt, quoted in Carl Oglesby and Richard Shaull, *Containment and Change: Two Dissenting Views of American Society and Foreign Policy in the New Revolutionary Age* (New York, 1967), p. 30.

10. Dean Rusk, quoted in Ronald Steel, *Pax Americana* (New York, 1967), p. 129.

11. John F. Kennedy, quoted in Arthur Schlesinger, Jr., *A Thousand Days: John F. Kennedy in the White House* (Boston, 1965), p. 507.

12. John J. McCloy, "Foreign Economic Policy and Objectives," in *Goals for Americans* (New York, 1960), p. 342.

13. For an insight into the way national-security bureaucrats looked at the Third World, even in the early Kennedy period when "uncommitted nations" were identified as a special concern of the new administration, see Schlesinger, *A Thousand Days*, p. 508, where a task of his fellow White House assistant, Robert Komer, is characterized: "Robert Komer . . . patrolled the gray areas from Casablanca to New Guinea."

14. James Bryce quoted in Irving Louis Horowitz, *Three Worlds of Development* (New York, 1966), p. 80.

15. For a compelling analysis of American perceptions of

violence, based on comparisons of U.S. and foreign films, see Nathan C. Leites and Martha Wolfenstein, *Movies: A Psychological Study* (Glencoe, Ill., 1950), especially pp. 176–179.

16. For accounts of prevailing U.S. views of development and how to achieve it, see W. W. Rostow, *Stages of Economic Growth: A Non-Communist Manifesto* (Cambridge, England, 1960), especially chs. II and VI; Edward S. Mason, *Foreign Aid and Foreign Policy* (New York, 1964); John Kenneth Galbraith, *Economic Development in Perspective* (Cambridge, Mass., 1962). See also Albert O. Hirshmann, *The Strategy of Economic Development* (New Haven, 1958).

17. Chester Bowles, "The Developing Nations' Greatest Need," *The New York Times Magazine*, April 12, 1964, p. 15.

18. For a discussion of official U.S. attitudes toward the role of the military in underdeveloped countries, see Horowitz, *Three Worlds*, pp. 420–425.

19. For discussions of the ideology of revolutionaries of the Third World, see *ibid.*, chs. 7–10; Paul Sigmund. *The Ideologies of the Developing Nations* (New York, 1964); Ho Chi Minh, *Oeuvres Choisis* (3 vols.; editions en langue étrangère; Hanoi, 1962); Kwame Nkrumah, *Neo-Imperialism*; Luis Taruc, *Born of the People* (New York, 1953).

20. The statistics on Brazilian universities are reported in David Nasatir, "University and Politics in Latin America," quoted in Horowitz, *Three Worlds*, p. 405.

21. The decline in the underdeveloped countries' share of exports is reported in *ibid.*, pp. 168–169. See also United Nations, Conference on Trade and Development, *Final Act* (E/Conf. 46/ L.28), June 16, 1964, Section III, p. 8.

22. The $20-billion gap is discussed in Horowitz, *Three Worlds*, p. 170. See also Raul Prebisch, *Towards a New Trade Policy for Development* (New York, 1964).

23. For a summary of Third World attitudes toward U.S. policy on development, see Horowitz, *Three Worlds*, pp. 164–192.

24. For an account of the fall of the price of raw materials see Albert-Paul Lentin, *La Lutte Tricontinentale: Impérialisme et Révolution après la Conférence de La Havane* (Paris, 1966), p. 100.

25. An account of U.S. voting at the conference can be found in Horowitz, *Three Worlds*, pp. 164–192.

26. Figures on concentration of landownership, like figures on per-capita income in underdeveloped countries, are only approximate. One half of the arable farmland in Brazil is owned by 1.6 percent of the population. I have relied on the figures of Peter Nehemkis, *Latin America: Myth and Reality* (New York, 1966), ch. IV. He bases his account on reports of the Inter-American Development Bank and the UN Department of Economic Affairs.

27. Address of John F. Kennedy at Punta del Este, March 13, 1961.

28. For figures on Brazilian economy, see Nehemkis, *Latin America*, pp. 143, 146.

29. For figures on payment of taxes, see Horowitz, *Three Worlds*, pp. 199-200.

30. In 1966 in the United States, federal and state tax revenues amounted to almost 30 per cent of the gross national product. (Department of Commerce, Bureau of the Census, *Statistical Abstract of the United States*, 1966, Washington, D.C., 1967, pp. 319, 396, 400.)

31. In the United States in 1965, the top fifth of the population received 41 percent of the aggregate income of the country. (*Statistical Abstract*, 1966, p. 333.)

32. For Taruc's own account of how he moved from reformer to revolutionary, see "Taruc-Roxas Correspondence," in *Far Eastern Survey*, XV (1946), pp. 314–317. See also Luis Taruc, *Born of the People*.

33. For an account of the recruitment of Vietcong guerrillas, see Douglas Pike, *Viet Cong* (Cambridge, Mass., 1966), p. 291.

34. For a psychological and political analysis of revolutionary elites, see Harold D. Laswell and Daniel Lerner, eds., *World Revolutionary Elites* (Cambridge, Mass., 1966), especially chs. VI and VII.

35. Peter Paret and John W. Shy, "Guerrilla Warfare and U.S. Military Policy: A Study," reprinted in Lieutenant Colonel T. N. Greene, ed., *The Guerrilla, and How to Fight Him* (New York, 1962), p. 40.

36. Quoted in Harold Laswell, *Politics* (Cleveland, 1958), p. 155.

37. Brian Crozier, *The Rebels: A Study of Post-War Insurrections* (Boston, 1960), p. 39.

38. The attempt by the NLF to explain its assassination is described in Pike, *Viet Cong*, p. 250.

39. Robert McNamara, quoted in Peter Paret and John W. Shy, *Guerrillas in the Sixties* (New York, 1962), p. 62.

40. Che Guevara, quoted in Paret and Shy, *Guerrillas*, p. 34.

41. Fidel Castro, quoted in Regis Debray, *Révolution dans la Révolution* (Paris, 1967), p. 103.

CHAPTER **3**

The Roots of Revolution

One

THE NATIONAL-SECURITY MANAGER and the Revolutionary view the conflict between them from such different perspectives that neither credits the other with believing his own rhetoric. "How can the leaders of the most powerful nation in the world, probably in the history of the world, see guerrilla bands in faraway places as threats to their national security?" the Revolutionary asks. The President of the United States can't be serious when he claims to fear that communists, once victorious in Vietnam, will pursue the U.S. army to Hawaii and San Francisco. If the Americans are dedicated to building democracy, why don't they start with the dispossessed of their own country? Completely skeptical of the layers of official explanation, he concludes that the real reason the United States opposes his attempt to seize power in his own country is economic imperialism.

The American bureaucrat asks, "How can the guerrilla leader really be the nationalist patriot he pretends to be when he is engaged in wrecking fragile new societies, killing government officials, and blocking government programs?" "If the guerrillas really represented the nation, they would not insist on a monopoly of power for themselves, but would be ready to work with coalitions and not subvert them." Since they regularly commit what Walt

Rostow calls "crude acts of international vandalism"[1] by getting outside aid from communist countries, since they are seeking to impose communism on the underdeveloped world, which is a "serious disease," they stand revealed as modern-day Quislings, ready to betray their countries into the hands of Russia, China, or some other predatory power.

On no issue is the ideological gulf wider than on the question of revolution itself. As we have seen, the American bureaucrat is reluctant to apply the term to modern guerrilla war, for "revolution" connotes an act of political violence that is both spontaneous and indigenous. Communist insurgency, he insists, is always manipulated violence. The local soil may be ripe for revolution, but the insurgent leader, if he is a communist, is the agent or dupe of a foreign power. He may call himself a patriot, a nationalist, a guerrilla, but he is really a fifth columnist, because his primary allegiance is not to the people he purports to lead.

In this chapter and the one that follows we will attempt to examine these assumptions. In this chapter we are looking for answers to several questions. How do revolutions start? Why does a man become a revolutionary? What is the role of foreign ideas, foreign arms, and foreign money? When is the revolution indigenous?[2] In the chapter following we shall look specifically at the role of communism in various revolutions and insurgencies during the past 50 years.

The romantic conception of revolution—an avenging whirlwind of popular feeling suddenly and spontaneously blowing up against unbearable oppression—is one that is hard for a democrat to be against. One cannot imagine a clearer expression of the popular will. But it is an unreal standard by which to judge political violence. Except for a few slave revolts, riots, and impromptu rebellions with limited consequences, revolutions do not happen spontaneously. They are products of organization and elite direction, and they always require some sort of outside intervention. Existential misery in itself is not sufficient to galvanize a peasant population into a revolutionary army. People do not normally make the desperate decision to cut themselves off from their own society, to make a sustained fight against the established order, and so to make the risk of death part of their daily life unless some event has convinced them that revolution is the only alternative and some person has shown them how it might be accomplished. For centuries men have lived in far worse conditions than the peasants of Cuba, Vietnam, Russia, or China without lifting a finger against the government. Even today in India and some parts of Latin America widespread starvation is a characteristic of so-called "stable" societies.

The evidence strongly suggests that most men do not take to the hills against the government unless they feel personally and deeply aggrieved.[3] In the absence of such disaffection, the most skilled revolutionary agitator cannot persuade a man to leave his family and the village of his birth to live the life of a guerrilla. In short, something extraordinary must happen to a peasant who has accepted the age-old exploitation and poverty of his village to convince him that these conditions now amount to intolerable injustice. It is a process that cannot be explained in terms of terror and propaganda, although both may be present. Nor can he be terrorized into supporting the guerrillas unless the area is in fact administered by the insurgents rather than the government. And for this to occur, the guerrillas must win the confidence of a significant part of the population, through patient organization of the villages and the demonstration of some immediate benefits, such as land reform or education.

The authorities of the established order themselves play a crucial role in turning peasants into guerrillas. Aristotle pointed out that "insult" is the primary condition that provokes rebellion. Men will put up with egregious exploitation as long as it seems dictated by the natural order. It is only when economic misery can be traced to human injustice that the possibility of a political remedy emerges. The man who turns to political violence has often suffered violence at the hands of the state. In 1947 William H. McNeill and his associates interviewed Greek guerrillas fighting in the hills during the civil war. They found a "notable upsurge in recruitment" of guerrillas after the government carried out "mass arrests and deportations without trial" in March, 1947:

> The men talked earnestly and quietly of the reasons why they had taken to the hills. Without exception they said the Rightist terror had driven them there. One by one they related details of violence against

themselves or members of their families, or imprisonment or killings by Rightists.[4]

In Vietnam and throughout Latin America and parts of Africa, the established authorities by bringing violence and repression to the villages have helped to create revolutionaries.

To become a revolutionary, a peasant must be attracted by some alternative vision. He must be convinced that fighting can lead to something better, no matter how vague the revolutionary program may be. Here foreign intervention plays an important role. The intrusion of wholly new ideas such as economic development or political democracy, many of which have been spread by American technology and propaganda, raises expectations and increases dissatisfaction. The disparity between promises and performance, between rhetoric and reality, creates the political climate in which men can perceive injustice.

Thus, by promoting the rhetoric of freedom and the vision of the abundant life around the world, the United States itself has helped stir up revolution. For the Revolutionary, however, communist countries provide a more obvious and directly applicable example. The American economic system is beyond emulation for most poor countries, because its essential elements—capital, technological skill, and a literate population—are missing. Russia and China, on the other hand, appear to offer a plausible technique for transforming backward countries into industrial nations.

Every revolution has derived inspiration from abroad. The French Revolution borrowed ideas from Thomas Jefferson and Thomas Paine. The Russian Revolution was inspired by German radicals. The major ideological components of communism are standard equipment in the revolutionary programs of the Third World. These subversive ideas figure prominently in the speeches of noncommunist nationalists as well as those revolutionaries who view themselves as part of a communist movement. Men like Senghor, Nasser, and U Nu have accepted many of the basic propositions of Marxist-Leninist analysis. Capitalism is responsible for colonial exploitation. Socialism with state planning is essential. A single party must rule. The collective must be favored over the individual. There is no doubt that the principal intellectual influences on the postwar generation of revolutionaries have been Lenin, Mao, and other theorists of communism.

The communists themselves learned in the midst of their success in Russia that revolution, contrary to what Trotsky believed, cannot be spread by example. Revolutionary ideas travel; revolutions do not. As we shall see in the next chapter, a successful revolution in one country may incite rebels in other countries to attempt to make their own, but the outcome will depend entirely on local conditions. What are the conditions that make revolution possible? Why is it that in some countries economic misery and political exploitation can continue for years without serious revolt?

In his study of peasant revolutions, Barrington Moore advances the thesis that the vulnerability of a society to revolution depends upon whether it is "highly segmented" or "depends on a central authority."[5] The more centralized the power, the more likely a revolution. He also suggests that where the landed aristocracy is unable to make the transition to a commercial society but tries to "maintain its style of life in a changing world by extracting a larger surplus out of the peasantry," a serious revolutionary potential exists.

Before a revolution actually breaks out, however, some outside catastrophe usually overtakes the state and undermines its ability to enforce the traditional law and order which support the privileges of the dominant classes. In most of the revolutions of the past fifty years war has served that function. World War I completed the process of demoralization and exhaustion of the czarist bureaucracy, leaving its short-lived successor, the Kerensky government, prey to an almost bloodless Bolshevik coup. The Japanese invasion disrupted the Kuomintang's weak political control over China and made Mao's victory possible. In the Philippines, Vietnam, Greece, Malaya, Indonesia. Yugoslavia, and elsewhere foreign invasion undermined the control of the old elites and opened the political process to new forces. Resistance movements against the Nazi and Japanese invader, flying the banners of nationalism and radical social change together, became the avenue to power for men who never participated in the political process under the prewar regime.

In many countries war liberated the disenfranchised from the oppressive rule of their governments and for the first time gave them the exhilarating idea that through organization and violence they could bring about political change. Other sudden disruptions of the old society, such as the precipitous end of a colonial administration, the defection of the army, or a natural disaster such as a massive crop failure, may also provide the sparks of revolution. But without organization and political direction the insurrection cannot maintain itself, much less succeed. The issue of leadership is the crucial one.

Two

The United States has based its opposition to revolutions in the postwar world on the character and allegiance of their leadership. Most of the coups, rebellions, and civil wars that have erupted in the last twenty years have concerned tribal, religious, or sectional rivalries and have not elicited an American response. Where, however, an insurgent group or a revolutionary regime has attempted radical social change, even suggesting a communist influence, the United States has sooner or later intervened against it on the grounds that the revolutionaries were acting for a foreign power.

Whether a revolutionary leader owes allegiance to an indigenous movement or to a foreign power is of the greatest political and legal significance. Under the present system of international law the constituted authority of the state can lawfully receive outside aid to put down a "rebellion," but not if the insurgents are strong enough to maintain a protracted "civil war." Then outside states must not intervene unless it can be shown that one of the factions in the "civil war" is really under the control and direction of a foreign state. In that case, as the United States has argued in the Vietnam war, what purports to be a locally based civil war is actually a sophisticated form of foreign invasion, which other nations have a right to oppose.[6]

But while the legal issues of intervention in civil war are rather murky, the political tradition on this question is much clearer. In democratic countries, at least, there is a strong feeling that intervention against local revolutions is a reactionary policy reminiscent of the Holy Alliance. Indeed, until the present era, popular sympathy in the United States has historically been with the revolutionaries. President Millard Fillmore gave Louis Kossuth his good wishes (but nothing else) when the Hungarian revolutionary called at the White House.

Despite the sweeping language of the Johnson Doctrine, which purports to obliterate the distinction between civil wars and international wars, no U.S. leader has yet declared that America has a mandate to suppress all revolution. On the other hand, the United States has chosen to treat virtually any insurgency with a radical leftist orientation as if it were an invasion by Trojan horse.

Let us look for a moment at the communist revolutionaries with whom the United States has been locked in combat. How and why did they decide to commit their lives to the overthrow of the old regimes? Several of them, including Luis Taruc, the Huk leader, and Vafiades Markos, the leader of the Greek insurgency of 1946-49, came to power in World War II resistance movements. Like most revolutionaries, each had spent some time in jail. Each had been a rebel before the war. But the war was the opportunity to transform personal feelings of disaffection into a political movement. The resistance movement gave them legitimate and easy access to weapons and to power over masses of their countrymen. None of these men began to act at the behest of a foreign power or international movement, although each received some help after he had made his own commitment to seize political power by force of arms. Castro became increasingly radical in the ten years before his guerrilla movement wrested power from the Batista government in 1959, a regime which the Cuban Communist party continued to support up to a few months before Castro installed himself in Havana. There is some evidence that as early as 1948 he was helping to incite riots in Colombia, where also he took the communists by surprise, and that beginning in 1955 he worked with some veteran communists like Alberto Bayo. But it does not appear that Castro's views were revolutionary until 1952, when he lost a bid for a Senate seat in a rigged election. The main support of his movement came from the Cuban middle classes and was distinctly noncommunist. Castro, who himself turned a small guerrilla operation into a spontaneous mass uprising, has always been more optimistic about exporting revolution than traditionally cautious old-line communist functionaries. He has outfitted and dispatched guerrilla expeditions to Venezuela, Bolivia, and Nicaragua and has found himself under growing attacks from the orthodox communist parties for these tactics.

Ho Chi Minh was a schoolboy rebel at fifteen, a participant in nationalist insurrectionary movements in Hue, years before he first came in contact with Marxism or the Communist party. He traveled to Europe at the time of World War I to agitate for Vietnamese independence from France. He describes his own earliest connections with Leninism:

> Immediately after the first world war I was working in Paris. . . . At this time I often used to distribute pamphlets denouncing the evils of colonialism. I supported the October Revolution simply out of a sort of spontaneous sympathy. . . . I liked and respected Lenin simply because he was a great patriot who had freed his people. I had not then read any of his works. . . . Thus it was patriotism and not communism that caused me to believe in Leninism and the third international. Little by little, progressing step by step, in the course of struggle in which I combined theoretical study and practical work, I came to understand that only socialism and communism can liberate the oppressed and the workers of the whole world.[7]

Despite years spent in Moscow, service as a Comintern agent in China, and participation in international communist meetings in the years before World War II, Ho never shifted his primary goal, the independence of Vietnam, nor his primary allegiance, the Vietnamese people. True, he was quite capable of eliminating political rivals who also called themselves nationalists. But in the course of his long career he came into direct conflict with the Russian and French Communist parties and openly opposed them when they did not support Vietnamese independence. In 1946 the French communists opposed Vietnamese independence. Returning from France, Ho denounced Maurice Thorez, the communist vice-premier of France, for his "most remarkable opinion" that the

French flag should continue to fly over Indochina. In the same years he often complained that the Soviet Union was not supporting his independence struggle, which of course was true. The difference between a nationalist revolutionary who embraces communism and a Communist-party agent are quite clearly revealed by comparing the subservience of, say, the French Communist party to the labyrinthine course of the Moscow line with Ho's singleminded pursuit of local political goals irrespective of major shifts in Kremlin policy.

Three

The Revolutionary, above all, is obsessed with the fate of a place. While he may have the incredible patience of a Ho Chi Minh and be prepared to fight for a generation, his eyes are firmly fixed on the here and now. He wants to liberate his country. Why one man makes the irrevocable commitment to radical change and leads a revolution while another accommodates himself to a corrupt society must be answered in terms of individual psychology rather than economic class. Most of the communist revolutionary leaders have come from middle-class professional families. Indeed, the leadership of the national-liberation movements around the world is filled with doctors, lawyers, and history teachers. Why do they do it? For the excitement of it, Robert McNamara has suggested. Perhaps. But the revolutionary leader is rather restricted in his future career opportunities. It is not easy to rejoin the society from which he has voluntarily exiled himself. Even after seizing power he must tread the tightrope that separates the palace from the prison. The stakes are supremely high. He must win, for the alternative is death. There is nothing we know of the character of the modern revolutionary leader to suggest that the decision to become one is frivolously made. It may well be, as some American scholars have suggested, that the underlying motives are far from heroic. A man may become a revolutionary because of a thirst for power, a search for personal identity, or a strong feeling of guilt. But whatever the personal reasons, the Revolutionary is filled with a sense of himself. To an extraordinary extent, the Titos, Castros, and Hos are their own men.[8]

In what sense, then, are they part of the communist movement? In seizing power, communist doctrine was a source of inspiration. Hardly a blueprint for local action, as each Revolutionary has found, the writings of the communist theorists proclaim the inevitability of revolution, which is no small boost to the morale of a ragged band of rebels hiding in the jungles or the hills. Communist doctrine also offers a dogma through which one can identify friends and enemies and can plan a strategy of revolution. Moreover, it offers a plausible vision of the good society. Finally, there is really no other body of theory to which to turn. For the last fifty years it has been hard to find writers on the practice of revolution who have not in some way been connected with communism. But each revolutionary leader has had to take communist dogma and adapt it to his own local conditions. As Regis Debray pointed out in *Révolution dans la Révolution,* the Russian Social Democrats "instinctively thought in terms of repeating the Paris Commune in Petrograd; the Chinese Communists in terms of repeating the Russian October Revolution in the Canton of the 20's; and the Vietnamese comrades, a year after the foundation of their party, in terms of organizing insurrections of peasant soviets in the northern part of their country."[9] Each Revolutionary began by applying the closest model of a successful revolution and ended by improvising.

As we shall see more clearly in the next chapter, the Revolutionary is not seeking advice, much less direction, from abroad so much as material aid. Once the revolution has been launched, and its leaders seek outside help to support and protect it, the situation becomes more complicated. Every insurgent movement has sought foreign assistance, and most have received it in some form or other. Lafayette and Kosciusko led contingents of French and Poles in support of the American rebels. Admiral de Grasse's fleet helped win the decisive victory. Ordinarily the Revolutionary must demonstrate his own power before outsiders will intervene on his side. Castro did not receive Soviet aid until he had successfully overthrown the Batista regime. Ho fought the French for almost three years

before he received substantial Soviet or Chinese aid. The
Greek guerrillas fought for almost two years before Yugoslav weapons and supplies became a critical factor. Indeed, revolutionary movements are outfitted at first with
weapons from the local enemy rather than outside friends.
In China, Cuba, and Vietnam the revolutionary armies
began their drives with weapons captured from the governments they were fighting. Mao Tse-tung attributed his
success to the fact that Nationalist troops trained and
armed by the United States "changed hats"[10] and joined
the rebel side. Hundreds of Vietminh soldiers received
training in guerrilla warfare during World War II at a
camp run by Chiang Kai-shek's army and secured most of
their weapons from that source. The late leader of the
Guatemalan communist guerrilla army, Luis Turcios, was
an honor graduate of the U.S. Army Ranger School at
Fort Benning, Georgia. Where a foreign government is
sending the legitimate authorities military aid, the Revolutionary makes greater efforts to enlist outside arms to
offset it. He also seeks the use of neighboring territory as
a sanctuary for his guerrilla forces. In Greece and Vietnam, neighboring communist governments have helped
local revolutionaries in this way.

But the relationship between the local Revolutionary
and the foreign power who gives him aid is a highly
ambivalent one. The Revolutionary always starts from a
position of great weakness and needs help. But unlike
the international communist bureaucrat, secret agent,
Quisling, or fifth columnist, his power base is indigenous.
Ultimately he will stand or fall on the support he is able
to get from the local population and the defections to his
cause. Quite different from the puppet who is installed by
a foreign invading army, as were early postwar regimes in
Eastern Europe and North Korea, the indigenous Revolutionary—Tito, Castro, Hoxa, or Ho—fiercely guards his
independence. Typically he is both more radical and more
militant than the Soviet communist leadership, but his
views are his own, for he has made his own revolution.

Why does one communist country of movement help
another? As we shall see in the next chapter, Russia has
been cautious in giving aid, providing it to local communists only when her political control was assured. China,
with relatively little to give, has also used assistance to
insurgents more as a weapon of foreign policy than as an
expression of ideological solidarity. The generation of

guerrilla leaders that has become active in the last five years have different attitudes toward cooperation. The split among the large communist powers has given smaller radical insurgent movements more flexibility to work out arrangements with one another and to give mutual aid. Castro has set the example for other revolutionary leaders by showing a strong ideological commitment to the spread of revolution and by helping to equip rebel bands in other countries. Committees which attempt to act as clearing houses for various guerrilla movements have been established. Representatives from many different movements meet each other from time to time at conferences, which are usually held in Havana. They also seek to learn from each other's war experiences. The Guatemalan National Liberation Front, for example, has appointed one of its leaders chairman of the "Guatemala Committee for Solidarity with Vietnam" and sent him to Hanoi to act as an observer. While such activity is increasing in many places around the world, insurgent movements with few exceptions are still very weak.[11]

The United States has succeeded in fulfilling its own prophecy. All radical insurgent leaders throughout Asia, Africa, and Latin America see the United States as the common enemy. Not only does America support the army and the police, but United States soldiers have been engaged in actual combat against rebels.[12] General Robert W. Porter, Jr., has reported to the House Foreign Affairs Committee that United States rangers have been in battle against the forces of Yon Sosa and César Montes, the two Guatemalan guerrilla leaders. Green Berets have also been in combat in Colombia and Thailand as "advisers," and the CIA has flown missions for the Portuguese in Mozambique.[13] The ubiquitous United States military presence has been the stimulus to revolutionary solidarity. Although hard to achieve in practice, a new theory of revolutionary internationalism is growing. One of Hugo Blanco's followers in Peru explained it this way to a *Newsweek* correspondent:

We wanted a quick victory. Now we know that the United States will never allow us that luxury, so we prepare for the long slow fight ahead. . . . We must coordinate our efforts, not just ourselves in Peru, but throughout Latin America. We are nationalists but the only way to win for us in Latin America is to become

internationalists. The United States cannot win Viet-
nams in eight different countries at the same time. We
must begin to think in new terms: that the poor of the
world are at war against the rich.[14]

NOTES—CHAPTER THREE

1. W. W. Rostow, "Guerrilla Warfare in Under-Developed
Areas," in Lieutenant Colonel T. N. Greene, ed., *The Guerrilla,
and How to Fight Him* (New York, 1962), pp. 54–63.

2. For discussions of the theory and dynamics of revolution,
see Hannah Arendt, *On Revolution*; Crane Brinton, *The Anat-
omy of Revolution* (rev. ed.; New York, 1952); Chalmers
Johnson, *Peasant Nationalism and Communist Power; The
Emergence of Revolutionary China* (Stanford, Calif., 1962).

3. For a discussion of the personality and background of
some of the leaders of postwar revolutions, see Brian Crozier,
The Rebels: A Study of Post-War Insurrection (Boston, 1960).

4. William H. McNeill and Elizabeth D. McNeill, *Report on
the Greeks* (New York, 1948), p. 155.

5. Moore's thesis is to be found in Barrington Moore, *Social
Origins of Dictatorship and Democracy* (Boston, 1966), ch. IX,
especially pp. 459–460.

6. For a discussion of the legal issues relating to intervention, civil war, and revolutions, see Richard A. Falk, "Janus
Tormented: The International Law of Internal War," in James
N. Rosenau, ed., *International Aspects of Civil Strife* (Princeton, 1964), pp. 185–240, especially pp. 197ff.

7. Ho Chi Minh, quoted in Jean La Couture, *Ho Chi Minh*
(Paris, 1967), p. 25.

8. For an attempt to relate revolutionary ideology to personal psychological need, see Lucian Pye, *Politics, Personality
and Nation Building* (New Haven, 1962).

9. Regis Debray, *Révolution dans la Révolution* (Paris,
1967), p. 16.

10. Interview of Mao Tse-tung with Edgar Snow, quoted in
Franz Schurmann and Orville Schell, *Communist China*, vol. III
in *The China Reader* (New York, 1967), p. 372.

11. For description of efforts at cooperation among revolutionary movements, see Albert-Paul Lentin, *La Lutte Tricontinentale: Impérialisme et Révolution après la Conférence de La
Havane* (Paris, 1966), pp. 265–310.

12. Peace Corps volunteers, newspapermen, and clergy returning from Latin America have reported observing contingents
of U.S. special-forces teams in several Latin American countries including Bolivia, Colombia, and Honduras. It appears to
be U.S. practice to employ Cuban and Puerto Rican soldiers for
clandestine military operations in Latin America, including a
widely reported napalm attack on a rebel headquarters in Peru.

(See French News Agency Dispatch, Oct. 16, 1965.) U.S. policy is to avoid the use of American personnel wherever possible for combat, reserving them for training and advice. (See testimony of General Robert W. Porter, Jr., U.S. Congress, House of Representatives, before the Committee on Foreign Affairs, 90th Congress, 1st session, 1967, pp. 535–562). The major thrust of U.S. counterinsurgency programs in Latin America has been extensive training operations for local military: "Dollar for dollar, we are getting more for our money out of these schools than anything else we are doing down there." (See testimony of Porter, p. 542.)

On January 16, 1968, the two top military advisers in Guatemala City were assassinated. According to a communiqué of the Rebel Armed Forces, insurgent groups arranged the assassinations because the U.S. mission had "ordered the Guatemalan army to create groups of assassins" to kill the insurgents. (*The Washington Post,* January 18, 1967.)

13. The CIA activities in Mozambique were revealed in a civil trial. See David Welsh, "Flyboys of the C.I.A.," in *Ramparts,* December 1966, p. 12.

14. John Gerassi, "Latin America—The Next Vietnam?", in *Viet-Report,* January–February 1967, p. 25.

CHAPTER 4

International Communism and the Export of Revolution

One

WHEN THE UNITED STATES began fighting a guerrilla movement in the Philippines shortly after the Spanish-American War, Lenin was an obscure pamphleteer living in exile. For fifty years, however, the specter of communism has been both the official pretext and the fearful inspiration for the growing American commitment to suppress revolution. The ideology of anticommunism strips rebellion of legitimacy by stamping it "made in Moscow" (or Peking or Havana) and exalts the suppression of revolution as an act of liberation. Since the justification of the American war on revolution rests on a view of communism, we shall in this chapter briefly explore communist theory and practice concerning foreign revolutions.[1]

When the Bolsheviks seized power in Russia in 1917 they came armed with Marx's vision of how revolutions happen and Lenin's strategy for assisting the process. Marx believed that the "class struggle" was the engine of radical social change and that the widening gulf between the successful and the failures in modern capitalist society would lead to its violent overthrow. Lenin stressed the need for organization and planning to make the inevitable happen. While Marx's analysis suggested that a "revolutionary situation" was present only in advanced industrial societies that had a proletariat, Lenin's singleminded concern was the liberation of peasant Russia from suffocation at the hands of the collapsing Romanov dynasty and the establishment of Bolshevik rule. "Give us an organization of revolutionaries," he cried, "and we shall overturn Russia."[2]

Events moved much faster than Lenin had dreamed. The World War snapped the last threads that held the czarist bureaucracy together. It appeared that the whole European state system might not be able to survive the convulsion of the first global war. The fall of the czar and the exhilarating confusion of the times convinced Lenin that Trotsky's idea of "permanent revolution" was correct. The bourgeois revolution would again be overturned and supplanted with a socialist revolution, which could survive the inevitable opposition of the rest of the capitalist states only if it spread beyond Russia. "Our task," Trotsky declared to the First Comintern Congress in 1919, is "to mobilize the forces of all genuinely revolutionary parties of the world proletariat and thereby hasten the victory of the communist revolution throughout the world."[3]

The ease of the October Revolution, an amazingly swift and relatively bloodless seizure of the state machinery, intoxicated the Bolsheviks with a euphoric vision of a wave of revolutions. Events soon intruded on the dream. In Germany in 1919, the country where the revolution was supposed to begin, two abortive communist coups were attempted. In Berlin the feeble "Spartacus Uprising" was easily suppressed by the Socialist government. In Munich a "Bavarian Socialist Republic" was established by the German Communist party. It lasted for about three weeks in April, 1919. Béla Kun's communist government in Hungary lasted a few weeks longer before invading Romanian and Czech armies, heavily supported by the French, brought it down later the same year. The "revolutionary situation" which Trotsky had prophesied was over.[4] His two major predictions had proved false. The revolution could not be pushed beyond Russia's borders. And within those borders it could be defended.

Long before Stalin took power the Soviet government moved rapidly to ensure that the Comintern, the international organization of communist parties, became an instrument of Kremlin policy. Foreign communist parties were to be elite and conspiratorial, not mass-based. They were expected to take orders. Comintern agents carrying out Moscow's instructions began to give disastrous advice to local communist leaders. In March, 1920, Béla Kun, now a Comintern functionary, pushed the reluctant German communists into another abortive putsch.[5] In 1923 the Russians encouraged another coup in Germany, which also failed after a few hours of street fighting in Hamburg. The next year the Soviets infiltrated Russians into Estonia, but these "insurgents" were eliminated by the Estonian government in a day.

The "world revolution" remained an important rhetorical goal for many years. Even Joseph Stalin, who grasped total control of the Soviet state with the help of the slogan "socialism in one country" and made communism an instrument of Russian power, could write a German communist in late 1923, "The victory of the German proletariat will undoubtedly shift the center of world revolution from Moscow to Berlin."[6] However, the preoccupation of Soviet leaders with the civil war, foreign intervention, and the staggering task of reconstructing a huge nation cooled any remaining enthusiasm for proletarian internationalism. Under Stalin the concept of the world revolution along with every other tenet of the communist faith was put at the service of the Soviet state.

"A revolutionary," wrote Stalin in 1927, "is one who is ready to protect, to defend the USSR without reservation, without qualification, openly and honestly. ... An internationalist is one who is ready to defend the USSR without reservation, without wavering, unconditionally; for the USSR is the base of the world revolutionary movement and this revolutionary movement cannot be defended and promoted unless the USSR is defended."[7]

The Stalinist conception of revolution reflected both his obsession with domestic weakness and the failure of the few early attempts to export revolution by force of arms. Besides the Estonian fiasco, the Russians fought a brief war with Poland (which the Poles started) under the banner of "revolution from without" and attempted to install a puppet regime.[8] Only in territories that had been part of the czarist empire or a Russian protectorate, such as Outer Mongolia, did the Soviets succeed in establishing a communist government. This was not the export of revolution but the consolidation of empire by military power. Popular uprisings, revolutionary ideology, or indeed internal politics of any kind had little to do with it.

Two

Beyond the reach of the Red army the Soviets soon abandoned the idea of exporting revolution. Indeed, a principal function of the Comintern was to cool revolutionary zeal where such activity would embarrass the Soviet government in its relations with other states.[9] Lenin would have nothing to do with local communists in Turkey and Iran because he was courting Ataturk and the Shah. Communist parties that acted independently, which usually also meant impulsively, were denounced or disowned. The Korean communists were abandoned after they demonstrated that they could not be effectively controlled. The Comintern tried unsuccessfully to dissuade the Indonesian communists from staging a series of uprisings in 1926 and 1927, which ended in disaster for them. Stalin's effort to guide the Chinese revolutionary movement in the 1920's also ended in failure.[10] He sent a Comintern agent, Michael Borodin, to China to advise the communists to cooperate with the Kuomintang until such time as they were strong enough to squeeze out the party of Sun Yat-sen "like a lemon." Some of the present bitterness of old-time Chinese leaders toward Russia can be traced to the fact that it was the Chinese communists who got squeezed. Shortly afterward, Mao Tse-tung rose to leadership of the Chinese party on an unorthodox ideological program which accorded to the peasantry, not the proletariat, the prime role in a revolution which would come about, not through a coup, but a prolonged armed struggle. Both ideologically and politically, Mao was determined to remain independent of Stalin's Russia and to make his own revolution.

In the Spanish Civil War, 1936–39, Stalin ordered the Spanish communists to abandon revolutionary goals and to support the Republican government. Under Stalin's direction the local party members sided with the government against Trotskyites, who were still dedicated to the establishment of a communist society. Stalin's prime interest, as the Hitler-Stalin pact made unmistakably clear, was to build and defend the power of the Soviet state at any cost. To this end local communists would be sacrificed unhesitatingly.[11] But in fact the abandonment or leashing of foreign communists was hardly a sacrifice for Stalin or his successors, for a truly independent communist revolution was a threat to Soviet interests. It is no accident, as the Soviets themselves like to say, that two of the three communist governments established by local revolutionaries independent of the Red army—China and Albania—became enemies of the Soviet state, and a third, Yugoslavia, once also an enemy, is now at best a wary neighbor.

There is little doubt that Stalin would have liked to manufacture revolutions if the revolutionary governments would have been reliably subservient. But the Russian dictator was a shrewd judge of the limits of his power. The prewar experience suggested that Russia lacked the capacity to bring about revolution in other countries. The postwar experience revealed that without the overwhelming power of the Red army on the scene, local revolutionaries, no matter how many years they had spent in Moscow, would not play the puppet role. Having risked their lives in the wartime resistance movements and with their own energy and skill thrown off the old regimes along with the Nazis, they were not prepared to exchange German masters for Russian.[12]

In country after country communists took a leading role in the resistance movements of World War II. Some had been party functionaries and had played a role in the Comintern. Others identified with communism because it represented the only radical alternative to fascist or collaborationist regimes or to decadent oligarchies. Stalin, who had been right in minimizing the possibilities of revolution in the interwar period, now underestimated the revolutionary implications of the upheavals of World War II. He discouraged the French resistance and told them to line up behind General de Gaulle. He directed the Italian communists, who were in a very strong position, to come to terms with the government of Marshal Badoglio. He gave the same advice to Mao Tse-tung, urging him to submit to the Kuomintang, despite the fact that Mao's armies controlled

vast portions of China and that Chiang twenty years
earlier had slaughtered the Communist-party leadership.[13]
Tito, he demanded, must agree to the restoration of the
Yugoslav monarchy. "The bourgeoisie is very strong,"
Stalin warned, "not only in Serbia but in China, Poland,
Romania, France, Italy—everywhere."[14] Even in countries
occupied by the Red army Stalin moved quickly to re-
move independent local revolutionaries, but slowly to im-
pose a social revolution. Stalin did not bring Hungary and
Romania under tight Soviet control until 1947. According
to Tito, these moves were in response to the Truman
Doctrine.

Three

In 1946 Stalin revived the Comintern, which he
had summarily disbanded in the war in a show of good
will to his capitalist allies. Outfitted with a new name, the
Cominform, and a newspaper with the world's longest
name—*For a Lasting Peace! For a People's Democracy!*—
the new bureaucratic organ of world communism was
even more subservient to Stalin's will than its predecessor.

The Soviet dictator now advanced the thesis of the "two
camps." The revolution had spread to the countries that
had been brought into the Soviet orbit as a result of the
war, and the Soviet Union no longer stood alone and
"encircled." World politics must now be understood as a
conflict between the capitalist camp and the communist
camp. For the Kremlin the decisive test of an enemy or a
friend was not how it organized its economy, but whether
it lined up behind the Soviet Union on international issues.
Stalin displayed the same sympathy and understanding for
the monumental upheavals in the colonial world as John
Foster Dulles expressed a few years later when he observed that neutralism was "immoral." Stalin, too, was
interested in Third World countries only if they could be
gathered under his tent.[15]

On the periphery of his expanding empire Stalin was

prepared to support local communists and to exert political and military pressure in their behalf. Characteristically, the two places where Stalin gave direct support to local coups, Azerbaijan and Czechoslovakia, were both contiguous to the expanded Soviet camp and had been occupied by the Red army in the war. Elsewhere local communists could count on receiving perfunctory, and usually unreliable, advice from Moscow—or express discouragement of revolutionary activities. In 1948 a series of communist-inspired rebellions broke out in Southeast Asia.[16] They were preceded by a communist-sponsored youth conference in Calcutta. The Soviets talked of global conflict, and the Chinese and Vietminh representatives reported on their own armed struggles. Within a few months unsuccessful insurrections were attempted in Burma, Malaya, the Philippines, and Indonesia. In each of them local leaders calling themselves communists played decisive roles. Each was a nationalist leader who had come to a position of power in the wartime resistance movements against the Japanese. Each miscalculated the difficulty of insurrection, although the situations in each country were quite different. No doubt the current rhetoric from Moscow influenced the direction of revolutionary planning. It may well be, for example, that Moscow's official policy of friendship and cooperation with the United States, which lasted until 1946, persuaded Luis Taruc, the leader of the Huks in the Philippines, not to take an anti-American position in the immediate postwar period. The decision in 1946 not to oppose the American plan for Philippine independence, Taruc later wrote, was a major error.[17] In other places, too, with whatever influence the Soviets could bring to bear, they stressed caution. With little understanding of the nature of the Asian revolutionary movements and little real interest in them, Stalin's bureaucrats had little useful advice to give.

Four

The most mysterious event in the long history of Stalin's dealings with foreign communists was the Korean War.[18] It is one of the essential assumptions of official Cold War history that Stalin ordered the war. Indeed, Korea being the only case in the postwar period of the overt use of communist armies across an international frontier (albeit a temporary one, located in the middle of what had been a nation), it has been used again and again as the prime example of communist aggression. Although the South Korean army also thrust north of the 38th parallel on the morning of June 25, 1950, it seems clear that the North Korean army struck first. But it was hardly the unprovoked attack from the blue that the State Department likes to recall. The events of June 25 were preceded by more than two years of guerrilla warfare, border raids initiated by both sides, and mounting threats by South Korean President Syngman Rhee to conquer the North. Like Vietnam, Korea was a nation divided as a result of the Cold War. As 1950 began, Rhee declared that he was prepared "to unify our territory by ourselves," even at the cost of "bloodshed and civil strife." He mobilized his armies. According to MacArthur's chief of intelligence, Charles A. Willoughby, at the time of the attack "the entire ROK army had been alerted for weeks and was in position along the 38th parallel."[19] In March Rhee broadcast to North Korea that the hour of their liberation was at hand. Threats to march north mounted throughout the spring.[20] Guerrilla warfare in the South also continued, and the Rhee government stepped up its arrests.

A consideration of these almost forgotten events is offered not to justify the North Korean attack—which was a monumental disaster for Korea and the whole course of the Cold War—but rather to attempt to put the extraordinary event in somewhat better perspective. It is certainly at least as plausible that the North Koreans

attacked to forestall an attack from the South as that this
was a case of Hitler-like aggression. For our purposes,
however, the crucial question is not whether communist
military forces attempted to conquer noncommunist military forces in a divided country, but whether the communist forces were directed by the Soviet Union.[21]

We do not know precisely what the Soviet role was in
connection with the invasion of June 25, 1950. The war
had been preceded by several years of guerrilla warfare,
strikes, and insurrections, which the South Korean government with American aid and advice had successfully suppressed. According to former Premier Nikita Khrushchev's
memoirs, the war was the idea of Kim il Sung, the North
Korean leader, and Stalin. Here is Khrushchev's account
of how the war broke out:

> About the time I was transferred from the Ukraine
> to Moscow at the end of 1949, Kim Il-sung arrived with
> his delegation to hold consultations with Stalin. The
> North Koreans wanted to prod South Korea with the
> point of a bayonet. Kim Il-sung said that the first
> poke would touch off an internal explosion in South
> Korea and that the power of the people would pre-
> vail—that is, the power which ruled in North Korea.
> Naturally Stalin couldn't oppose this idea. It appealed
> to his convictions as a Communist all the more be-
> cause the struggle would be an internal matter which
> the Koreans would be settling among themselves . . .
> I remember Stalin had his doubts. He was worried
> that the Americans would jump in, but we were in-
> clined to think that if the war were fought swiftly—
> and Kim Il-sung was sure that it could be won swiftly
> —then intervention by the USA would be avoided . . .
> I must stress that the war wasn't Stalin's idea, but
> Kim Il-sung's. Kim was the initiator. Stalin, of course,
> didn't try to dissuade him. In my opinion, no real
> Communist would have tried to dissuade Kim Il-sung
> from his compelling desire to liberate South Korea
> from Syngman Rhee and from reactionary American
> influence.[22]

Once the North Korean's invasion ran out of steam and
Stalin realized that contrary to Kim's prediction the people of South Korea were not about to greet the invaders
as liberators, he pulled back:

It's incomprehensible to me why he did it, but when Kim Il-sung was preparing for his march, Stalin called back all our advisors who were with the North Korean divisions and regiments, as well as all the advisors who were serving as consultants and helping to build up the army. I asked Stalin about this, and he snapped back at me, "It's too dangerous to keep our advisors there. They might be taken prisoner. We don't want there to be evidence for accusing us of taking part in this business. It's Kim Il-sung's affair." So our advisors were recalled. As a result, the North Korean army was in trouble from the very start.[23]

Stalin's successors arranged for the end of the Korean War within four months of the old man's death and began to develop a new policy toward revolutionary movements in the former colonial areas of the world. Under Stalin, Soviet foreign policy analysts lumped Asia, Africa, and Latin America together as "the East," much as their United States counterparts classified them as the "Gray Areas." Now the Soviets, no doubt in part because the Chinese began to woo the new nations at the Bandung Conference of 1955, started to differentiate noncommunist governments of the decolonizing world. Under Stalin they were all dismissed as imperialist lackeys. Now the Soviets made an effort to grade their performance and to influence it. But the criterion for judging whether the "national bourgeoisie" of a "neutralist" country still part of the international economy was "progressive" or not had little to do with their faithfulness to the Marxist classics, their policies on collectivization, or the position of the local communist party, but whether they would join "the fight against imperialism and military blocs."[24] Soviet doctrine continues to insist that the neutralist countries can be shepherded toward communism, and official Soviet interest in them is justified by this goal. Yet the Soviets have lavished the most aid and given major political support to those regimes which have shown independence of the United States but have outlawed the communist party or have imprisoned local communists—Egypt, Iraq, Indonesia, and India. While Soviet ideologists have worked out a doctrine of support (mostly moral support) for Wars of National Liberation, again and again—in Algeria, Cyprus and Egypt, among others—the Kremlin has demonstrated that it is not interested in encouraging local revolution but in enlisting allies for Russia and, where possible, spreading the Russian sphere of influence.

Soviet policy toward the Third World has been so clearly in the tradition of self-serving Great Power politics that the Kremlin has difficulty in posing as a champion of revolution. Thus, for example, by giving military aid in countries like Indonesia and Iraq, the Soviet government has strengthened the professional military, who are generally the strongest opponents of communist revolution. As Peter Paret and John Shy report in their study of guerrilla movements, ". . . the communists have never organized and dominated a foreign guerrilla movement from the outset."[25] In his detailed survey of Soviet activity in the Middle East and North Africa, Manfred Halpern concludes that the U.S.S.R. "through the requirements of its foreign policy has become a major brake on communist revolutions. . . ."[26] In Latin America the communist parties have traditionally had good working relations with some of the worst oligarchic and dictatorial regimes. The Cuban Communist party supported Batista and did not make formal contact with Castro until a few months before his seizure of Havana. Communists cooperated with Trujillo in the Dominican Republic and with Jiménez in Venezuela.

Five

The Chinese have exploited the obvious inconsistencies between Soviet revolutionary pretensions and their counterrevolutionary practice in the deepening struggle with the Kremlin for ideological leadership of the world communist movement. Let us look first at the basic differences in theory between the Chinese and the Soviet Communist parties on revolution in the Third World and then consider how these differences are reflected in actual practice.

The leaders of every successful revolution have been free with advice. The makers of the Chinese Revolution, having seized the most populous country in the world more swiftly than anyone had thought possible, and having produced a radical social, economic, and political transformation in a generation, have been strongly intoxicated with missionary zeal. Partly because their own revolution was such a towering achievement, made without outside help or even encouragement, partly because of age-old Chinese chauvinism, and partly because the U.S.S.R. long ago abandoned a serious commitment to revolution, the communist leaders of China believe that they have a monopoly on revolutionary truth.

As they look at the world, they are the only revolutionary power with the credentials to advise the Third World. In his famous article "Mao Tse-tung's Theory of People's War,"[27] Lin Piao points out that prerevolutionary China was "semicolonial and semifeudal," while prerevolutionary Russia was "imperialist." The October Revolution began with armed uprisings in the city, while the Chinese Revolution grew out of a protracted struggle in the countryside. "The people's war led by the Chinese Communist party, comprising the War of Resistance and the revolutionary civil wars," Lin Piao writes, "lasted for twenty-two years. It constitutes the most drawn out and most complex people's war led by the proletariat in modern history, and it has been the richest in experience." Revolutionaries in the Third World should, therefore, listen respectfully, for only China has had comparable experience on which to draw; and only China is sufficiently outside the Great Power system to be able to identify with and support true wars of liberation.

Throughout its history the ideologists of communism have struggled with the question of violence. Lin Piao points out that Mao's "vivid" phrase, "political power grows out of the barrel of a gun," is an updated version of Marx's observation that "force is the midwife of every old society pregnant with a new one." A social revolution that takes power from old hands unwilling to give it up and passes it to new ones is by definition violent. Yet in every age there have been leading communists who have denied the necessity of violence. Kautsky, Bernstein, Marx himself, Lenin, and Stalin have all been the authors of "revisionist" statements conceding the possibilities of peaceful revolution. For obvious practical reasons the Soviet Union in its campaign for acceptance as a Great Power in a world of hostile, powerful capitalist states has been increasingly driven to downplay the role of violence in revolution, and particularly to deny its own responsibility for promoting violence within other societies. The Chinese, on the other hand, adhere to the original Leninist view that since those who oppose revolution always resort to violence, the struggle to overcome them must necessarily be violent. "This is called," Lin Piao adds, "doing unto them what they do to us."[28]

"The experience of the Chinese Revolution shows," Lin Piao states, that revolution can be successful only through "long and tortuous struggle."[29] The world revolution "hinges on the revolutionary struggles of the Asian, African, and Latin-American peoples who make up the overwhelming majority of the world's population."[30] These are the "rural" areas of the world, which will eventually encircle and defeat the developed imperialist countries, which are the "cities." The socialist countries have "an internationalist duty to support the people's revolutionary struggles in Asia, Africa, and Latin America."[31]

The Soviets refuse to climb into the box the Chinese have prepared for them. In their polemics with Peking they point out that they are not pacifists, but have "always recognized armed as well as peaceful forms of struggle."[32] But to emphasize armed struggle "as the only way of revolution," the Soviet Central Committee taunted the Chinese in 1966, is "ultrarevolutionary phrasemaking" designed to cover up China's "extraordinary caution in their own practical deeds." If the Chinese score points on the Soviets by demonstrating that their behavior is actually counterrevolutionary, the Soviets can win a few for themselves by showing that the Chinese have devoted much talk to the support of independence movements but little else. Mao entered the Korean War only when MacArthur approached Manchuria. He gave medical supplies to the Algerian rebels, and after late 1960, arms. (Arms also flowed in to the rebels from West Germany, Tunisia, and Egypt and many other countries.) The Chinese have given far less aid to North Vietnam than have the Soviets. Some Chinese arms and money have found their way to Thailand, Laos, and Indonesia and to insurgent movements in Latin America and Africa, but they have been insignificant amounts. Compared to the United States investment, or even the Soviet investment, in military aid, the Chinese performance, as one would expect of an undeveloped country absorbed with massive internal problems, has been unimpressive. If their role in Algeria is at all typical, they have, according to a leading member of the Algerian resistance, behaved correctly toward the local revolutionaries and have refrained from seeking to dominate the local movements, as the Soviets have often tried to do.

Chinese doctrine includes an explanation for its verbal extravagance and practical caution. Lin Piao emphasizes that no national-liberation movement can rely on external support. Although the revolutionary forces throughout the world give "one another support and encouragement," each country is "liberated as a result of its own efforts."[33] Again and again the Chinese leaders have told local revolutionaries, "Go make your own revolution. You have our example and our continuing encouragement."

Dean Rusk has referred to the Lin Piao doctrine as a "do-it-yourself kit"[34] for promoting revolution. Conceding that the Chinese have been "more cautious in action than in word,"[35] he has warned that Lin's exhortation to local revolutionaries must be regarded as a latter-day *Mein Kampf*. China, according to the official Washington view, threatens to expand, not by sending its armies swarming across its borders, but through the use of "the power of subversive organization." The assumption behind these remarks is that the country with the revolutionary model will control the country that puts the model into practice, that revolutionary governments installed by local insurgents will be subservient to the land of revolutionary inspiration.[36] There is nothing in the history of communism or revolution to suggest that this is really the case.

Both the Soviet Union and China have demanded ideological purity from revolutionary governments and insurgent movements. But they have both been rebuffed. Castro has publicly quarreled with both major communist powers and has shown an unwillingness to subscribe either to Peking's world view or to the Soviets' self-serving conception of coexistence. In March, 1965, Castro publicly rejected the Chinese thesis of U.S.-Soviet collusion, and the Chinese retaliated by cutting their rice shipments to Cuba almost in half. Castro denounced this act as a "rice bomb."[37] At the Tricontinental meetings at Havana in January, 1966, the Cuban delegate lashed out at interference from foreign communist parties. "We Cubans, who have struggled for seven years against the United States, only ninety miles from her shores, don't need to receive lessons on anti-imperialism from anyone."[38]

Since the Bandung Conference of 1955 the left-wing neutralist governments and the leaders of insurgent movements have sought to build a "militant solidarity" against the vestiges of colonialism and neoimperialism. Revolutionary leaders have been attempting to devise institutions through which they might help each other. At the Havana Conference of the Tricontinental, a "Committee to Assist National Liberation Movements and the Struggle Against Neocolonialism" was established at the initiative of Third World revolutionaries, not Russia or China. The Conference heard various appeals from guerrilla leaders for material aid. A Venezuelan insurgent leader told the Conference pointedly, "Often there are peasants who are ready to join the guerrillas but cannot be used because there are no arms or equipment. . . . Instructors, money, and arms are vital for a revolutionary movement, and rifles are more useful than pronouncements or moral appeals."[39] The Conference proclaimed the right to send "military aid necessary for armed struggles, means of transporting it, financial aid," as well as technical assistance, food, and medical supplies. "The most important expression of solidarity,"[40] Turcios, the Guatemalan insurgent leader declared, is to expand the armed revolutionary struggle. Every new war of liberation "is an expression of effective solidarity with each of the peoples of the three continents."

The strategists of the Third World revolutions believe that only a wave of revolutions can overcome the American commitment to the maintenance of reactionary governments in Asia, Africa, and Latin America. Encouraged by the enormous drain on U.S. military and financial resources involved in America's unsuccessful efforts to suppress the Vietnamese National Liberation Front, Third World revolutionaries are putting increasing faith in Lin Piao's strategic formula:

> Everything is divisible. And so is this colossus of U.S. imperialism. It can be split up and defeated. The peoples of Asia, Africa, Latin America and other regions can destroy it piece by piece, some striking at its head and others at its feet. That is why the greatest

fear of U.S. imperialism is that people's wars will be launched in different parts of the world.[41]

No one knows better than the leader of a small guerrilla band in the hills that revolution cannot be exported. It cannot even be orchestrated. Conscious of their present weakness but confident that after long struggles they will prevail, the new generation of guerrilla leaders is looking for outside support, but he will not bargain his independence for it. Until now the communist powers have not been generous with material aid for independent revolutionary struggles. Where they have poured in arms and money, it has been either to support a puppet regime, as in Korea, or to respond to a major commitment from America, as in Vietnam.

NOTES—CHAPTER FOUR

1. Containment of communism, or, in Prime Minister Churchill's words, the effort to "strangle Bolshevism in its cradle," was an important motivation for the U.S. and allied interventions in Russia after World War I. The charge of communist inspiration was made by members of the State Department in 1933, when the United States opposed, by diplomatic show of force rather than armed intervention, the Grau San Martín regime in Cuba. See, for example, telegram 527 from Ambassador Jefferson Caffrey, December 21, 1933, in Department of State, *Foreign Relations of the United States: 1933* (Washington, D.C., 1952), V, p. 544. See also Bryce Wood, *The Making of the Good Neighbor Policy* (New York, 1961), p. 217, for an account of State Department officials' views of the Cuban revolutionary regime as "communistic." Most concern with revolution has come in the postwar period. For an excellent statement of the official analysis of guerrilla warfare as a weapon of the Kremlin, see Roger Hilsman, "Internal War: The New Communist Tactic," in Lieutenant Colonel T. N. Greene, ed., *The Guerrilla, and How to Fight Him* (New York, 1962), pp. 22–26: "The new tactic is internal war—using military force not across national boundaries but inside them . . . the Communists have found what they regard as a new chink in our armor."

2. For an account of Leninist theory and strategy on revolution, see Robert V. Daniels, *The Nature of Communism* (New York, 1962), ch. II. See also Franco Venturi, *Roots of Revolution* (New York, 1960). The quotation from Lenin can be found in Daniels, p. 21.

3. See *Kommunisticheskiy internatsional v dokumentakh,* 1919–1932 (Moscow, 1933), p. 17.

4. For a description of early communist revolutionary activity, see Thomas P. Thornton, "The Emergence of Communist Revolutionary Doctrine," in C. E. Black and T. P. Thornton, eds., *Communism and Revolution* (Princeton, 1964), pp. 43–57.

5. See Paul Levi, *Unser Weg in den Putschismus* (Berlin, 1921), p. 46, for an account by the former head of the German Communist party of his attitude toward the "antics" of Comintern functionaries who try to give advice to experienced nationalist leaders.

6. Joseph Stalin, in *Rote Fahne,* October 10, 1923, quoted in Thornton, "Emergence of Communist Revolutionary Doctrine," p. 51n.

7. Joseph Stalin, *Works* (Moscow, 1927), vol. X, pp. 53–54.

8. According to P. A. Golub (in "Pol'skiye revolyutsionnye voyska v Rossii v 1917-1920 godakh," in *Voprosi Istorii* No. 3, 1958, pp. 44–63), the Soviets enlisted some 5,700 Poles into the Red army to lend some revolutionary legitimacy to the Polish operation.

9. See Thornton, "Emergence of Communist Revolutionary Doctrine," pp. 62–63, for an account of Comintern efforts to cool revolutionary zeal in Iran, Turkey, Korea, etc. Also, in Indonesia, where an independent revolutionary party was organized which then joined the Comintern, agents of the Comintern appear to have "argued for caution."

10. A summary of early activities of Stalin with respect to the Chinese Communist party and its relations to the Kuomintang is found in *ibid.,* pp. 63–66.

11. The Soviets "ruthlessly purged" local communists in Poland and elsewhere in Eastern Europe who were not wholly subservient to Moscow's interests. See Daniels, *The Nature of Communism,* p. 207.

12. For an account of the communist role in the Yugoslav resistance movements, see Chalmers Johnson, *Peasant Nationalism and Communist Power: The Emergence of Revolutionary China* (Stanford, California, 1962). My own understanding of the relations between Moscow, the West, and West European resistance movements has been helped by discussions with Professor Gabriel Kolko, whose book, *The Politics of War,* includes an account of the wartime left-wing partisans in occupied Europe.

13. Stalin's conservatism concerning revolutionary prospects in China, Yugoslavia, France, Italy, and elsewhere has been attested to by Dedijer and Djilas. See V. Dedijer, *Tito Speaks* (New York, 1953), p. 322; Milovan Djilas, *Conversations with Stalin,* translated by Michael B. Petrovich (New York, 1962), p. 114.

14. Conversation between Stalin and Tito recorded by Ded-

ijer and quoted in Isaac Deutscher, *Russia, What Next?* (New York, 1953), p. 101.

15. Official Soviet attitudes toward the Third World during the Stalin era, when, according to the line laid down by Andrej Zhdanov, there were only "two camps" and no neutrals, are discussed in T. P. Thornton, "Communist Attitudes Towards Asia, Africa, and Latin America," in Black and Thornton, *Communism and Revolution,* p. 245. See also T. P. Thornton, ed., *The Third World in Soviet Perspective* (Princeton, 1964), for examples from Soviet writing on their changing views. A typical Soviet view of the Stalin period is found in Ye Zhukov, "Obostrenije Krizisa kolonialnoy sistemy," in *Bol'shevik,* No. 23 (1947), pp. 51–64.

16. For an account of the Soviet attitudes toward and involvement with the Southwest Asian insurrections of the late 1940's, see Ruth T. McVey, "The Southeast Asian Insurrectionary Movements," in Black and Thornton, *Communism and Revolution,* pp. 145–184. See also J. H. Brimmell, *Communism in South East Asia* (London, 1959), pp. 249–263; Gene D. Overstreet and Marshall Windmiller, *Communism in India* (Berkeley, 1959), pp. 252–275.

17. Taruc's analysis of his failure is in *Born of the People* (New York, 1953), p. 199.

18. The Korean War is discussed in Glenn D. Paige, "Korea," in Black and Thornton, *Communism and Revolution,* pp. 215–242. Of particular interest is the discussion of the guerrilla war period of 1948–1950 (pp. 223–227). See also Alan S. Whiting, *China Crosses the Yalu: The Decision to Enter the Korean War* (New York, 1960); I. F. Stone, *The Hidden History of the Korean War* (New York, 1952); David Rees, *Korea: The Limited War* (New York, 1964).

19. Charles A. Willoughby's statement is found in Denna Frank Fleming, *The Cold War and Its Origins (1917–1960)* (2 vols.; Garden City, New York, 1961), vol. II, p. 599.

20. On May 30, 1950, Rhee had been decisively defeated in elections. He stepped up his threat against the North declaring his readiness to "take Pyongyang within a few days." This statement is quoted in *ibid.,* p. 654.

21. For some evidence that American leaders at the time of the attack thought that it might have been provoked, see John Gunther, *The Riddle of MacArthur* (New York, 1951), p. 166; Fleming, *The Cold War,* vol. II, p. 654.

22. See *Khrushchev Remembers,* by Edward Crankshaw (Boston, 1970), p. 367.

23. *Ibid.,* p. 370.

24. A discussion of changing Soviet attitudes toward the "East" and their evolving definition of a "progressive" national bourgeoisie can be found in T. P. Thornton, "Communist Attitudes," in Black and Thornton, *Communism and Revolution,* especially pp. 247, 254.

25. Peter Paret and John W. Shy, *Guerrillas in the 1960's* (rev. ed.; New York, 1965), p. 17. The full quote is as follows:

> The third use of the guerrilla—that of fighting in his native country as an agent of a foreign power—is more difficult to pin down. This may seem surprising, since Communist agitation and subversion are well-known facts of contemporary life. But until today, the communists have never organized and dominated a foreign guerrilla movement from the outset. It most nearly happened in Indochina, where the rebel Vietminh were trained in China and equipped by the Chinese very early in the game. . . . Here too, though the guerrillas clearly helped advance the interests of a foreign power and received its active support, their basic strength derived from identifying with their own compatriots.

26. Manfred Halpern, "The Middle East and North Africa," in Black and Thornton, *Communism and Revolution*, p. 324.

27. Lin Piao's article, published in 1965, is reprinted in an official Chinese translation in Franz Schurmann and Orville Schell, *Communist China*, vol. III of *The China Reader* (New York, 1957), pp. 347–359. The comparison of the Soviet and Chinese revolutions is found at pp. 347–348. The discussion of revolutionary violence is at p. 348.

28. Lin Piao, quoted in *ibid.*, p. 349.

29. Lin Piao, quoted in *ibid.*, p. 353.

30. Lin Piao, quoted in *ibid.*, p. 352.

31. Lin Piao, quoted in *ibid.*, p. 352.

32. Letter of the Central Committee of the Communist party of the Soviet Union to the Chinese Communist party, quoted in *ibid.*, pp. 494–499, especially p. 498.

33. Lin Piao, quoted in *ibid.*, p. 342.

34. Dean Rusk, Statement before the House Subcommittee on Far Eastern Affairs on United States Policy Toward Communist China, April 16, 1966, quoted in *ibid.*, p. 510.

35. Dean Rusk, quoted in *ibid.*, p. 511.

36. For an explicit statement of these assumptions, see speech of William P. Bundy, "The United States and Communist China," February 12, 1966, quoted in *ibid.*, pp. 378–385: "But essentially we are dealing here not with the power of ideas but with the power of subversive organization—perhaps the one field in which Communist China has shown real innovation and skill" (p. 385). Chinese activities in Africa are described in Fritz Schatten, *Communism in Africa* (New York, 1966). See also William Attwood, *The Reds and the Blacks: A Personal Adventure* (New York, 1967).

37. Castro made the statement about the "rice bomb" on January 2, 1966; see Albert-Paul Lentin, *La Lutte Tricontinentale* (Paris, 1966), p. 49.

38. The Cuban delegate who is quoted in the text was Osmani Cienfuegos, the chairman of the "Foreign Relations Commission" of the Cuban Communist party. He is quoted in *ibid.*, pp. 49–50. *Pravda* attacked the conference on several occasions.

39. Quoted in Lentin, *La Lutte Tricontinentale*, p. 275.

40. Turcios, quoted in *ibid.*, p. 276.

41. Lin Piao, quoted in Schurmann and Schell, *The China Reader*, vol. III, p. 357.

CHAPTER 5

The Road to World Leadership: The Police Idea in U.S. Foreign Policy

One

THE POSSESSION OF GREAT POWER has led those responsible for protecting America to devote ever-increasing energy and resources to the quest for physical security in a world that has less and less of it to offer. Since 1945 the national-security bureaucracy has assumed for the first time in over one hundred years that the United States is vulnerable to attack. Since 1955 the Pentagon and the State Department have carried on their daily work in the shadow of charts which show that in a nuclear war American society as we have known it will be destroyed along with one-third to two-thirds of her people. Thus, the impulse to keep war as far as possible from our shores has grown ever stronger as technology has increasingly undermined the foundations of national security. Presidents and generals have popularized the idea that if battles can be fought in Asian or African villages, they will not have to be fought over American cities.

Official explanations for the policy of opposing violent

revolution and guiding underdeveloped nations into approved paths to development rest heavily on such strategic considerations. The outbreak of violence among remote peoples is usually noticed only when some economic or military interest of the United States is discerned. In general, a small underdeveloped country has a hard time attracting the State Department's attention unless it either is located on the periphery of what used to be called the "Sino-Soviet bloc," is a victim of an insurgency with communist connections, or has become the target of Soviet or Chinese diplomacy.

Yet America has always tried to explain its relations to the rest of the world in terms of ideological principles which transcend parochial economic or military interests.[1] There is a messianic idea running through American history that this nation has something to give the world beyond the example of the Affluent Society and that the spread of American civilization abroad is the ultimate vindication of the American political experiment. From the earliest involvement of the Republic in foreign adventures, Americans have wrapped the desire for more land, more power, more respect, more bases, more raw materials, and more markets in an ideological mantle. So also the postwar effort to push ever farther from our own shores the ramparts of Fortress America.

It is easy enough to dismiss the role of ideology in foreign policy as a pretext or mask for the normally unattractive motivations that drive men to seek power or to expand their influence. Yet while we are well advised to cast a cold eye on statesmen who claim they are killing foreigners only to uplift them, it is too easy to dismiss ideological masks as pure hypocrisy. Ideas do play a critical independent role in arousing men in the national-security bureaucracy to action, in attracting the support of public opinion, and, above all, in setting what Whitehead called the "mental climate" within which statesmen grapple with the definition of the national interest and how to achieve it.

In this chapter we shall briefly review the ideological tradition surrounding America's conception of her world role and, in particular, how she has viewed her "responsibilities" for using force beyond her shores.

Two

The men who founded America, believing that they had devised a more perfect instrument for the realization of human freedom than had ever existed, hoped and expected that the American system would spread to other lands. Thomas Jefferson declared that America was to be a "standing monument and example" which would "ameliorate the condition of man over a great portion of the globe."[2] Joel Barlow, one of America's early poet-diplomats, believed that "the example of political wisdom and felicity here to be displayed, will excite emulation throughout the kingdoms of the earth, and meliorate the conditions of the human race."[3] Many of the Founding Fathers were internationalists, or "citizens of the world," a fact which Gouverneur Morris, an uncomplicated nationalist, held against them. For Jefferson it was important that freedom should blossom in other lands. It was "not very important to the happiness of either party"[4] that societies undergoing revolutionary change abroad have some political connection with the United States.

From the earliest days of the Republic expansionists and antiexpansionists struggled with each other over the proper role of force in spreading American civilization. During the Revolutionary War there was strong sentiment for the invasion and annexation of Canada. "We shall never be on a solid footing," Samuel Adams demanded, "till Britain cedes us what Nature designs we should have, or till we wrest it from her."[5] The "natural" requirements of security also extended to Nova Scotia and Florida. The dispossession of the Indians was justified, as Indiana's Governor Harrison put it, because "one of the fairest portions of the globe" could not remain "the haunt of a few wretched savages" when "it seems destined by the Creator to give support to a large population and to be the seat of civilization, of science, and of true religion."[6]

But the expansionist ideology, which served as a drumbeat to accompany restless Americans across the continent and beyond, was opposed by the cautious counsel of men like John Quincy Adams, who warned against using foreign policy as an instrument of regeneration for others. The attempt to spread freedom to other lands, as some of the expansionists urged, would mean changing the basis of American policy "from liberty to force." America might become "the dictatress of the world" but she would "no longer be the ruler of her own spirit." Adams continues:

> Wherever the standard of freedom and independence has been or shall be unfurled, there will be America's heart, her benedictions, and her prayers. But she goes not abroad in search of monsters to destroy. She is the well-wisher to the freedom and independence of all. She is the champion and vindicator only of her own.[7]

Despite such warnings, the idea grew that "manifest destiny" meant not only filling up an "empty" continent with American energy but also using America's "inherent power . . . to regenerate mankind."[8] Mexico, the *United States Democratic Review* declared in 1858, "is in a state of suspended animation. She is in fact dead. She must have resurrection. . . . This American Republic is strong enough to do anything that requires strength. It is vital enough to inject life even into the dead."[9] The United States also had begun to perceive a mission that extended beyond the continent, to "civilize, fertilize, and regenerate." The New World would breathe life into the Old, like it or not. For the expansionists, the annexation of Hawaii, the Philippines, and Cuba was made inevitable by the wheel of fortune. "Whether they will or no," Captain Mahan declared, "Americans must now begin to look outward."[10] The Cuban intervention in 1898, President McKinley declared, was based on "the large dictates of humanity." It was now "the duty and the manifest destiny" to "civilize and Christianize" the Filipinos, who were not, as Senator Albert Beveridge liked to point out, "of a self-governing race."[11]

The march toward colonial empire reached its highwater mark in the McKinley era. Strong anti-imperialist forces developed in the early twentieth century which rejected the ideology of the "white man's burden" and the jingoism of the Beveridges and the Mahans. The long and difficult pacification of the Philippine insurgency with its mounting American casualties and financial drain had a good deal to do with cooling enthusiasm for General Arthur MacArthur's brand of jungle philanthropy.

The moving ideology of American interventionism soon shifted from "manifest destiny" to the new concepts of "international police power" and "world leadership." Theodore Roosevelt developed the idea that the United States had a special role to exercise police power in the Western Hemisphere in the name of the community of nations—a responsibility to intervene against "wrongdoing or impotence."[12] The United States had no "land hunger," only a passion for order. "Disorganization and disorder will not be long permitted in a world grown as small as ours,"[13] was a professorial comment around the turn of the century. As he moved into Panama, Roosevelt compared himself to a policeman jailing a blackmailer.[14] The Taft administration continued what is called a "moral protectorate" of Nicaragua, and Wilson ordered the Marines to assume the entire functions of government in the Dominican Republic for five years to restore "internal order." Wilson also moved against Mexico and Coolidge against Nicaragua, again to forestall revolutionary movements which appeared to endanger American interests. "We are not making war on Nicaragua," President Coolidge explained, "any more than a policeman on the street is making war on passers-by."[15]

John Bartlow Martin, the special envoy to the Dominican Republic at the time of the 1965 intervention, describes the activities of his predecessors on that island:

> In a dozen years from 1904 to 1916, the United States moved from the Roosevelt Corollary to full-scale Marine occupation of the Dominican Republic. First we collected customs, then we forbade insurrection in order to maintain stability, then we held elections with warships in the harbor and sailors—or Marines—at the poll, then we demanded full control over internal revenues and expenditures as well as over customs, then we demanded the disbanding of the Army and establishment of a Guardia Nacional (Constabulary); then we sent the Marines.[16]

As the commanding U.S. admiral explained as he took over the Dominican occupation, the United States had no intention "to acquire by conquest any territory nor to attack its sovereignty, but our troops will remain until all revolutionary movements have been stamped out"[17] and necessary reforms put into effect.

Three

Outside the Western Hemisphere, where, each President reiterated, the United States held the only warrant to police, the rules were different. Woodrow Wilson emphasized that manifest destiny demanded not the dispatch of troops, which he hoped to avoid, but the exercise of "the moral leadership that is offered us." By the time of the armistice, the President, who in 1915 had been so opposed to war as an instrument of politics that he had been shocked to learn that the War Department had contingency plans for fighting Germany, was now convinced that military power must be the ultimate basis of collective security. Around this issue there rallied that strange coalition of populists, humanists, pacifists, fascists, militarists, and xenophobes who were tagged as "isolationists." Some, like Senator Lodge, thought the assumption of "world leadership," as lobbyists for the League of Nations liked to call it, would leave America "with our country's vigor exhausted" and "her moral force abated by everlasting meddling and muddling in every quarrel great and small, which afflicts the world."[18] Others, like John Dewey, Herbert Croly, and Oswald Villard, attacked the League as an instrument for freezing the imperialist prewar status quo and for defending it by a resumption of war. Still others believed that "world responsibility" was an exercise in altruism and would have none of it. "It makes a mighty difference," the Veterans of Foreign Wars cried, "whether America continues to quick-step to 'Yankee Doodle' or takes to marking time to 'God Save the

King.' "[19] The American Legion in 1919 demanded legislation for "taking the profits out of war." In Chicago "Big Bill" Thompson prepared to run for mayor against King George V; and John Bassett Moore and Elihu Root, the leading American international lawyers of the day, worried that the League might mean the end of the Monroe Doctrine. On the other hand, many church, civic, and peace groups joined the ranks of the isolationists only to demand a system of world order resting on disarmament and conciliation instead of coercion.

As the 1920's wore on, there developed a growing disillusionment in war as a method of settling political problems. The world had manifestly not been made safe for democracy. The allies wouldn't pay their war debts. The Kellogg-Briand Pact to "outlaw war," an attempt to substitute promises for military coercion as a guarantee of peace, reflected the growing popular mood. When the depression struck, many Americans were quick to blame it on "the tragic heritage that has come down to us from this so-called war to end war."[20]

The findings of the revisionist historians, led by Sidney B. Fay, that the issues surrounding the 1914 war were muddier than Americans had been led to believe, reinforced by the more sensational revelations of the Nye Committee about the role of the "merchants of death" in getting the United States into the war, helped to create a climate in which the commitment of military power overseas was looked upon not as a moral crusade but as a cynical expression of "power politics." In 1932 Rabbi Stephen S. Wise stood up in the pulpit and apologized for his support of the 1914 war and promised "without reservation or equivocation"[21] never to sanction another resort to arms. A large number of Christian ministers publicly espoused pacifism.

Four

Franklin D. Roosevelt came to the White House with the backing of isolationists like William R. Hearst, to whom FDR gave assurances that the United States did not belong in the League. Strengthening the forces of "international morality," as Cordell Hull liked to talk about, and the observance of neutrality in the wearisome quarrels of Europe was the new President's prescription for peace. While some, like Henry Stimson, were increasingly worried about the radical militarist regimes that had come to power in Japan, Italy, and Germany and proposed that America "no longer draw a circle about them" but "denounce them as lawbreakers,"[22] the prevailing sentiment was against assumption of police responsibilities. Most Americans did not see how the United States could play that role without courting war. And war was unthinkable.

The early New Dealers were in tune with the national feeling. In 1936 Jerome Frank, the young chairman of the Securities and Exchange Commission, wrote *Save America First* and coined the watchword of the isolationists. Roosevelt himself supported the Neutrality Act of 1935. In August, 1936, at Chautauqua he made it clear that American boys were "not coming back" to Europe, that confronted with "the choice between arms profits and war"— a reference to the Nye hearings—the nation "will answer—must answer—'we choose peace.' " By the next year Hitler's invasion of the Rhineland and his stepped-up persecution of the Jews had caused some defections from the isolationist majority. Roosevelt now took his first major step away from neutrality in the direction of asserting world police responsibility for the United States by calling for a "quarantine of aggressors":

It seems to be unfortunately true that the epidemic of world lawlessness is spreading. When an epidemic of physical disease breaks out, the community approves and joins in a quarantine of the patients in order to protect the health of the community against the spread of the disease.[23]

While the speech was opposed by both *Business Week* and *The New Republic*, it set the tone for a series of accelerating moves toward involvement in the war—repeal of the neutrality acts and the arms embargo, Lend-Lease, and, finally, after Pearl Harbor, fighting itself. Much of the pressure toward intervention came from the Committee to Defend America by Aiding the Allies and the more militant Fight for Freedom Committee. Increasingly Roosevelt began to welcome their pressure to offset the strength of the "America Firsters," a group in which liberals like Robert M. Hutchins and Chester Bowles found themselves sharing the organization's letterhead with old-fashioned populists like Senator Burton Wheeler, German sympathizers like Charles Lindbergh, and fascist ideologues like Father Coughlin.

"Why didn't they call me pusillanimous?"[24] FDR once asked a leading interventionist upon seeing a full-page advertisement attacking his isolationist policy. Strong propaganda was needed, for until the moment when bombs fell on Hawaii, close to thirty percent of the country, according to a succession of Roper polls, still felt that the United States should "have nothing to do with any warring country."[25]

Five

The coming of the war eventually transformed public opinion and created a new interventionist consensus among American leadership. The bitter fight between the interventionists and the isolationists had taught Roosevelt three major lessons. First, the maintenance of peace rested inevitably on the use of force. Second, the commitment of American power to the maintenance of peace could never again be left to the vicissitudes of domestic politics. Some prior commitment of America's responsibilities to world order must be given. Third, the United States, whose intervention in World War II meant the difference between victory and defeat for the aggressors, would have the dominant role in keeping order in the postwar world.

Even before Pearl Harbor, Roosevelt began to think about how the United States would play its police role after the war. In August, 1941, when he met Prime Minister Churchill at Argentia Bay to sign the Atlantic Charter, he was persuaded of the need for an international police force composed of the United States and Britain. As Sumner Welles, who attended the meeting, recalls, he "would not be in favor of the creation of a new Assembly of the League of Nations,"[26] at least not until after the police force had been functioning for a while. He wrote his personal representative at the Vatican, Myron C. Taylor, that his ultimate goal was universal disarmament, but since disarmament "by uniform voluntary methods" might take "generations" to accomplish, the nations interested in preserving peace "must be in a position to enforce nonaggression."[27]

By 1943, at the Tehran Conference, the idea of a U.S.-British police force was out of the question, for Russia's survival seemed assured. The President now proposed that "four policemen"—Britain, Russia, China, and the United States—should enforce the future peace. When Stalin asked FDR whether his proposal meant sending U.S. troops overseas, the President replied that America could limit its contribution to air and naval units. He envisaged that the real power of the police force would be its air squadrons, located at semiautonomous bases throughout the world, which would deter or punish aggressors primarily through air raids on population centers.[28] At Yalta a year later he told Stalin that American troops would leave Europe within two or three years of the victory. His interest in building a strong, friendly China was in large part motivated by a wish to find a political justification for withdrawing the American military presence from Asia. Conscious of her overwhelming power, Roosevelt saw the United States, much like the watchmaker God of the eighteenth-century rationalists, as the prime mover of a security system which would no longer require the day-to-day attention of the American government. Like a well-run town, this was a world where the policeman was always on call but not much in evidence.

An efficient, neutral gendarmerie was far more important to him than the various political and institutional structures for world organization that Cordell Hull and others were urging upon him. "Aren't you at least in favor of a world secretariat?"[29] Hull asked him early in the war. With a laugh he replied, "I'll give you the Pentagon or the Empire State Building. You can put the world secretariat there." Supremely confident of his personal capacity to charm adversaries into cooperation, he generalized his preferred method of doing business into a prescription for a future world system. The problem was "getting along" with Stalin. "What helps a lot," Admiral Ross McIntire, the President's physician, recalls his saying, "is that Stalin is the only man I have to convince. Joe doesn't worry about a congress or a parliament. He's the whole world."[30]

Roosevelt envisioned the United States as the power able to usher in the postimperial era. It was an idealistic, rather vague vision, tempered with the instincts of a Dutch trader. In Richard Hofstadter's words, "The ruthless imperialism of the older colonial powers ... might be replaced by a liberal and benevolent American penetration that would be of advantage both to the natives and to American commerce."[31] Roosevelt was intrigued by the thought of a vast China trade, an activity, he once reminded Rexford Tugwell and Raymond Moley, in which his ancestors had been much involved. He was thrilled at the possibilities open to American oil companies in Saudi Arabia as a result of the concessions obtained during the war from Ibn-Saud, and in Churchill's presence he raised the possibility with the sultan of Morocco of obtaining similar concessions. He talked about an irrigation project in Tunisia that would make the Imperial Valley in California look "like a cabbage patch," and an artificial lake that would make the Sahara bloom for hundreds of miles. British and German bankers had had world trade "pretty well sewn up in their pockets for a long time."[32] Now, he told Churchill, the British must give up preferential trade agreements within their empire and admit "healthy competition."

The United States, as he clearly saw it, would emerge

from the war as the supreme economic power. The State Department, according to Harry C. Hawkins, the director of its Office of Economic Affairs, looked upon the United Nations to provide the political structure within which a satisfactory system of international trade could be established.[83] Cordell Hull's most passionate conviction was that the only satisfactory system was one resting on free trade and convertible currencies. Only if the nations could compete economically on equal terms could the disastrous autarchy of the depression years be avoided. Happily, such an enlightened policy also best served U.S. interests as a whole, since the world's strongest economic power was likely to win the competition.

Politically the United States would seek the stance of the mediator or referee between the declining imperialism of Britain and the expanding power of Russia. It was not only his distaste for what he thought was Churchill's "selfish politics" but also his desire to preserve this impartial role for the United States that prompted him to avoid siding with the prime minister in Big Three meetings on such matters as the proposed second front in the Balkans. Roosevelt thought that he could establish a "give-and-take" relationship with Russia which would satisfy Stalin's security interests in Europe without disturbing America's role of unquestioned global political and economic leadership.

Six

The idea that the war had thrust upon the United States the responsibilities of world leadership was now promoted in many different quarters in the United States. Many different conceptions of that responsibility emerged.

Outside the Western Hemisphere the "Four Policemen" —essentially the United States and Russia—would oppose threats to security and peace. Within the Western Hemisphere the United States would continue to insist on the right to play this role alone. In short, influential planners thought that the United States should demand the right to take police responsibility for the Western Hemisphere but not accord the same privilege to any other power for any other region. As the war in Europe ended, Assistant Secretary of War John J. McCloy remarked that the United States ought to be free to operate a regional arrangement under its control in South America and at the same time be free to intervene promptly in Europe; that it ought not give away "either asset." Secretary of War Henry Stimson agreed, suggesting that it was not asking too much to have "our little region over here which never has bothered anybody."[34]

Henry Luce, early in 1941, first in an article, then in a series of widely distributed newspaper advertisements and booklets, developed the thesis that this was to be The American Century. "The other day," he wrote, "Herbert Hoover said that America was fast becoming the sanctuary of the ideals of civilization. For the moment it may be enough to be the sanctuary of those ideals. But not for long. It now becomes our time to be the powerhouse from which the ideals spread throughout the world. . . . It is the manifest duty of this country to undertake to feed all the people of the world who as a result of the world-wide collapse of civilization are hungry and destitute—all of them, that is, whom we can from time to time reach consistently with a very tough attitude toward all hostile governments."[35] Walter Lippmann warned in 1943 that America stood now at the center of Western civilization. She must assume the role of guarantor of the "Atlantic Community" or face the prospect that Europe would fall under the pressure of an expanding Soviet Union and the "emerging peoples of Asia."[36] Henry Wallace predicted that "The English-speaking peoples of the world will have to take the lead in underwriting world prosperity for a generation to come."[37] Frank Knox, the Secretary of the Navy, declared that the United States and Britain, having crushed the Axis, should "police the seven seas."[38] In the 1943 hearings on Lend-Lease, Republican congressmen Karl Mundt and Charles Eaton found themselves in agreement with the old New Dealer Adolph Berle, that the United States must now seek world power "as a trustee for civilization."[39]

It was the conduct of the war itself, however, that

began to give concrete meaning to the concept of police responsibility, which virtually all now agreed had been thrust upon the United States. (In 1943, in order to neutralize the Willkie internationalists in the party, the GOP drew up the Mackinac Charter, calling for "responsible participation by the United States in postwar cooperative organization among sovereign nations to prevent military aggression. . . ."[40]) In North Africa and the liberated portions of Italy the American forces found themselves in a position to choose the local government.

The dominant role of the communists in the French and Italian resistance movements was a source of increasing concern for the Americans. President Roosevelt expected a civil war to break out in France after liberation.[41] On January 23, 1945, Eisenhower's military headquarters issued a "Directive on Internal Security," which alerted American troops to the possible danger of "internal disorder and strife" due to "economic and political factors" and instructed them in procedures for putting down any such revolt.[42] General de Gaulle, who was head of the provisional government, requested that any such internal security forces be assigned to him, but the State Department did not have confidence that he could keep the communists from coming to power. He had already appointed communists to the Ministries of Health and Industrial Production. Thus the U.S. Army assumed responsibility for the public order. In Italy, too, under the terms of the Italian surrender instrument, as well as in the Far East, in accordance with President Truman's General Order No. 1, U.S. military authorities took over the task of disarming resistance groups who appeared to pose a threat to the return of the established order. Italian communists had thousands of men under arms and were in physical control of Milan and the other major cities of northern Italy. The U.S. Army moved in swiftly to disarm the communists. They offered little resistance and were quickly dislodged from control of city governments and factories which they had seized when the Germans withdrew.[48]

As the war ended, the U.S. government began to clarify the official conception of police responsibilities in the postwar world. The Truman administration conceived its global role as resting on two basic propositions. The first was that U.S. power—chiefly military power—was the essential guarantor of peace. The United States, President

Truman declared shortly after the Japanese surrender, would hold the atomic bomb as a "trustee" for civilization until an agreed system of international control was put into effect. "We must," wrote General George C. Marshall in his final report as chief of staff in September, 1945, "if we are to realize the hopes we may dare to have for peace, enforce our will to peace with strength."[44] From the early days of the war the civilian leaders of the military establishment who would become the key foreign-policy figures in the immediate postwar period had come to an identical conclusion. "The cornerstone in any plan which undertakes to rid us of the curse of war," James Forrestal told the Bond Club in 1943, "must be the armed might of the United States."[45]

The second proposition was that Roosevelt's hope that the United States might exercise its police power over the postwar world in cooperation with the Soviet Union was a vain one. Stalin's intransigence, according to the leading foreign-policy advisers—Averell Harriman, Admiral William Leahy, James Byrnes, and James Forrestal—made it impossible to regard Russia as a proper policeman. Indeed, she was the prime outlaw. The Soviets had rejected the United States position on Poland, which called for the retention of a degree of Western influence, guaranteed by free elections and coalition governments. The Soviets installed a subservient government in Romania and refused to broaden the puppet Polish provisional government to include noncommunists from abroad. While some members of the Truman administration, like Admiral Leahy, thought the Yalta agreements were "so elastic that the Russians can stretch it all the way from Yalta to Washington without ever technically breaking it,"[46] the official administration attitude was one of outrage. The Soviets had deliberately and deceitfully violated their Yalta pledge to put the Polish government on "a broader democratic basis."[47] The United States, all through the war, had insisted upon "access, on equal terms, to such trade, raw materials and industry"[48] as remained in Eastern Europe, and the violation of the American understandings of the Polish agreements was regarded as an extremely serious challenge to American interests. The Soviets fed U.S. suspicion and anger by opposing U.S. positions on Germany, the organization of the United Nations, and nuclear disarmament, among many others, and by asking for occupation rights in

Japan. By April, 1945, when Roosevelt died, the tone of the diplomatic exchanges was already acrimonious. In his last messages to Stalin, Roosevelt spoke of his "concern" and "astonishment"[49] at Stalin's actions, particularly the Soviet charge that Allied military commanders had conspired with the Germans for a separate surrender in Italy.

Within two weeks of Roosevelt's death the most influential members of the new administration had concluded that America was headed for a global test of strength with a new hostile force in the world, which was variously analyzed as Soviet Imperialism, the ideology of Communism, or "the East." "We might well have to face an ideological warfare just as vigorous and dangerous as fascism or Nazism,"[50] Ambassador Averell Harriman told Navy Secretary Forrestal in late April, 1945. "Hitler's greatest crime," Harriman, Forrestal, and General Clay agreed at lunch in Berlin a few weeks later, was "opening the gates of East Europe to Asia."[51]

In February, 1946, George F. Kennan, counselor of the Moscow Embassy, sent an eight-thousand-word dispatch from which he later developed his famous article on "containment." The rulers of the Soviet Union would:

> stand before history, at best, as only the last of that long succession of cruel and wasteful Russian rulers who have relentlessly forced the country on to ever new heights of military power in order to guarantee the external security of their internally weak regimes . . . we have here a political force committed fanatically to the belief that with the United States there can be no permanent *modus vivendi*, that it is desirable and necessary that the internal harmony of our society be disrupted, our traditional way of life destroyed, the international authority of our state be broken, if Soviet power is to be secure.[52]

The U.S. naval attaché in Moscow appended the comment that the American people, with their democratic tradition, could not remotely understand the "utter ruthlessness and complete unscrupulousness of the Soviet ruling clique."[53] President Truman himself soon became convinced that the Soviets were embarked on a major challenge to U.S. supremacy. "There isn't a doubt in my mind," he wrote Secretary of State Byrnes in 1946, "that

Russia intends an invasion of Turkey and the seizure of the Black Sea straits to the Mediterranean. Unless Russia is faced with an iron fist and strong language, another war is in the making. Only one language do they understand—'How many divisions have you.' "[54]

As the United States now saw it, the principal problem of world order was the containment of Russia not only as a "national entity" but also as a "missionary religion." According to the prevailing official view, the two premises that undergirded the prewar policy of noninvolvement had been destroyed by two crucial events. At Pearl Harbor, it became clear that indefinite coexistence with evil was impossible. Sooner or later an enemy who regarded "honesty," "honor," "trust," and "truth" as negative virtues (Churchill's description of the Russian leaders to members of the Truman cabinet in 1946[55]) would strike. At Munich the world learned that conciliation and accommodation, admirable techniques of diplomacy when dealing with reasonable men, are used by Hitlers as weapons to crush gullible adversaries. "Appeasement," which in the prewar dictionaries meant "conciliation," now meant something very close to "surrender."

The men of the Truman administration who set the course of national-security policy for a generation formed their basic political judgments under the impact of these two events. They added up to new and seemingly limitless police responsibilities to protect the world from communism. As the postwar world opened, the United States prepared to take the lead in demanding "international law with teeth."[56] As far ahead as American leaders could see in the convulsing world of 1945, the United States would supply both the teeth and the law.

NOTES—CHAPTER FIVE

1. For a description of the role of idealism in U.S. foreign policy, see Robert E. Osgood, *Ideals and Self-Interest in America's Foreign Relations* (Chicago, 1964), especially pp. 34–35, 51–52, 369–377.

2. Thomas Jefferson, in A. A. Lipscomb and A. E. Bergh, eds., *Writings of Thomas Jefferson* (20 vols.; mem. ed.; Washington, D.C., 1903), vol. X, p. 217.

3. Joel Barlow, July Fourth Oration, delivered in Hartford, Conn., 1789, quoted in Albert K. Weinberg, *Manifest Destiny* (Chicago, 1963), p. 102.

4. Thomas Jefferson, quoted in *ibid.*, p. 103.

5. Samuel Adams, quoted in *ibid.*, p. 22.

6. William Henry Harrison, quoted in *ibid.*, p. 79.

7. John Quincy Adams, Address given on July 4, 1821, quoted in Ronald Steel, *Pax Americana* (New York, 1967).

8. *United States Democratic Review*, quoted in Weinberg, *Manifest Destiny*, p. 183.

9. *Ibid.*

10. Alfred Mahan, quoted in *ibid.*, p. 25.

11. Albert Beveridge, quoted in *ibid.*, p. 307.

12. Theodore Roosevelt, quoted in *ibid.*, p. 428.

13. Talcott Williams, *Annals of the American Academy of Political and Social Science*, XVI (1900), p. 240.

14. Theodore Roosevelt's "blackmailer" reference, referred to in Weinberg, *Manifest Destiny*, p. 426.

15. Calvin Coolidge, quoted in *ibid.*, p. 441.

16. John Bartlow Martin, *Overtaken by Events: The Dominican Crisis from the Fall of Trujillo to Civil War* (New York, 1966), p. 28.

17. Quoted in Sumner Welles, *Naboth's Vineyard: The Dominican Republic, 1844–1924* (2 vols.; New York, 1928), vol. II, p. 777.

18. Henry Cabot Lodge, quoted in Weinberg, *Manifest Destiny*, p. 472.

19. Quoted in Selig Adler, *The Isolationist Impulse: Its Twentieth Century Reaction* (New York, 1961), p. 87.

20. From a letter of P. O'Gara to Senator George W. Norris, April 8, 1932, quoted in *ibid.*, p. 228.

21. Rabbi Wise, Sermon in 1932, quoted in *ibid.*, p. 229.

22. Henry Stimson, quoted in Kenneth Thompson, *Political Realism and the Crisis of World Politics: An American Approach to Foreign Policy* (Princeton, 1960), p. 190.

23. Franklin D. Roosevelt, quoted in Foster Rhea Dulles, *America's Rise to World Power* (New York, 1954), p. 176.

24. Franklin D. Roosevelt's comments were reported to me in a personal communication with James P. Warburg.

25. Polls cited in Robert E. Sherwood, *Roosevelt and Hopkins* (New York, 1948), p. 128.

26. Franklin D. Roosevelt, quoted in Frank Donovan, *Mr. Roosevelt's Four Freedoms* (New York, 1948), p. 128.

27. Franklin D. Roosevelt, quoted in *ibid.*, p. 41.

28. Franklin D. Roosevelt's wartime thinking on a postwar police force is described in *ibid.*, pp. 81–94.

29. Cordell Hull, quoted in Richard Hofstadter, *American Political Tradition* (New York, 1945), p. 348.

30. Franklin D. Roosevelt, quoted in *ibid.*, p. 348.

31. Franklin D. Roosevelt, quoted in *ibid.*, p. 349.

32. Franklin D. Roosevelt, quoted in *ibid.*, p. 349.

33. For an account of economic thinking in the State Department and its relationship to strategic considerations, see Warren Hickman, *Genesis of the European Recovery Pro-*

gram (Geneva, 1949), pp. 91–166. See also Joseph M. Jones, *The Fifteen Weeks* (New York, 1964), pp. 93–95.

34. For the full text of the telephone conversation of May 8, 1945, from which these remarks were taken, see Gabriel Kolko, *The Politics of War.*

35. Henry Luce, quoted in Charles A. Beard and Mary R. Beard, *The American Spirit* (New York, 1962), pp. 497–498.

36. Walter Lippmann, quoted in Adler, *The Isolationist Impulse,* p. 305.

37. Henry Wallace, quoted in Beard and Beard, *The American Spirit,* p. 496.

38. Frank Knox, quoted in *ibid.,* pp. 494–495.

39. See remarks of these congressmen in U.S. Congress, House of Representatives, *Extension of Lend-Lease Act, Hearings,* before the Committee on Foreign Affairs, 78th Congress, 1st session, 1943.

40. Mackinac Charter, quoted in Adler, *The Isolationist Impulse,* p. 308.

41. President Roosevelt's concerns about a civil war in France are discussed in Walter Millis, *Arms and the State* (New York, 1956), p. 123.

42. See *Directive on Internal Security,* January 23, 1945, quoted in Hickman, *Genesis,* p. 155.

43. For a description of U.S. attitudes toward and relations with European resistance movements, see Kolko, *The Politics of War,* especially ch. II.

44. George C. Marshall, *Biennial Report of the Chief of Staff of the United States Army, July 1, 1943–June 30, 1945* (Washington, D.C., 1945), p. 6.

45. James Forrestal, quoted in Arnold Rogow, *James Forrestal* (New York, 1963), p. 125.

46. Admiral William D. Leahy, *I Was There* (New York, 1950), pp. 315–316.

47. See the text of the Declaration of the Crimean Conference on Poland, calling for "universal suffrage," "free and unfettered elections," and the "right" of "all democratic and anti-Nazi parties" to take part in the election, quoted in H. L. Trefousse, ed., *The Cold War* (New York, 1966), p. 68.

48. This language is based on Article VII of The Atlantic Charter, quoted in Hickman, *Genesis,* p. 68. See also U.S. Department of State, *Papers Relating to the Foreign Relations of the United States: The Conference of Berlin (Potsdam),* (Washington, D.C., 1960), vol. I, pp. 262–264. This document is cited in Walter Le Feber, *America, Russia, and the Cold War (1945–1967)* (New York, 1967), p. 10n.

49. See letter of President Roosevelt to Marshal Stalin, April 1, 1945, quoted in Trefousse, *The Cold War,* p. 34.

50. Averell Harriman, quoted in Walter Millis, ed., *The Forrestal Diaries* (New York, 1951), p. 47.

51. Quoted in *ibid.,* p. 79.

52. Kennan's dispatch is quoted in *ibid.,* pp. 137–139.

53. Quoted in *ibid.*, p. 140.

54. Harry S. Truman, *Year of Decisions*, vol. I of *Memoirs* (New York, 1955), p. 606.

55. For a description of Churchill's visit with members of the Truman cabinet, see Millis, *The Forrestal Diaries*, p. 145.

56. The expression was used publicly by Bernard Baruch in his speech on atomic energy before the United Nations, June 6, 1946. See *The New York Times*, June 7, 1946.

Part
TWO

CHAPTER 6

The Truman Doctrine and the Greek Civil War

One

IN THE NAME OF THE TRUMAN DOCTRINE the United States supplied the military and economic power to enable the Greek monarchy to defeat an army of communist-led insurgents in 1947–49 and won a victory which has become a model for U.S. relations toward civil wars and insurgencies. Almost twenty years later the President of the United States was defending his intervention in Vietnam by pointing to his predecessor's success in Greece. The American experience in Greece not only set the pattern for subsequent interventions in internal wars but also suggested the criteria for assessing the success or failure of counterinsurgency operations. Greece was the first major police task which the United States took on in the postwar world. One of the most important consequences of the American involvement in Greece in the 1940's was the development of new bureaucracies specializing in military assistance, police administration, and economic aid, committed to an analysis of revolution and a set of responses for dealing with it that would be applied to many different conflicts in the next twenty years.

In this chapter we shall look into the fateful series of

decisions that culminated in the Truman Doctrine and its execution in Greece. To start this inquiry, we need to ask a basic question: Why did those in charge of the national security of the United States happen to define the problem in Greece in the way they did, and why did they use the power of the United States in the ways they did? To some the answer may be so obvious that the question itself is startling. Official history, as it always does, records these decisions as more or less inevitable responses to clear-cut challenges. There was no other practical or honorable choice.

To understand this turning point in American foreign policy, however, we must attempt to reconstruct the scene as it was seen through contemporary eyes. If we turn to Winston Churchill as chronicler, we find him, a few years after these events, expressing great surprise that the American intervention turned out the way it did. Alluding to Roosevelt's strong opposition to British military activities against the Greek communists during the war, the former prime minister wrote, "I little thought . . . that the State Department, supported by overwhelming American public opinion, would in a little more than two years not only adopt and carry on the course we had opened, but would make vehement and costly exertions, even of a military character, to bring it to fruition."[1]

The continuation of Britain's role in Greece was a highly accurate description of the American intervention, but it was hardly an inevitable one, especially in view of the bad press accorded the British Empire in the United States. Tradition suggested other definitions of the American Responsibility toward Greece. In late 1946 and early 1947 there were at least three other plausible ways for U.S. National-Security Managers to look at the Greek crisis. Each would have dictated a form of intervention different from the Truman Doctrine. Each would have required a different definition of the American national interest. One was to continue to regard Greece primarily as a relief problem. At the end of September, 1946, the Food and Agriculture Organization reported that Greece urgently needed a minimum of one billion dollars from the United States and British governments. The United States had already provided most of the three hundred and forty-five million dollars spent on Greek relief in 1945 and 1946, and the Truman administration was planning to spend sixty million dollars more, but the Republican-controlled Eightieth Congress, elected on the economy slogan "Had Enough?", appeared unwilling to support a major project of international charity. Greek officials argued that raids by insurgents, which resumed in September, 1946, were a major factor in preventing economic recovery. But a U.S. mission under Paul Porter, which arrived in January, 1947, found that the most pressing crises were due to the collapse of the Greek currency, the resultant panic over the disappearance of gold reserves, and a strike by the entire Greek civil service.

The problem of Greece might, alternatively, have been regarded as a traditional crisis of Balkan politics. The Peace Conference held in the summer and fall of 1946 dramatized the depth and bitterness of the conflict between Greece and her Balkan neighbors, particularly Bulgaria and Yugoslavia, over disputed territories. The prime minister devoted most of his opening speech to parliament in 1946 to Greece's territorial claims. When the United States refused to back Greece's demands for northern Epirus and for certain adjustments of the frontier with Bulgaria, Greek politicians from left to right called the settlement "a most cruel injustice" and an occasion for "deepest mourning."[2] Bulgaria and Yugoslavia made no secret of their desire to annex parts of Macedonia and Thrace. In conversations with Americans, Greek officials stressed the danger that the Soviet Union might encourage the newly communist Balkan regimes to satisfy their territorial ambitions and thereby at the same time extend the area of Soviet influence. Thus the problem might have been seen principally as one calling for international mediation. In effect, the United States, Britain, and the Soviet Union might have continued their informal agreements during the war, establishing zones of respective "responsibility" in the Balkans and jointly guaranteeing the frontiers. However, the Great Powers would have had to agree on what their respective roles in the Balkans were to be, and it was the lack of agreement on this very issue that fanned the growing East-West suspicion into the Cold War.

The third way to look at Greece in 1946–47 was as a problem of internal political collapse. The ultrarightist government of Constantine Tsaldares, established after the British army had helped put down the communist-led ELAS rebellion in 1945, attempted to root out opposition by force. The government ousted the leadership of the Greek

Federation of Labor and replaced it with government appointees. In October, 1946, the Greek government dismissed seventeen university professors and twenty-six senior civil servants on purely political grounds, although most of them were not communists. "The internal situation is much worse than it has ever been. Law and order are nonexistent,"[3] a former Liberal premier told a group of visiting British M.P.'s. Like the Diem government in Vietnam ten years later, the Tsaldares regime conducted what the U.S. correspondents for the *Herald Tribune* and Associated Press termed "a desperate effort to halt a growing rebellion and wipe out not only Communists but all democratic, liberal, and republican elements."[4] The government armed right-wing supporters, and often with the collaboration of the police, encouraged them to terrorize political opponents. "This tactic," a former Progressive (moderate) party minister wrote in October, 1946, "drives the people to the hills, since no Greek is willing to be beaten without reason, only because he is an opponent of the party in power."[5] The government was rapidly polarizing the country by limiting the expression of political choices either to wholehearted support of Tsaldares' reactionary policy or to wholehearted opposition by joining communist-led guerrilla bands in the hills. A British parliamentary delegation, made up of Labour, Conservative, and Liberal members, visiting Greece in late summer 1946, condemned the government terrorism and urged sweeping reforms,[6] including the restoration of constitutional liberties, an amnesty, the reestablishment of an independent labor movement, the end of political deportations, and the formation of an "all-Party Government . . . to include all sections with the possible exception of the Extreme Left." The establishment of a regime which "resembled a dictatorship," the report observed discreetly, "would have fatal consequences."[7] As these observers saw it, the government should attempt to accommodate the mounting political opposition in Greece, not repress it.

The United States made a few modest efforts in late 1946 to persuade the Greek government to move in the direction of reform. On October 18, Ambassador Lincoln MacVeagh showed King George II a letter from the President suggesting that the United States was prepared to grant "substantial aid and supplies"[8] but that "the Greek Government should help persuade American public opinion that the rulers of Greece constituted no oligarchy of reactionaries, bent on exploiting U.S. aid in order to tyrannize their political opponents."[9] The government should be broadened so that Americans might come to see that all Greeks, except the communists, were united.

However, in the minds of the U.S. National-Security Managers, the Greek crisis soon took on a very different significance. Greece was still a relief problem, still a point of tension in age-old Balkan rivalries, and more than ever, a revolution with deep domestic political roots. But more than any of these, Greece was now seen as a pawn in a global struggle. Keeping Greece noncommunist had become the central concern of the United States.

When President Truman announced the decision to help the Greek monarchy win the civil war, he stressed that the commitment was prompted by the "terrorist activities of several thousand armed men, led by communists."[10] The United States was to use its power to put down violence. But, clearly, violence itself was not the issue, for throughout 1946, according to correspondents of the London *Times* and other U.S. and British papers, the Greek government itself had been carrying out mass arrests, tortures, beatings, and other retaliation against those who had been on the wrong side of the earlier civil war that ended in January, 1945. The foreign minister had resigned in early 1946, charging "terrorism by state organs."[11] In Greece, as elsewhere, the violence of constituted authorities, however oppressive their rule, was judged by one criterion and the violence of insurgents by another. President Truman alluded to the corruption and brutality of the Greek government by conceding that it was "not perfect." But while the fascist character of the government genuinely bothered some members of the U.S. government, most National-Security Managers shared the judgment of former Secretary of State James Byrnes: "We did not have to decide that the Turkish Government and the Greek Monarchy were outstanding examples of free and democratic governments."[12]

It was enough that the guerrillas were communists and as such constituted, according to Joseph Jones, the State Department official who drafted the original Truman Doctrine message, an "instrument" of Soviet "expansionism." What was happening in Greece was important to officials in Washington only as it affected U.S. interests, as the State Department saw them. This is, of course, the standard by which governments customarily judge internal

developments in other countries. The interesting question
is why the Truman administration saw the mounting insurgency in Greece as a threat to the American national
interest.

Two

To understand the commitment to Greece, one
must try to grasp the picture of the world which the U.S.
National-Security Managers carried around with them in
their heads. As 1947 opened, the magnitude of the fundamental changes wrought by the war was becoming
clearer. Looking back at the whirlwind of events that had
spun around them in the last two years, President Truman
and his advisers could discern three general trends. First,
the effort to oppose Soviet domination of Eastern Europe
had failed. The breakup of the London Conference of
September, 1945, the chief cause of which, according to
Secretary of State Byrnes, was the refusal of the Russians
to broaden the governments of Bulgaria and Romania and
to permit free elections, marked for him and for John
Foster Dulles, his Republican adviser, the onset of the
Cold War. The effort to remove Poland from exclusive
Soviet control, which Truman had vigorously taken up in
his first encounter with Molotov eight days after assuming
office, had also failed. The atomic bomb, which Byrnes
had suggested "might well put us in a position to dictate
our own terms at the end of the war,"[13] had not produced
the intended result. Churchill had called for an end to
the "police governments" and the "iron curtain" across
Eastern Europe. President Truman had declared that
"these nations are not to be spheres of influence of any
one power." In January, 1946, the President had insisted,
"I'm not going to agree to the recognition of those governments unless they are radically changed."[14] It is true
that Stalin acceded to certain American demands relating
to elections in Hungary and temporarily postponed the
Bulgarian elections in the summer of 1945. But Byrnes's

policy of "patience and firmness" had by the end of 1946 resulted not in a relaxation but in a drastic tightening of the Soviet grip on Eastern Europe.

"This war is not as in the past," Milovan Djilas, former Vice-President of Yugoslavia, remembers Stalin saying in April, 1945. "Whoever occupies a territory also imposes on it his own social system. Everyone imposes his own system as far as his army can reach. It cannot be otherwise."[15] By early 1947 Stalin had removed his armies from Czechoslovakia and Hungary. But in every country of Eastern Europe he had established the basis for undisputed control. With the breakdown of the London Conference in December, 1945, the communists in Poland moved swiftly and brutally to crush the opposition Socialist party. By 1947 Stanislaw Mikolajczyk, the opposition leader supported by the West, had fled the country. It was not until October, 1946, that Bulgaria fell under the control of the communist-dominated Fatherland Front. In Hungary the communists did not obtain control until the elections of August, 1947. (In November, 1945, they had polled only seventeen percent of the vote in a free election.) In Romania the communist daily *Scinteia*, as late as November 8, 1946, was wishing King Michael "a long life, good health, and a reign rich in democratic achievements."[16] A few months later Romania, too, had become a People's Republic.

The second trend Truman and his advisers had observed was that outside of Eastern Europe a tough American line had succeeded in producing a series of Soviet retreats. On June 7, 1945, the Soviet foreign minister asked Turkey for the return of the province of Khars, a former czarist conquest, and for a share in the administration of the Dardanelles. These demands prompted the Turkish Foreign Office to send a message to Washington warning that "the Soviets, like Hitler, have become victory drunk and are embarking on world domination."[17] When, later, Soviet troops moved up to the border, Under Secretary of State Acheson told the President that "it was the view of the State Department that the Russian note and its last three demands on Turkey reflected a desire to control and dominate that country."[18] Acceding to these demands, he argued, "would be followed next by infiltration of Greece by Russia with the obvious consequences in the Middle East and the obvious threat to the line of communications

of the British to India." President Truman agreed that
"this trial balloon" should be firmly resisted even at the
risk of war. "We might as well find out whether the
Russians are bent on world conquest now as in five or ten
years."[19] In February, 1946, Secretary Forrestal arranged
to have the body of the Turkish ambassador, who had
died in Washington fifteen months earlier, taken home on
the *Missouri*, the largest battleship of the fleet and the
scene a few months earlier of the Japanese-surrender
ceremony.

Secretary Byrnes thought that this bit of battleship
diplomacy had "produced most satisfactory results,"[20] for
the Russians appeared to be easing their pressure on the
Turks. He supported Forrestal's ideal that the United
States should "establish the custom of the American Flag
being flown in these waters."[21] (Indeed, Forrestal favored
American naval forces sailing "in any waters in any part
of the globe.") During the next year the United States
dispatched on "courtesy calls" to the Mediterranean an
additional two aircraft carriers, seven cruisers, eight destroyers, and four other military vessels. In September,
1946, the Navy Department announced that units of the
American fleet would be permanently stationed in the
Mediterranean to "carry out American policy and diplomacy." In the face of this commitment of American
power, the Soviets dropped their demands on Turkey.

The Soviets further convinced U.S. leaders of the effec-
tiveness of the "get-tough" policy in their response to
American diplomacy over the Iranian crisis of early 1946.
This was another piece of territory adjacent to the Soviet
Union into which Russian military power had flowed during the war. In January, 1942, Britain, Russia, and Iran
had signed a treaty which called for joint occupation of
Persia for the duration of the war, provided all foreign
troops would be withdrawn within six months of the end
of hostilities. When the day prescribed for the evacuation
of Soviet troops arrived, U.S. intelligence reports revealed
that the Russians were reinforcing rather than withdrawing their garrisons.

Since the end of 1944 the Soviets had been attempting
to negotiate mineral and oil rights in the northern provinces of Iran, but the pro-British government had termi-
nated the negotiations. The Soviets thereupon directed the
communist-controlled Tudeh party to agitate for an au-

tonomous provincial government, with which it hoped to complete the concession arrangements. With the aid of Soviet troops, which prevented the central Iranian government from intervening, the rebels formed a "Provisional Assembly of Autonomous Azerbaijan," which began to pressure the central government to accede to Soviet demands. These included a 51½-percent interest in a Russian-Iranian stock company to exploit the oil in the northern provinces (the British concessions left the Iranians about 20 percent) and a right to keep troops in portions of Iran indefinitely. The Iranians warned the State Department that a communist coup in Tehran was imminent.

While the Iranian premier was in Moscow attempting to negotiate the withdrawal of the Russian troops, Secretary of State Byrnes delivered a speech which a State Department official of the time has characterized as "virtually an ultimatum."[22]

> We have joined with our allies in the United Nations to put an end to war. We have covenanted not to use force except in the defense of law. . . . But as a great power and as a permanent member of the Security Council, we have a responsibility to use our influence to see that other powers live up to their covenant. And that responsibility we also intend to meet. . . . Though the status quo is not sacred and unchangeable, we cannot overlook a unilateral gnawing away at the status quo. The Charter forbids aggression to be accomplished by coercion or pressure or by subterfuge such as political infiltration.[23]

Byrnes's speech strikingly foreshadowed the Truman Doctrine speech of a year later. Though the tone was less strident, all the basic elements of that doctrine were already present. Indeed, the Truman speech incorporated some of the language of the earlier Byrnes declaration. The United States announced that it intended to enforce the law of nations and to make other nations behave. Changes in the status quo brought about by "pressure," "coercion," or "political infiltration" amounted to "aggression." To meet the threat of aggression, Byrnes reiterated a few days later, "our military strength will be used."

These strong statements, supported by former Prime Minister Churchill's "Iron Curtain" speech at Fulton, Mis-

souri, a few days earlier, persuaded the Russians to withdraw their troops. The Soviets had already secured many
of the concessions they had demanded, including Tudeh
participation in the Tehran government, a continuation of
the revolutionary Azerbaijan regime, and the oil concessions. But once the troops were gone and British troops
moved in across the border at Basra, Iraq, they lost them
all. A Tudeh-led general strike in July, 1946, provided the
occasion to remove the communists from the central government, crush the Azerbaijan regime, and, a few months
later, cancel the oil concessions. Ten months later Brigadier General H. Norman Schwartzkopf, formerly head of
the New Jersey State Police, arrived with twenty-five
million dollars' worth of small arms to take charge of the
Iranian police. Once again a show of force had paid off.

The third trend of international life which haunted the
Truman administration was the decline and impending fall
of the British Empire. During World War II the British
imperial system had been viewed in Washington as an
institution which not only was an offense against the
Wilsonian vision inherited by Roosevelt and Hull of a
decent world moral and legal order but also was a threat
to the global economic system which the United States
wanted to see in the postwar world. Throughout the war
the State Department planned on facing a Britain which
would continue to play her prewar role. Thus the problem
for the State Department was how to combat the imperial
preference and other devices for excluding American
trade and investment in the colonial areas and how to
extend American influence into strategic areas under British control. In short, the British Empire was seen as the
principal rival to United States economic power.[24] However,
when the war came to an end, the United States reas-
sessed its view of the British Empire, for it soon became
evident that British economic and political power had
collapsed throughout the world.

In India, Thailand, Burma, Ceylon, and Malaya, British
rule was being challenged by nationalist independence
movements that had been triggered by war and the Japanese occupation. In the Mediterranean, too, British supremacy was coming to an end. Now the National-Security
Managers in the State Department and in the Pentagon
began to see the decline of British power not only as an

economic opportunity but also as a threat to U.S. security. They argued that with the end of the robust British Empire, the United States must "fill the vacuum." That is, either the United States or a dependent ally must continue to exercise a clear preponderance of power throughout the world or a hostile power would. In the chaos of the postwar world, the concept of imperial order looked better and better to the professionals in the State Department. "Half the world was held together and protected and removed from the white heat of great power rivalry by a force that was both skillful and benign,"[25] was the wistful comment on the disappearing empire by a policy-planning-staff member at the time. But the colonials were having increasing doubts about the benignity of the British Empire, and Churchill's successor, facing bankruptcy, had begun to preside over its liquidation.

On January, 20, 1947, the Attlee government issued a White Paper which contained the stark admission, "The position of Britain is extremely serious."[26] The American loan was running out. The shortage of coal was "calamitous." Following the unusually brutal blizzards of February, 1947, more than half of British industry came to a complete standstill. "The biggest crash since the fall of Constantinople—the collapse of the heart of an Empire—impends,"[27] *The New York Times* intoned. "It has projected before our imagination the picture of a world without Britain. The consequences to us of such a void in the economic and political universe are alarming."

Three

In itself the struggle for power in a barren Balkan land would not have triggered the massive American response which the Truman administration mounted in the spring of 1947. Against the background of a collapsing world order, however, the Greek civil war convinced

American National-Security Managers that here was an object worthy of a great commitment.

The Nazi invasion of Greece, like the Japanese occupation of Southeast Asia, shook a traditional society. As in Vietnam and Indonesia, so also in Greece, a brutal occupation undermined the established holders of power and opened the way for new forces in the society to enter politics through violence. In Greece several rival underground organizations sprang up to resist the Germans. One was EDES (National Republican Greek League), headed by antimonarchist but conservative army officers, notably Colonel Napoleon Zervas. In 1942 British intelligence agents parachuted into Greece with funds to subsidize the EDES if it would carry out certain prescribed acts of sabotage against the Nazis. Earlier the British had made contact with ELAS, a guerrilla army organized in the mountains in the winter of 1941–42 primarily by Greek communists; but the ELAS leaders had been suspicious of the British and unenthusiastic about the particular sabotage efforts the British were urging on them. By July, 1943, ELAS had sixteen thousand guerrillas in the field, EDES about three thousand. The noncommunist guerrillas were badly split among rival groups. The communist forces, under the leadership of the Greek National Liberation Front (EAM), were better organized.

When the resistance began in 1941–42, the communist-led guerrillas had no contacts at all with Moscow. The prewar links between the Greek Communist party and Moscow, "tenuous and unreliable" as they were,[28] had been completely cut off by the Axis occupation. In July, 1943, eight Soviet officers arrived at the ELAS headquarters to assess the prospects of the guerrillas. The Soviet military mission reported that ELAS was "just a rabble of armed men, not worth supporting."[29] Requests for Soviet aid went unanswered; Bulgarian guerrillas operating just over the border with Soviet support also ignored the struggle in Greece. As the Italians and then the German occupation forces withdrew in 1944, the rival guerrilla forces began to attack each other. The British supported EDES; ELAS captured most of its arms from the retreating Axis armies. General Scobie, the British commander, sought to reconcile the various guerrilla bands and to persuade them to operate in separate areas. Meanwhile he installed a government in Athens under George Papandreou, a monarchist politician.

The Soviet-satellite Bulgarian army occupied parts of Macedonia and Thrace. The Soviets, consistent with their agreement with Churchill to leave Greece primarily to British influence, ordered the Bulgarian troops to evacuate Greek soil. By the end of 1944 ELAS controlled most of the countryside of Greece and occupied all cities, towns, and villages except for Athens, Salonika, Piraeus, and a few other centers where British troops were stationed. EAM, the political arm of the communist-guerrilla movement, began to administer large areas of the country, making use of secret police and their power over the distribution of UNRRA supplies. Openly agitating against the Papandreou government and the government secret police, they charged, accurately, as it turned out, that the government was killing and imprisoning leftist partisans while protecting former Nazi collaborators.[30] The civil war began when ELAS, still in political control of far more of Greece than the Athens government, refused to surrender its arms unless EDES also agreed to disarm. The revolt which flamed over the whole peninsula required a British force of seventy-five thousand to crush it.

In February, 1945, the British arranged a cease-fire at Varkiza. The guerrillas agreed to surrender their arms, provided an immediate plebiscite on the return of the king was held, to be followed by free elections. ELAS did surrender far more weapons than anyone in the British army thought they had had, but they hid most of their small arms and automatic weapons in the mountains. The government, which had yet to condemn a single Nazi collaborator, carried out wholesale arrests and executions of former ELAS fighters.[31] EAM charged that at least five hundred had been murdered and twenty thousand arrested in the first five months after the cease-fire. The government countered with a discovery of the bodies of eighty-eight hundred hostages allegedly murdered by the ELAS during the fighting. In the civil war both sides had taken hostages and practiced terrorism. Now, with ELAS disarmed, the government and the bands of royalist guerrillas who supported it were responsible for most of the terror and political murder.

The Greek government was not only repressive but also hopelessly corrupt. Tsaldares spent about fifty percent of the budget on the army and the police, six percent on reconstruction. Capital was fleeing the country. The rich knew how to escape taxation, and inflation was rampant. At the end of the war the drachma was valued at one hundred and forty-nine to the dollar. A year later it was five thousand to the dollar. Much UNRRA aid was diverted to the black market. In 1947 an American investigating team found huge supplies rotting in warehouses at a time when seventy-five percent of Greek children were suffering from malnutrition. The British proceeded to reconstruct the army, which they put in the hands of monarchist officers, including, as Ernest Bevan admitted in the House of Commons, two hundred and twenty-eight former officers of the Nazi security battalions in Greece. They also strengthened the police, leaving it under the direction of the police chief, who for three years had served the Nazis.

In 1945 and 1946 the British installed, successively, a general and an admiral as prime minister of Greece. Both filled provincial administrative posts with monarchist sympathizers before the British replaced them with an aged Liberal politician, Themistokles Sophoulis. On March 31, 1946, an election was held, which resulted in a clear-cut victory for the monarchists. Although termed a fair election by numerous Allied observers, this verdict, as Howard K. Smith, the CBS correspondent who visited Greece shortly after the elections, concluded, is open to doubt:

> With all power and armed force in the hands of the right and with the countryside under the terror of ubiquitous and merciless rightist bands, the Greek peasant was in no mood to be heroic; . . . I visited a village outside Athens and was told by peasants through a neutral Greek interpreter that they had been threatened with having their village burned down if they did not yield a majority monarchist vote in the elections. In this village the newspaper of the Liberal Party—the party of the Premier of Greece [Sophoulis]—was forbidden to be read on pain of beatings.[32]

Meanwhile the EAM was in the throes of an internal debate between those who favored attempting a slow political route to power and those who wanted to resume the fight. As the government repression mounted, the militants in the EAM grew stronger. Noncommunist politicians from the six parties that made up the original Liberation Front resigned. Many ex-ELAS leaders, "spurred on by what would happen to them if they were arrested, took to the hills and began collecting former comrades around them."[33] According to Major Edgar O'Ballance's recent account of the civil war, this trend was "spontaneous rather than centrally organized or inspired,"[34] although the Greek Communist party tried to keep control over these fast-moving events.

At the end of 1945 ELAS was reorganized as the "Greek Democratic army" with the help of members of the Bulgarian and Yugoslav general staffs. In the beginning Stalin apparently approved of the cooperation, although Soviet promises of assistance were never fulfilled. The relationship between the other Balkan communist regimes and the Greek communists was ambivalent from the first. Relations with Albania were the best, probably because the Greek Communist party had renounced the claim still pressed by the Athens government to annex the Albanian province of northern Epirus. In 1946 a communist government was established in Tirana which permitted the Greek Democratic army to build camps on its soil near the border to be used as rear bases for incursions into Greece. A Radio Free Greece was set up on Albanian soil. Actual military aid, however, was small.

Tito, in Yugoslavia, was more uncertain about aiding the Greek rebels. His political plans at the time called for a Balkan federation under his own control, and particularly a communist Slav Macedonia, which would in all events be detached from Greece.[35] In 1946 he did offer food, use of army camps, and a few transport vehicles, but little else. The question of Yugoslav aid provoked dissension within the Greek Communist party between nationalists, who were suspicious of Tito's territorial aims, and those party leaders who put ideological solidarity above all else.

In late 1946 Bulgaria also came under the full control of a communist government. Dimitroff, the party chief, was also a nationalist with an interest in annexing Thrace as well as the city of Salonika.

By October, 1946, the Greek Democratic army, which had reached the level of six thousand men, was carrying on hit-and-run raids throughout northern Greece. The government, unable to deal with them either by using the thirty-thousand-man police force or by arming loyal villagers, secured British permission to use the national army, now at a strength of one hundred thousand men. The domestic political life of the country was moving toward a new crisis when Tsaldares, against all the pressures of the British to broaden his extreme-right-wing government, eliminated all the opposition parties from the cabinet and closed down two communist newspapers.

The Balkan neighbors now agreed to step up their aid to the communist rebels, but at a price. General Markos, the commander of the Greek Democratic Army, made agreements with Albania, Yugoslavia, and Bulgaria for the detachment from Greece of its Slavic areas and for other territorial adjustments most unfavorable to Greece. By March, 1947, when the Truman Doctrine was announced, the rebel force stood at about seventeen thousand men. Making increasing use of Yugoslav territory for regrouping and medical care, the rebels carried out raids of mounting intensity, using terrorist techniques in the countryside, including the taking and executing of hostages. General Zervas, the former head of the EDES, who was appointed minister of public order in early 1947, carried out an extensive program of political murder of his own.

By the time President Truman asked Congress for military aid for Greece, the communists had developed a political and intelligence network that included about fifty thousand active workers who were engaged in collecting information and supplies and carrying out sabotage and other acts of terrorism. An additional two hundred and fifty thousand sympathizers gave the rebels assistance from time to time.

A Yugoslav general was now attached to the headquarters of the Democratic army at Bulkes, Yugoslavia. The Soviet Union, which had recognized the Greek government almost immediately, withdrew its ambassador in April, 1947. Stalin gave no aid to the rebels, however. The Soviets limited their involvement to a handful of military liaison officers whose function was to observe the arrangements worked out between the Yugoslavs and the Greek guerrillas. A Balkan joint staff was formed under Yugoslav domination. Tito agreed to give more weapons and supplies in return for the right to veto any changes in the high command of the Greek Democratic Army. The Greeks were unhappy about the arrangement and distrustful of the Yugoslavs, but they had nowhere else to turn. The International Brigade of communist volunteers, of which some of the rebels had dreamed, and some had, indeed, been promised, never materialized. By 1948 about seventy-five percent of the rebels' small arms were coming from the Balkan neighbors, mostly Yugoslavia; none came from the Soviet Union directly, nor, so far as one can determine, did Stalin transmit weapons to the Greeks through the Balkan satellites.[36]

On February 21, 1947, the British first secretary called on the director of the U.S. State Department's Office of Near Eastern and African Affairs and the deputy director of European affairs and handed these two senior foreign-service officers a note. What the note said was that Britain could no longer maintain her forces in Greece or continue her economic support to that nation. What the note meant, as one of the career men in the State Department comprehended it, was that "Great Britain had within the hour handed the job of world leadership, with all its burdens and all its glory, to the United States."[37]

The next eighteen days leading up to the President's enunciation of the Truman Doctrine before a joint session of Congress was a time of feverish activity for the State Department. But plans for giving military aid to Greece were well advanced long before the British note arrived. At the Paris Peace Conference on the Balkans, Byrnes had begun thinking about making a major United States commitment to Greece. But during October and November of 1946 most of the planning and negotiating on the question was in the hands of the Pentagon and middle-level officers in the State Department Office of Near Eastern and African Affairs. In mid-October, Loy Henderson, the director of that office, remarked to the Greek ambassador in Washington that "the integrity of Greece was a basic point of U.S. policy in the Mediterranean."[38] On November 2, a U.S. military officer attached to the American delegation at the Paris Conference told the Greek military attaché "that the speediest strengthening of the Greek State, in order to enable it to withstand pressures," had become "a positive line in U.S. policy."[39] He promised military and economic aid if the Greeks presented a clear-cut program of their needs. While the President had stressed the importance of broadening the

Greek government in his message to the king, the reaction
in Athens to these indications of growing U.S. interest in
Greece was to move in the opposite direction. Two days
after the Greek officer reported that the American officer
had "spoken with authority" when he invited a request for
aid, Tsaldares eliminated all opposition-party ministers
from the cabinet. Shortly thereafter the United States
promised to send an economic mission and dispatched the
aircraft carrier *Randolph* on a well-publicized "courtesy
call" to Athens.

Sporadic incursions of Albanian and Yugoslav guerrillas
into Greek territory had begun in September. All but a
few of the guerrillas who staged these initial raids marking
the resumption of the civil war, however, were Greeks. In
December the Security Council voted to send an investigating commission to the Balkans to investigate the charge
that the Albanians and Yugoslavs were fomenting rebellion in Greece. When the commission was later denied
access, U.S. diplomats took this to be a tacit admission of
the charges.

At about the same time, Tsaldares came to Washington
to ask for aid and once more to press the Greek claim to
northern Epirus. The prime minister reported back that he
had found the President and Byrnes, the secretary of
state, sympathetic, but that Acheson, the under secretary,
seemed cool to the idea of economic aid and indifferent to
Greece's territorial claims. Senator Vandenberg, whom
the prime minister also met, was reported to have shown
"great sympathy and understanding for the Greek
cause."[40] Tsaldares returned to Athens encouraged. On his
return the cabinet was reshuffled again. Maximos became
premier and Tsaldares took over as vice-premier and
foreign minister. But the cabinet was not broadened to
include moderate or liberal politicians who favored
dealing with either the government crises or the growing
insurgency in other ways.

The political life of the United States was also undergoing some rapid changes. A few weeks before the British
first secretary "handed the job of world leadership" to his
American counterpart, the Eightieth Congress had taken
its seats in what Speaker Sam Rayburn called a "beefsteak
election." The Republicans had won the Senate 51 to 45
and the House 245 to 118. In the autumn of 1946, Harry
Truman's personal popularity had fallen to the un-

precedented low level of thirty-two percent (it had been as high as eighty-seven percent during the war). During the campaign the mere mention of the President's name had elicited boos, and after the election a senator of his own party, J. W. Fulbright, had publicly called for the President's resignation. There was a gathering mood in the country of frustration and resentment, fed by increasing impatience with lingering wartime controls, shortages, strikes, and racial disturbances. The Republicans, in control for the first time in eighteen years, were adamant for cutting six billion dollars from Harry Truman's "astounding" 37.5-billion-dollar budget. They also demanded that tariff cutting under the Reciprocal Trade Agreements be halted and that the Export-Import Bank toughen its lending policies and restrict its loans to low-risk projects that "directly promoted American exports." At the same time, Republican leaders were charging the administration with being "soft on communism."

This congressional mood, characterized by a blend of economic isolationism and political belligerency, had a considerable effect on the tone and direction of the Truman Doctrine. The President told Arthur Krock in an exclusive interview,[41] a week after he announced the new policy, that he had wanted for several months to "proclaim the new doctrine when a fitting moment arose." He said he had been talked out of it on previous occasions by some of his advisers. This time, however, the National-Security Managers moved with breathtaking speed toward a unanimous recommendation for a dramatic break with history.

The first reaction of George C. Marshall, who had just taken office as secretary of state, to the British note was annoyance that the responsibility for Greece had been "dropped in America's lap." However, the career foreign-service officers in the Office of Near Eastern and African Affairs were, as Joseph Jones recalls, "quite openly elated"[42] at the possibility that the United States would create a "Greek-Turkey-Iran barrier" to keep the Soviet Union out of the Middle East. Within four days they had prepared a paper, "Position and Recommendations of the State Department Regarding Immediate Aid to Greece and Turkey," which called for the transfer of military supplies to Greece and the establishment of an American administrative organization for Greece "that would con-

trol the Greek economic program in order to assure
proper use of the funds and supplies furnished by the
United States."[43] A day later Secretary of War Patterson
and Secretary of the Navy Forrestal, as well as Chief of
Staff Dwight D. Eisenhower, had "signed off" on the
paper and by the afternoon Secretary Marshall and Dean
Acheson, the under secretary of state, were discussing it
with the President. He "required no convincing"[44] and
summoned a bipartisan group of congressional leaders to
the White House the following day to get their reaction.

Secretary of State Marshall began the briefing. With the
crisp, assured delivery that impressed President Truman
that the general was the greatest living American, he
outlined the facts of the British decision to withdraw, and
their implications. But the reaction was not what the
National-Security Managers in the State Department and
the Pentagon had hoped. Some of the congressional leaders thought that Marshall was recommending the giving of
aid on grounds of humanitarianism or loyalty to Great
Britain. "Isn't this pulling British chestnuts out of the
fire?" one asked. "How much is this going to cost?"
demanded another.

Acheson was worried about the direction of the conversation. "Is this a private fight or can anyone get into it?"
he asked his chief, and when Marshall with evident relief
motioned him to proceed, the under secretary took off on
a wholly different tack. He did not talk about Greece, the
rebels, or the decline of Britain. He talked about the
Soviet Union. The Russians were out to "encircle" Turkey
and Germany. According to the reports of Mark
Ethridge, traveling in Greece on a United Nations investigating team, and Paul Porter, also there as head of the
American economic mission, Greece might collapse in
three weeks. Communist activities in Western Europe,
Iran, Turkey, and Greece, Acheson implied, were bril-
liantly orchestrated. If their campaign succeeded, the Soviets could then control the eastern Mediterranean and the
Middle East. "From there the possibilities for penetration
of South Asia and Africa were limitless."[45] Finally, he
turned to Europe. After painting a bleak picture of a
continent in ruins, with a communist sitting as minister of
defense in the French cabinet, Acheson, as Jones has
described it, proceeded to "pull out all the stops":[46]

Only two great powers remained in the world, the
United States and the Soviet Union. We had arrived

at a situation unparalleled since ancient times. Not since Rome and Carthage had there been such a polarization of power on this earth. . . . It was clear that the Soviet Union was aggressive and expanding. For the United States to take steps to strengthen countries threatened with Soviet aggression or Communist subversion was to protect the security of the United States.[47]

With an "or" Acheson took a massive intellectual leap and lumped two quite different political phenomena.

The flow of Soviet power into the vacuums left by the British collapse was not only a threat to the security of the United States, it was a threat to "freedom anywhere in the world." The two great powers "were divided by an unbridgeable ideological chasm." For the United States, "democracy and individual liberty were basic; for them dictatorship and absolute conformity." Acheson gambled that he could move American politicians not with the chessboard language of balance of power, the stock in trade of the professional diplomat and the soldier, but with the rhetoric of crusade that had twice in his lifetime stirred the whole nation to do battle on foreign shores.

His instincts were correct. Vandenberg, deeply impressed by Acheson's presentation, told the President that he must lay these same facts before the American people if he wanted to get congressional support for the program. The President must "scare hell"[48] out of the Congress and the people. Vandenberg was particularly impressed by the concept of an ideological struggle.

A few days later he wrote to a fellow member of Congress:

I am frank in saying that I do not know the answer to the latest Greek challenge because I do not know the facts. I am waiting for all the facts before I say anything. . . . But I sense enough of the facts to realize that the problem in Greece cannot be isolated by itself. On the contrary it is probably symbolic of the world wide ideological clash between eastern communism and western democracy.[49]

The day after the White House meeting, intensive work on the Truman Doctrine message began at the State

Department. We were "the most privileged of men,"[50] Jones wrote later of the feverish days in which the new foreign policy was being drafted, "participants in a drama such as rarely occurs even in the long life of a great nation." Acheson told his staff of Vandenberg's condition for congressional support. Nothing was to be done to soften the picture of conflict which Acheson had conveyed at the White House. The presidential speech should be drafted, Acheson told the staff, "without any regard to the effect it might have" on the Moscow Conference about the future of Germany which Secretary Marshall was about to attend. Jones recalls thinking that other secretaries of state would almost certainly have reversed the priorities and softened the tone of the Truman Doctrine in the hope of improving the prospects of success at the bargaining table. But Marshall saw "what was important, and what was relatively less so . . . *all* barriers to bold action were indeed down."[51]

The first formal request from the Greek government for military aid arrived on March 3, 1947, about a week after the decision had been made in Washington to supply it. The Greek government had for several weeks let Washington know of its interest in military aid, but it was only after the basic lines of U.S. policy were decided that the request was prepared—and in Washington, not Athens. "The message was drafted in the State Department and suggested to the Greek government,"[52] Jones reveals.

Greek archives shed further light on this crucial stage in the commitment to Greece. On February 23, Loy Henderson summoned the Greek chargé d'affaires. As the Greek diplomat reported to Athens, the director of the Office of Near Eastern and African Affairs was smiling "as though experiencing some sort of glowing inner satisfaction."[53] Henderson informed the Greek that the United States had decided to take historic measures to aid his country. He then outlined the text of a draft letter of request, and after "protracted discussion" the American and Greek diplomats "prepared in common" a draft, which, the chargé reported, "I was requested to submit urgently, as soon as I got your approval, to the State Department in the name and at the instructions of the Greek government." Henderson stressed that the text "had been drafted with a view to the mentality of Congress. . . . It would also serve to protect the U.S. Government against internal and external charges that it was taking the initiative of intervening in a foreign state or that it had been persuaded by the British to take over a bad legacy from them. The note would also serve as a basis for the cultivation of public opinion which was under study."[54]

When the note incorporating the State Department's language arrived, it contained a request for "the aid of experienced American administrative personnel," economic and technical, to assure "effective and up-to-date utilization" of the assistance program. Exactly two weeks later, President Truman mentioned these provisions for American supervision, and the Congress burst into applause. In the congressional hearings a few weeks later, administration witnesses put great stress on the "request" from the Greek government as evidence for the fact that the United States was not engaging in an unwarranted "intervention."

As a result of the reaction of Vandenberg and others at the White House meeting, the National-Security Managers decided unanimously to present the new policy in global terms. "We should couch it in terms of a new policy of this government to go to the assistance of free governments everywhere,"[55] one policy paper stated. "The only way we can sell the public on our new policy," the representative of another department declared, "is by emphasizing the necessity of holding the line: Communism vs. democracy should be the major theme."[56] Acheson decided, however, to keep the actual requests for military and economic assistance limited. "If FDR were alive I think I know what he'd do," he told one of his assistants. "He would make a statement of global policy but confine his request for money right now to Greece and Turkey."[57]

Four

Two other ideas which had been crucial to the development of official thinking in important parts of the national-security bureaucracy were carefully excised from the Truman Doctrine message as it made the circuit of government in successive drafts. One was that the struggle in Greece was part of a global battle between economic systems. Six days before the Truman Doctrine message, the President had delivered a speech at Baylor University in Texas in which he declared that the United States was "the giant of the economic world,"[58] with the responsibility for setting "the future pattern of economic relations." Posing the fundamental split in the world between "free enterprise" and "planning," he strongly implied that the one led to peace while the other meant war. Two days before the President's scheduled appearance before Congress, Clark Clifford came to Acheson with a revision suggested in the White House to the effect that "continued chaos in other countries and pressure exerted upon them from without would mean the end of free enterprise and democracy in those countries and that the disappearance of free enterprise in other nations would threaten our economy and our democracy."[59] Acheson opposed the insertion of this ideological language on the grounds that it might embarrass American relations with the Socialist government of Great Britain. But a number of major advisers in the administration attached considerable importance to this point.

If Clifford's articulation of the economic conflict was too ideological for Acheson's taste, his second suggestion smacked too much of *realpolitik;* Clifford wanted a reference in the speech to Greece's strategic importance and to "the great natural resources of the Middle East."[60] When British Marshal Montgomery had asked the U.S. chiefs of staff in the fall of 1946 what value they attached to Middle Eastern oil, "their immediate and unanimous answer was—vital."[61] Forrestal was almost obsessed with the strategic importance of the area to the United States. But the State Department concluded that it would create an unfortunate impression if it appeared that the enunciation of the American Responsibility had something to do with oil. The administration anticipated enough problems in distinguishing the new American relationship to the Mediterranean from Britain's imperial role. As it was, Acheson was asked some pointed questions in the hearings about possible connections between the President's dramatic announcement of America's new "responsibility" for the Eastern Mediterranean and the authorization two days earlier of the trans-Arabian pipeline. Acheson replied that there was none. The charge made by leftist critics and a few disappointed British imperialists that the Truman Doctrine was principally a piece of petroleum diplomacy is a serious distortion. Nevertheless, there is no doubt, as Stephen Xydis observes in his exhaustive study of the relevant documents, that one motive for the United States' intervention was to stabilize the area so as to "contribute to the preservation of American oil concessions there."[62]

While the final version of the Truman Doctrine avoided these pitfalls, it was couched in a rather strident, global rhetoric which drew a good deal of criticism. Offering a Manichaean view of world politics, the President once again invited Americans to join a moral crusade. But this time it was a crusade against revolution as well as outside aggression.

At the present moment in world history nearly every nation must choose between alternative ways of life. The choice is too often not a free one.

One way of life is based upon the will of the majority, and is distinguished by free institutions, representative government, free elections, guarantees of individual liberty, freedom of speech and religion, and freedom from political oppression.

The second way of life is based upon the will of the minority forcibly imposed upon the majority. It relies upon terror and oppression of controlled press and radio; fixed elections, and the suppression of personal freedoms.

I believe it must be the policy of the United States to support free peoples who are resisting attempted subjugation by armed minorities or by outside pressures.[63]

Two other basic criticisms of the new policy which had been raised during the early weeks of incubation persisted after the public unveiling. "We have considered how the United Nations might assist in this crisis," President Truman declared in the final version of the speech. This passing reference was inserted a few days before delivery at the urging of Dean Rusk, then director of the Office of Special Political Affairs, which handled relations with the United Nations. But as Jones's authoritative account reveals, his office was not consulted during the development of the policy, and in fact played no part in the decisions.

No one in the administration or in Congress took the United Nations seriously enough to give any thought as to how it might be used. "To turn this problem over to the UN, which isn't constituted to handle it,"[64] observed Tom Connally, ranking Democrat on the Senate Foreign Relations Committee, recipient of a number of medals honoring him as a "father of the United Nations," would be a "buckpassing arrangement." The responsibility belonged to the United States alone. Senator Vandenberg, another father of the United Nations, wrote to a colleague while the Truman speech was being drafted, "I think Greece could collapse fifty times before the United Nations itself could even hope to handle a situation of this nature."[65] But when public attacks on the Truman Doctrine for bypassing the United Nations mounted, Vandenberg concluded that from a public-relations standpoint the administration had made "a colossal blunder in ignoring the UN"[66] and offered an amendment of the original bill providing for the international organization to assume "principal responsibility" whenever all the Great Powers agreed that it should.

The other criticism concerned the nature of the Greek government. In what sense was this ultrarightist, repressive regime "free"? Secretary of Labor Lewis Schwellenbach raised this question at the cabinet meeting held on March 7, suggesting that reform should be a precondition for aid. Walter Lippmann greeted the Truman speech with the observation that the United States was "not rich enough to subsidize reaction all over the world or strong enough to maintain it in power."[67] In an attempt to forearm himself against such criticism, Truman had pointed out in the speech that the government of Greece had "made mistakes." The National-Security Managers developed a rationale to justify a moral crusade in behalf of an inefficient and reactionary government. The argument, as Joseph Jones recalls it, went like this: "The United States had to make a choice between supporting temporarily a bad democratic government [democratic in form] and allowing an armed minority under Soviet direction to fasten a Communist dictatorship permanently upon Greece."[68]

Crucial to this analysis besides the dubious use of the term "democratic" was the assumption of "Soviet direction." As we have seen, the Soviets in fact were giving neither aid nor direction. A few months later they would vainly seek to persuade Yugoslavia to cut off the substantial aid which they were giving. "What do you think," Stalin exclaimed to the Yugoslav vice-premier in early 1948, "that Great Britain and the United States—the United States, the most powerful state in the world—will permit you to break their line of communication in the Mediterranean? Nonsense. And we have no navy. The uprising in Greece must be stopped, and as quickly as possible."[69] Indeed, the Soviet attitude toward Greece conformed perfectly to the Stalinist pattern. Since the Greek guerrillas had taken action independent of the Red army and Stalin's direction, the Kremlin viewed them as a nuisance and a possible threat to the diplomatic relations of the Soviet Union. Stalin saw them as potential clients of the Yugoslavs, whose claims to a role of independent political leadership in the Balkans he was already attempting to crush.

During the feverish days of preparation for the Truman Doctrine speech, no one in the national-security bureaucracy appears to have ventured a political analysis of the Greek rebels, their relations with Russia, Yugoslavia, or the other Balkan neighbors. The fifth-column analogy from World War II dominated official thinking. The possibility that men had taken to the hills for reasons of their own and not as agents of a foreign power was never seriously considered. "The President has determined to take a stand to 'aid' Greece, as a counter-Russia move,"[70] David Lilienthal wrote in his diary for March 9. Writing a grocery-store executive in Michigan, Senator Vandenberg made it clear that he had the same understanding of the purposes behind the new policy. It was a holding action to prevent the sweep of Soviet power in a "chain reaction" from the Dardanelles to the China Sea. "I think the adventure is worth trying as an alternative to another 'Munich' and perhaps to another war. . . ."[71]

Five

The press and the public immediately grasped that the Truman Doctrine was a watershed. The *Washington Post* clearly heard what the President was saying, and they thrilled to it. "He was asking America to be Atlas, offering to lead his country in that tremendous role." "The epoch of isolation and occasional intervention is ended," was the exultant judgment of *The New York Times.* "It is being replaced by an era of American Responsibility." The next day the *Times* put the message even more clearly: "A new and positive foreign policy of worldwide responsibility for the maintenance of peace and order."

Most press comment, even from the Middle West and the South, was favorable. But Robert Taft, echoing the editorial judgment of the *Chicago Tribune,* was immediately skeptical. "I do not want war with Russia," he told newsmen. He was troubled not by the economic aid but by sending American military missions to Greece. Other conservatives, including Senator Harry Byrd, spoke out against the cost of the program. Walter Lippmann warned that by defining the foreign-policy task of the United States as a worldwide ideological struggle, the country was taking on unlimited commitments. Senator Pepper, Henry Wallace, and the press on the left blasted the anti-Soviet cast of the policy, the bypassing of the United Nations, and the support for the reactionary Greek and Turkish governments. The day following the President's speech to Congress, Wallace charged in a radio talk that Truman had betrayed "the great tradition of America" by plunging into a "reckless adventure" that would usher in a "century of fear." Foreign reaction in noncommunist and anti-communist newspapers was on the whole cautious or openly critical. The first reaction of the Labour party newspaper *Daily Herald* was "uneasiness." "Our second thoughts are no happier," the paper concluded a week later.

A Gallup poll taken shortly after the President's message showed that about seventy-five percent of the people were aware of his proposal—an extraordinary high figure even for an important foreign-policy statement—and that most supported economic aid to Greece and Turkey. There was considerably more reluctance to accept military aid. Nonetheless, forty-seven percent of the respondents favored "a general policy" of helping governments "put down such revolts," where communists in foreign countries "try to seize control of the government by force." For most Americans the Truman Doctrine meant neither humanitarianism nor old-fashioned balance-of-power politics but anticommunism and Soviet containment. Senator Walter George, a conservative, unflappable southern politician who had built a career on a reputation for fiscal responsibility, reflected the prevailing reaction: "I deliberately place my support of this bill," he declared after returning from a secret briefing with the U.S. ambassador to Turkey, "on the belief that it is vital to us to check Russian expansion now. If unchecked, Russia will inevitably overrun Europe, extend herself into Asia and perhaps South America ... this process may go on for a full century."[72]

President Truman encouraged this sort of analysis. On April 6, two days before debate on the aid program opened in the Senate, he had observed, "We know how the fire starts. We have seen it before—aggression by the strong against the weak."[73] The leaders of the Republican Eightieth Congress seized upon the rhetoric of containment in the President's statements and made it their own. "Two worlds are in collision,"[74] declared Charles Eaton, chairman of the House Foreign Affairs Committee, a week before the House took its final vote on the bill. "One of them is going to survive." Only sixteen Republicans and seven Democrats in the Senate, ninety-three Republicans and thirteen Democrats in the House (and Vito Marcantonio of the American Labor party), voted against the new consensus.

The new consensus demanded not only a major commitment of American power and what an administration spokesman termed a "calculated risk" of war with Russia, but it thrust the United States into a role, new in peacetime, of supervising the politics of countries beyond the Americas. Paul Porter, who had been appalled by the corruption of the Greek government during his fact-finding mission to Athens a few months earlier, told the Senate Foreign Relations Committee that U.S. plans called for the establishment of an Office of Foreign Trade Administration, "with final power over all imports and exports" and extensive powers over the tax structure, industrial development, wages, and prices. The head of this superagency would be an American. All specific projects under the aid program would be selected by "the American recovery mission." When asked whether it was planned to send an American military mission, administration spokesmen replied in the negative. Only a few officers would be needed to make sure "the equipment reaches its proper destination."[75] Training would continue to be the responsibility of the British mission, which would remain.

The American military role quickly turned out to be more than routing supplies. By the end of 1947 a Joint U.S. Military Advisory and Planning Group was drawing up battle plans for the Greek army and insisting that "all its recommendations be carried into effect, at once and in full."[76] By early 1948 over two hundred and fifty U.S. officers were "advising" the tactical operations of the Greek army at the division level under the direction of General James A. Van Fleet.

The Americans also attempted to take direction of the political scene. Shortly after the first U.S. military equipment arrived, in late summer, 1947, the American mission demanded that the communist newspaper *Rizospastis* be closed, the right to strike be abolished, and all government employees suspected of communist sympathies or of passing communist propaganda be purged. At the same time, Dwight Griswold, the former governor of Nebraska whom Truman had appointed head of the Mission for Aid to Greece, tried to curb corruption and end the mass deportations, arrests, and executions. (On one night in the summer of 1947 the Greek government arrested five thousand people, many of whom were sent off to prison islands without trial.) In late summer Loy Henderson arrived in Athens amid mounting crisis to force the increasingly vicious Maximos-Tsaldares government to resign and to replace it with a coalition of Royalists and Liberals under the Liberal octogenarian Themistokles Sophoulis. Henderson returned to the United States for a round of speeches, describing the Greek problem not as civil war but as the heroic defense of democratic Greece against "the red tide of Communist invasion."[77] Before heading the government, Sophoulis had criticized the military orientation of the Truman Doctrine, maintaining that "economic reform and reconstruction are the ways to fight Communism, not spending money for killing Greeks." But now he felt forced, as a contemporary survey by the Council on Foreign Relations put it, to take "as drastic repressive measures as the preceding government had taken."[78] He invited the guerrillas to surrender and promised an amnesty but refused to bargain over the composition of a future government. Hardly any guerrillas gave themselves up. They did not trust the government, since the police and the army were still in the hands of the same rightists who had violated the amnesty promises of the Varkiza armistice, which had brought the first civil war to an end. They now stepped up their terrorist activities, including the kidnapping and relocation of thousands of children.

The initial effect of the American intervention had been to strengthen the terrorist bands of the right, known as "X-ites," for the American interpretation of the crisis as a foreign invasion rather than a domestic political confrontation exactly fitted their own ideology. While the Greek government fought the X Organization in the Peloponnesus, some army commanders turned American equipment over to small groups of them in the provinces and gave them a free hand to decide who were communists and what should be done with them.

When the Truman Doctrine was launched, some members of the State Department believed that a massive infusion of American power and money could establish a stable, moderate, reasonably democratic government and that the military operations should be regarded as instruments to set up the preconditions for bringing about political and social change. But by 1943 it had become clear that the military and political goals were incompatible. In supplying weapons and characterizing the struggle primarily as a Hitler-like fifth-column operation rather than as a conflict among Greeks over the sharing of political and economic power, by stressing the external rather than the internal aspects of the problem, the United States strengthened those forces in Greece with the least interest in reform.

When the conflicts became apparent between democratization and reform, on the one hand, and military security, on the other, those in Washington genuinely interested in reform lowered their sights. Ports and railroads were repaired; the Corinth Canal was repaired. The distribution of food prevented thousands from starving. A remarkable antimalaria campaign started under UNRRA was brought to a successful conclusion. A thousand miles of good highways were built. No progress, however, was made on the basic economic and political problems that were tearing apart the country. "Even as we undertook to bolster the economy of Greece to help her combat Communist agitation," Harry Truman records ruefully in his memoirs, "we were faced with the desire of the Greek Government to use our aid to further partisan political rather than national aims."[79] By the end of 1947 the United States had transferred substantial funds earmarked for economic reconstruction to the military effort, and most of the "reconstruction" programs that remained were road and port programs for the direct support of the counterinsurgency campaign. In the year following the arrival of the U.S. economic mission, the cost of living jumped fifty-three percent. In March, 1948, the Greek government announced that thirty-two percent of the population was on relief.

With the help of substantial American military equipment—seventy-four thousand tons arrived in the last five months of 1947—including artillery, dive-bombers, and stocks of napalm, the strength of the Greek National army was brought up to one hundred and thirty-two thousand and the National Guard to about fifty thousand. They faced a guerrilla force, which, despite heavy casualties, remained at about twenty-three thousand men. The guerrillas had no armor, no aircraft, and little artillery. While the first U.S. aid was pouring into Greece, Tito stepped up his aid, including much needed artillery, but for it he extracted a price. Substantial parts of Greece were to be detached and joined to a Yugoslav federation. The other satellite countries encouraged the rebel leader General Markos to announce a Free Democratic government, but when he did on Christmas Eve, 1947, not one communist country, including the Soviet Union, ever recognized it.

Despite the overwhelming superiority of the government forces, the guerrillas were achieving considerable successes with a series of raids throughout 1947 and the first six months of 1948. In 1948 they lost almost thirty-two thousand men under increasing air bombardment, but, remarkably, they managed to replenish their force and to maintain it at about the same level as before.

The expulsion of Tito from the Cominform in June, 1948, did not result in the immediate end of Yugoslav aid or in the closing of the border between Greece and Yugoslavia. But it did promote a split in the Greek Communist party between those, like General Markos, who thought Tito's guns were more valuable than Stalin's dubious good wishes, and the old political functionary, Zakhariadis, who believed that allegiance to Stalin could somehow be translated into something more helpful than an occasional surveillance by Soviet officers. The Stalinist faction won, and the defeat of the guerrilla movement began.[80]

In July, 1949, Tito announced that he would close the border, but for the last six months he had already drastically curtailed his assistance. More important, Zakhariadis, growing desperate at the defections of the communist neighbors and the mounting guerrilla casualties, took charge of the military operations himself. He gambled that he could blunt the impact of American aid by switching from insurgent raids to full-scale conventional warfare. The results were disastrous for the communists.[81] The rebels, in large battles for the first time, suffered major setbacks and on May 3, 1949, they broadcast an offer for a cease-fire. While they had offered twenty such proposals since 1946, this one contained substantially softer terms. However, it too was ignored by Greece and the United States.[82]

In the final six months of the war General Van Fleet initiated a campaign for "the systematic removal of whole sections of the population" in an effort to separate the guerrillas from the supporting population. In his recent analysis of the war Major Edgar O'Ballance attaches great importance to this tactic.

> This was more far-reaching than is generally realized. It removed the people; it demarcated a "front line," it prevented "back infiltration" and it caused a blanket of silence to descend. . . . The harsh policy of displacing thousands of people was a difficult decision for a democratic government to take, even in wartime, and the Greek Government hesitated for a long time. However, once this policy was put into effect it paid handsome dividends. . . .[83]

On October 16, 1949, with rebel resistance almost at an end, the guerrilla radio announced that the "Greek Democratic army" had decided to "cease-fire" in order "to prevent the complete annihilation of Greece." The civil war was over.

For the next twenty years the Greeks struggled to solve the staggering economic and social problems that had led to the bloody civil war. Despite massive U.S. economic and military aid the Greek government has remained unable to feed its own population. In his exhaustive review of contemporary Greek economics and politics, *Les Forces Politiques en Grèce*, Professor Jean Meynaud documents the continuation of economic stagnation and political chaos in Greece.[84] Despite improvement in the economy, the same basic conditions of the forties— widespread poverty, illiteracy, shortage of foreign exchange, repressive and ineffective government—remained in the sixties, leading to a series of constitutional crises and, most recently, to a particularly brutal and backward military dictatorship.

The United States continued to be deeply involved in Greek politics. For over one hundred years it had been traditional for Greek politics to be dominated by a foreign power, for the most part, Britain. Now the United States assumed that role. Just as there had been a "British party" in the nineteenth century, there was now an "American party." The U.S. ambassador, especially John Peurifoy when he held the post immediately after the civil war, habitually intervened in Greek affairs, as, for example, when he openly supported Marshal Papagos for premier against a rival faction. U.S. military attachés built close relations with segments of the Greek officers corps. Greek politicians charged in the Parliament that the Greek Central Information Agency, outfitted with American equipment and financed by the United States, had become in effect an arm of the CIA, carrying out such missions as the Americans directed. From 1944 to 1964 the United States gave Greece almost four billion dollars, of which a little over two billion dollars was in military aid and most of the remaining sums were to cover current budget deficits and to support agriculture. In the 1960's exports to the United States declined. Although private U.S. capital had flowed into Greece from such U.S. companies as Esso, Reynolds Metal, Dow Chemical, and Chrysler, and large sections of the economy are effectively controlled by U.S. capital, the financial health of the country remains precarious. Two decades of U.S. aid and a dominant American role in Greek politics and economics have averted or, as it now increasingly appears, postponed revolution and civil war, but they have not brought the country much closer either to a just and workable economy or to a stable political structure.[85]

NOTES—CHAPTER SIX

1. Winston Churchill, quoted in Joseph M. Jones, *The Fifteen Weeks* (New York, 1964), p. 73. This book contains many quotations from draft documents at the time, which have not yet been made public in any other source. The accuracy of his account is attested to by George Kennan, who was director of the Policy Planning Staff at the time (see his *Memoirs*, New York, 1967, p. 317:

> Mr. Joseph Jones, in his excellent book, *The Fifteen Weeks*, has described in great and faithful detail the various discussions, consultations, clearances, and literary struggles that took place within the government in the ensuing days before the President was in a position to present to the Congress. . . .)

and by Louis Halle, another member of his staff, in *The Cold War As History* (New York, 1967).

2. Quoted in S. G. Xydis, *Greece and the Great Powers* (Thessaloniki, 1963), p. 375.

3. Quoted in Leften Stavros Stavrianos, *Greece: American Dilemma and Opportunity* (Chicago, 1952), p. 173.

4. Quoted in *ibid.*, p. 177.

5. Quoted in *ibid.*, p. 178.

6. See *Report of the British Parliamentary Delegation to Greece* (London, 1946), pp. 15–16.

7. *Ibid.*

8. Harry S. Truman quoted in Xydis, *Greece*, pp. 400–401.

9. *Ibid.*, p. 401.

10. Harry S. Truman, Address before a Joint Session of Congress, March 12, 1947.

11. Foreign Minister John Sofianopoulos, quoted in Todd Gitlin, "Counter-Insurgency: Myth and Reality in Greece," in David Horowitz, ed., *Containment and Revolution* (Boston, 1967), p. 161.

12. James Byrnes, quoted in Jones, *The Fifteen Weeks*, p. 179.

13. James Byrnes, quoted in Gar Alperovitz, *Atomic Diplomacy* (New York, 1965), p. 202.

14. Harry S. Truman, *Year of Decisions*, vol. I of *Memoirs* (New York, 1955), p. 605.

15. Joseph Stalin, quoted in Milovan Djilas, *Conversations with Stalin* (New York, 1962), p. 114.

16. Quoted in Zbigniew Brzezinski, *The Soviet Bloc* (New York, 1962), p. 16.

17. Quoted in Walter Millis, ed., *The Forrestal Diaries* (New York, 1951), p. 97.

18. Dean Acheson, quoted in *ibid.*, p. 192.

19. Harry S. Truman, quoted in *ibid.*, p. 192.

20. James Byrnes, quoted in *ibid.*, p. 171.

21. *Ibid.*, p. 184.

22. Quoted in Jones, *The Fifteen Weeks*, p. 53.

23. James Byrnes, quoted in *ibid.*, p. 54.

24. For a discussion of Anglo-United States economic rivalry, as seen by the British, see Sir Ernest Llewellyn Woodward, *British Foreign Policy in the Second World War* (London, 1962). See also Walter Le Feber, *America, Russia and the Cold War* (New York, 1967), pp. 9–10.

25. Quoted in Jones, *The Fifteen Weeks*, p. 44.

26. Quoted in *ibid.*, p. 78.

27. Quoted in *ibid.*, p. 80.

28. For an account of Great Power relations with Greece during the war, see Xydis, *Greece*. Edgar O'Ballance, *The Greek Civil War* (New York, 1966), discusses the "tenuous and unreliable" relations of the Greek Communist party and Moscow at p. 53. Major O'Ballance is a British military writer. See also André Kédros, *La Résistance Grecque, 1940–1944* (Paris, 1966), for an account of the resistance movement during the Second World War.

29. Quoted in O'Ballance, *The Greek Civil War*, p. 78.

30. Charges and countercharges of executions are described in *ibid.*, p. 116. See also Howard K. Smith, *The State of Europe* (New York, 1949), pp. 238–239.

31. Corruption and remaining Nazi influence in the Greek government is discussed in Smith, *The State of Europe*, pp. 227–228, 233, 236, 238.

32. *Ibid.*, p. 235.

33. O'Ballance, *The Greek Civil War*, p. 116.

34. *Ibid.*

35. For an account of Tito's efforts to set up a Balkan federation, see Brzezinski, *The Soviet Bloc*.

36. The relations between the Greek rebels, the Yugoslav army, and the Soviet liaison officers is described in O'Ballance, *The Greek Civil War*, pp. 18, 78, 122, 131.

37. Jones, *The Fifteen Weeks*, p. 7.

38. Loy Henderson, quoted in Xydis, *Greece*, p. 401.

39. Quoted in *ibid.*, p. 406.

40. Tsaldares, quoted in *ibid.*, p. 447.

41. The Arthur Krock interview appeared in *The New York Times*, March 23, 1947. The account of the development of U.S. policy on the Truman Doctrine is described in Jones, *The Fifteen Weeks*.

42. Jones, *The Fifteen Weeks*, p. 133.

43. Quoted in *ibid.*, p. 137.

44. *Ibid.*, p. 138.
45. *Ibid.*, p. 140.
46. *Ibid.*, p. 143.
47. Dean Acheson, quoted in *ibid.*, p. 141.
48. Arthur Vandenberg, quoted in William A. Williams, *The Tragedy of American Diplomacy* (New York, 1962), p. 270.
49. Arthur Vandenberg, *The Private Papers of Senator Vandenberg* (Boston, 1952), p. 340.
50. Jones, *The Fifteen Weeks*, p. 146.
51. *Ibid.*
52. *Ibid.*, p. 77.
53. Xydis, *Greece*, p. 478.
54. Loy Henderson, quoted in *ibid.*, p. 479.
55. Quoted in Jones, *The Fifteen Weeks*, p. 151.
56. Quoted in *ibid.*
57. Dean Acheson, quoted in *ibid.*, p. 159.
58. Harry S. Truman, quoted in *ibid.*, p. 166.
59. Clark Clifford, quoted in *ibid.*, pp. 156–157.
60. Clark Clifford, quoted in *ibid.*, p. 156.
61. Xydis, *Greece*, p. 348.
62. *Ibid.*, p. 496.
63. Harry S. Truman, Address before Joint Session of Congress, March 12, 1947.
64. Tom Connally, *My Name Is Tom Connally* (New York, 1954), p. 319.
65. Arthur Vandenberg, quoted in Jones, *The Fifteen Weeks*, p. 160.
66. Vandenberg, *Private Papers*, p. 345.
67. *New York Herald Tribune*, March 27, 1947.
68. Jones, *The Fifteen Weeks*, p. 186.
69. Joseph Stalin, quoted in Djilas, *Conversations*, p. 164.
70. David Lilienthal, *The Lilienthal Diaries* (2 vols.; New York, 1965), vol. I, p. 159.
71. Vandenberg, *Private Papers*, p. 342.
72. Walter George, quoted in Alfred Steinberg, *Harry S. Truman* (New York, 1962), p. 293.
73. *The New York Times*, April 7, 1947.
74. Charles Eaton, quoted in Denna Frank Fleming, *The Cold War and Its Origins* (New York, 1961), vol. I, p. 470.
75. U.S. Congress, House of Representatives, Hearings on H.R. 2616, 80th Congress, 1st session, 1947, pp. 123–129.
76. O'Ballance, *The Greek Civil War*, p. 156.
77. *Department of State Bulletin*, February 29, 1948, p. 272.
78. Council on Foreign Relations, John C. Campbell, ed., *United States in World Affairs*, 1947 (New York, 1948), p. 476.
79. Harry S. Truman, *Years of Trial and Hope*, vol. II of *Memoirs* (New York, 1955), p. 132.
80. For an account of the internal politics of the Greek Communist party, see Dmitrios George Kousoulas, *Revolution*

and Defeat: The Story of the Greek Communist Party (London, 1965).

81. The Greek economic plight is described in Stavrianos, *Greece*, p. 193.

82. The appeals for a "cease-fire" are described in O'Ballance, *The Greek Civil War*, p. 214.

83. *Ibid.*, p. 215.

84. Jean Meynaud, *Les Forces Politiques en Grèce* (Montreal, 1965), p. 407.

85. For an account of subsequent U.S. involvement in Greece, see Maurice Goldbloom, "What Happened in Greece," in *Commentary*, December 1967, pp. 68–74. See also Stephen Rousseas, *The Death of a Democracy* (New York, 1967), for an account based on "smuggled documents" alleging U.S. involvement in the 1967 Greek coup.

CHAPTER 7

The Lebanese Civil War
and the Eisenhower Doctrine

One

ON JULY 14, 1958, in response to an urgent telegram from Lebanon's President Chamoun requesting the landing of U.S. troops in his country, President Eisenhower dispatched fourteen thousand Marines to the tiny nation, a force twice the size of the Lebanese army. By October of the same year the troops had been withdrawn virtually without firing a shot. A U.S. negotiator had helped to settle the civil war that had prompted the Lebanese president to call for the Marines by arranging to ease the president out of office. The brief encounter appeared to be the model of a successful intervention.

To understand the meaning of the Lebanese incident, one must go back a long time. The crucial event which set the stage for the assertion of America's "peacekeeping" role in the Middle East was the ill-fated Anglo-French invasion of Egypt in response to Nasser's nationalization of the Suez Canal. In his *Vision of History,* Hourani has given a good account of the political significance of these events:

157

The British action against Egypt, whether those who were responsible were aware of it or not, was an attempt to reassert British strength as the final decisive factor in Near Eastern politics: to say, in effect, that when interests or ideas of policy clashed, it was British interests or British conceptions of policy which should be supreme. It was an action which could succeed only if the other powers were willing to allow the Near East to be, in the last resort, a British preserve; if they were willing not to use their strength, or to use it only in support of England. Quite apart from the moral repugnance aroused by the manner of the action, it was a challenge to the essential interests of Russia and also of the United States; for it implied that, on issues which were bound to affect the whole network of American relations with all parts of the world, the final decisions should be made not by the United States but by England. It therefore led inevitably to the intervention of the two greatest powers.[1]

Suez, however, was only the precipitating crisis. It too was the product of forces unleashed by World War II that had been swirling in the Middle East for more than a decade. The two towering events in the recent history of the Middle East were the national independence of a number of Arab states and the creation of the State of Israel. During World War II Arab nationalists in Syria and Lebanon demanded independence and secured a promise from the British and Free French forces, which invaded both countries in 1941, that the French mandate over the area would end with the victory. England and France evacuated their troops but signed an agreement in which "each Government affirms its intention of doing nothing to supplant the interests or responsibilities of the other in the Middle East."[2] This determination to retain "responsibilities" clashed directly with the rising tide of nationalism in the area.

The British too began to relinquish political control of their mandate in Iraq, but "behind the shield of the monarchy and the astute political leadership of Nuri es-Said, British interest remained safe."[3] In Egypt the British troops stationed there under a prewar agreement forced the selection of a cooperative prime minister who agreed to a declaration of war. But this show of imperial strength

helped create the political pressures which forced Britain
to agree to withdraw her troops after the war from all
but the Suez Canal. In 1952 Gamal Abdel Nasser and the
"Free Officers," apparently with the support of the CIA,
ousted King Farouk in a coup designed to launch a social
revolution, although the ideology of the young officers
who brought down the old regime was quite unformed.[4]

The creation of the state of Israel backed by the
Western powers and the Soviet Union, the second event
which stamped the postwar Middle East, gave direction to
the forces of Arab nationalism. The new state became the
unifying issue of Arab politics. Nasser's reactions to the
fighting in Palestine in 1948 are typical of the symbolic
connection Arab nationalists have made between Israel,
the West, and the perpetuation of the old order of weakness and exploitation:

> We were fighting in Palestine but our dreams were
> in Egypt. Our bullets were aimed at the enemy lurk-
> ing in the trenches in front of us, but our hearts were
> hovering round our distant Mother Country, which
> was then a prey to the wolves that ravaged it. . . . We
> spoke of nothing but our country and how to deliver
> it.[5]

Haunted by the humiliating defeat in the Palestine war,
Nasser began to preach Arab unity as a means of over-
coming internal weakness and driving out foreign influence:

> One region, the same factors and circumstances,
> even the same forces opposing them all. It was clear
> that Imperialism was the most prominent of these
> forces; even Israel itself was but one of the outcomes
> of Imperialism. . . . Imperialism is the great force that
> throws around the whole region a fatal siege. . . . As
> long as the region is one, and its conditions, its prob-
> lems and its future, and even the enemy are the same,
> why should we dissipate our efforts?[6]

The idea of using the drive for Arab unity as a political
weapon had already occurred to the British, who at the
end of the war encouraged the creation of the Arab
League. After the war, Nuri es-Said, the pro-British prime
minister of Iraq, also tried to build an Arab coalition

that would remain allied to the Western powers. With the
decline of British and French power after the war, the
United States began to think in the same terms. The
United States asserted its new interest in the area in the
Truman Doctrine, and after the Korean War it turned its
attention to the creation of a defense network. Assistant
Secretary of State George McGhee toured the Arab capi-
tals with a British general seeking to enlist them in a
Western alliance. "Neutralism," he told them, "works only
for the enemy."[7] The Arab leaders, for whom, as Patrick
Seale puts it, "the West had been their enemy for their
whole political life,"[8] could not be convinced that neutrality was immoral. "We wish neither to support Communism nor to defend imperialist democracy," declared the
chairman of the Society of Muslim Youth in a statement
typical of nationalist sentiment of the time. But undaunted
by bombs, demonstrations, and angry denunciations, the
United States pressed on with its defense plans. The lease
for the air base in Saudi Arabia was renewed. On October
13, 1951, Britain and the United States proposed that
Egypt become a "founder member" in a Middle East alliance in return for the "internationalization" of the Suez
Canal.

One reason for the coolness of the Arabs to these
proposals, besides their suspicion of the West, was their
failure to grasp the Soviet threat. President Truman talked
of Stalin's "steady and relentless pressure" on the region as
a justification for giving five hundred and forty million
dollars in military assistance, mostly to the non-Arab nations Iran, Turkey, and Greece. But by 1952 it was hard
to assess the Soviet threat in these terms. Once the approaches to Turkey had been rebuffed and the Iranian
crisis had been settled on Western terms, Stalin adopted a
passive role in the Middle East. He had no aid program.
The official communist line was that Arab nationalism was
a reactionary force, unworthy of attention, much less
assistance. The communist parties in the Arab countries
were weak and divided. Sometimes they participated in
the many coups, riots, and demonstrations of the period,
but they never led them or had much influence over them.
In Syria and elsewhere the communists found themselves
far less adept at political intrigue than the other parties
who frequently managed to turn communist-sponsored
"united fronts" into anticommunist coalitions. In the early
fifties neither Stalin, who was occupied elsewhere, nor his

agents in local parties had much prospect of success. A policy that was pro-Israel and an ideology grounded in atheism were not very marketable in the Arab world.[9]

As Patrick Seale has concluded in his study of Arab politics for the Royal Institute of International Affairs, "western defense plans in the Middle East revived Soviet interest in the area."[10] Although after Stalin's death Soviet theoretical journals began to talk of the "Egyptian bridge with the liberation movement of the Near and Middle East,"[11] the Kremlin made it clear that once again it was looking to promote not revolution but Soviet influence. Hardly an objection was raised when Nasser arranged for the merger of Syria and Egypt and thereby succeeded in outlawing the growing Communist party in Syria just as he had in Egypt. The Soviet Union was at first concerned with preventing a hostile coalition in the Middle East. When it found that its influence grew as hatred of the West increased, it pressed ahead. In 1954 the Soviets began to show interest in Syria, and that year the Syrian army bought some tanks from the Czechs, thus breaking the Western monopoly on arms shipments in the Middle East. When the Bagdad Pact was announced in early 1955, Moscow issued a sharp warning charging that it was aimed at her, a conclusion fully supported by official explanations of the Pact before the U.S. Congress. On February 28, 1955, Israeli forces launched a raid on Gaza. A few months later Egypt concluded a much larger arms deal with Czechoslovakia. The thinking of the Egyptians at the time is contained in the reminiscences of one of Nasser's officers:

I was in Damascus when the Israelis launched their attack on Gaza on the night of 28 February 1955. You can imagine the tone of the talks on our military situation in Cairo where I returned early in March. I will be very frank with you: We were desperately weak. Our armed forces were short of everything. At the time of the Gaza raid, Egypt had six serviceable planes; about thirty others were grounded for lack of spare parts. Britain had stopped deliveries. We estimated that our tank ammunition would last for a one-hour battle. Nearly sixty per cent of our tanks were in need of major repairs. Our artillery was in the same deplorable state. We were even short of small arms.

We had tried to buy arms from Britain and America—but in vain. . . .

Our view was that the West was using Israel as a constant challenge to our leadership. The western powers knew that if faced with the choice of defeat by Israel or yielding to the West, we should have to choose the latter. This was the blackmail to which we were subjected. We felt that the only way to restore our freedom of action and liberate ourselves from Western subjection was to build up a real army able to face Israel on equal terms.

At Bandung, 'Abd al-Nasir asked Chou whether he was prepared to sell us arms. Chou replied that he would find it very difficult to let us have heavy equipment seeing he was still dependent on the Russians for such supplies. He promised to think it over.

I met him again a couple of days later when, after further discussions, he asked me whether we would agree to accept arms direct from the Soviet Union. I replied that, for my part, I would say yes, but that I had to discuss it with 'Abd al-Nasir. Chou then said that, in any event, a reply to our request would reach us through the Soviet Ambassador in Cairo. We then returned home.

On 6 May 1955 Mr. Daniel Solod, the Soviet Ambassador, called on me at the Ministry of National Guidance. He informed me that he had received a reply from his Government to the request for arms which we had made to the Chinese. His reply was verbal and consisted of two points. First, that his Government was prepared to supply us with any quantity of arms, including tanks and planes of the latest design, against deferred payment in Egyptian cotton and rice. Secondly, that his Government was ready to help us with any industrial project, including the High Dam at Aswan.[12]

The Soviet Union had reasserted the claims of the czars to a role as a major Middle East power. Responding to a whole series of Western moves, the post-Stalin leaders began to make a major play for the support of Arab governments by becoming a partisan of Arab nationalism and discouraging independent revolutionary activity of local communists. The Soviets, having established new embassies in Sudan and Libya and elsewhere, began a campaign to alienate the Arabs from the West. In the best tradition of the Middle East, they circulated false diplomatic reports implicating the British and Americans in various nefarious schemes. In March, 1955, the Soviets gave a guarantee of protection to Syria when Turkish troops massed on her frontier. At the Bandung Conference in 1955 Nasser was wooed by the Russians and Chinese. When Dulles announced that the United States would not finance the high dam at Aswan in retaliation for the growing ties with Russia, the Soviets stepped in with an attractive offer.

Within the next ten years Egypt received almost two billion dollars in military and economic assistance from the Soviet Union.[13] The Soviet's boldest moves in the Middle East came in response to the British-French-Israeli invasion of Egypt in October, 1956. The Soviet foreign minister informed the Security Council of the Soviet Union's readiness to dispatch "the air and naval forces necessary to defend Egypt and to repulse the aggressors." Khrushchev warned that "missiles would fly" against London and Paris if the invasion were not halted.

Two

When the Suez crisis subsided, U.S. relations with the countries of the Middle East were in bad need of repair. On the one hand, the American effort to fill the "power vacuums" left by the decline of Britain and France as Middle East powers by erecting an anticommunist alliance had succeeded in strengthening Egypt and the Soviet Union. Nasser now found "positive neutralism," i.e., opposition to Western intrusion, a convenient rallying cry for extending his own influence over the region. Dulles had demanded that the Arab nations take sides in the Cold War. Most preferred, however, to take Egypt's leadership even with Russian help in preference to close ties with the United States, now seen not only as the mainstay of Israel but also as the successor to the Western imperial powers. On the other hand, U.S. relations with England and France had been seriously damaged as a result of opposing the invasion. To the allies, Dulles' invocation of the UN Charter to condemn the intervention looked like a highly capricious application of a principle.

The United States had found itself in the unhappy position of defending Nasser, a man whom Eden had compared to Hitler and who, himself, had threatened to carry on a guerrilla war against the West throughout the Middle East. By siding momentarily with the Egyptian leader and cooperating with the Soviets in stopping the invasion, the United States had inadvertently given a boost both to "positive neutralism" and to Russian power in the Middle East.

The Eisenhower Doctrine was the instrument through which Dulles hoped to reverse this trend. On New Year's Day, 1957, the President tried out the Doctrine on the congressional leadership. "The existing vacuum in the Middle East must be filled by the United States before it is filled by Russia,"[14] the President declared. On January 5, 1957, in a speech to Congress, he emphasized that "all this instability" in the Middle East had been "heightened and, at times, manipulated by International Communism." Russia's interest in the area, the President declared, "is solely that of power politics. Considering her announced purpose of communizing the world, it is easy to understand her hope of dominating the Middle East."[15] Therefore, he proposed, the United States should increase economic, and particularly military, aid. The critical portion of the Doctrine was a request for a blanket authority for the President to use the "armed forces of the United States to secure and protect the territorial integrity and political independence of such nations, requesting such aid, against overt armed aggression from any nation controlled by International Communism."

Although the Congress had strongly supported a somewhat similar resolution two years earlier, authorizing the President to defend Formosa and the Pescadores, the situation was different, for China had laid explicit claim to this territory. Democratic congressional leaders, particularly Lyndon Johnson, could not see a similar urgency requiring the same blank check for the Middle East. Dean Acheson, the principal architect of the Truman Doctrine, treated the proposed Eisenhower Doctrine with contempt. It was "vague, inadequate and not very useful."[16]

By proposing to maintain all noncommunist governments in the region against either outside invasion or internal subversion, the United States was applying the Truman Doctrine to a new and wider geographical area. "The United States will have to accept an increasing responsibility to assist the free nations of the Middle East and elsewhere to maintain their freedom and their welfare," Secretary Dulles observed a few days before the Eisenhower Doctrine was presented. "We must live by the Golden Rule. By serving others, we serve ourselves."[17]

After three months of deliberation the Eisenhower Doctrine was passed as a joint resolution on March 9, 1957. In the preceding three months Dulles had been sharply questioned about how the Doctrine would work. "Would it apply to Syria?" one senator asked. The danger to Syria, Dulles replied, is "primarily one of subversion and indirect aggression, not of overt attack." The United States would be prepared to help Syria, and Egypt too, but not "if it merely supports governments which are subservient to or sympathetic to International Communism."[18] The President would have to decide, he told Senator Fulbright, whether in fact the country was communist-dominated. Thus the complex politics of the Middle East were squeezed into the familiar Cold War mold.

Raising the communist issue with such vigor, Dulles hoped, would please Britain and help heal the breach left in the wake of the Suez invasion, for it would divert attention from the overt aggression of the Western allies to the more obscure activities of Russia and her sympathizers. It seemed to lend credence to the British foreign minister's justification of the Suez invasion as a response to "Soviet mischief making." Instead, the British attacked the Eisenhower Doctrine as an attempt to crowd them out of the Middle East,[19] and the nationalist Arabs denounced it as an effort to restore a Western presence in the area. On January 19, Nasser, Hussein of Jordan, Ibn Saud of Arabia, and Al-Quatli of Syria issued a communiqué resolving "never to allow their countries to become a sphere of influence for any foreign power."[20] Even Hussein, who personally favored an alliance with the United States, was forced by the pressure of neutralist sentiment to reject the Eisenhower Doctrine. King Saud, who had been courted in Washington, also opted for "positive neutralism" when the issue was forced. Since the Doctrine offered protection only against communist aggression, and the Arabs were far more concerned about Israeli aggression, there was little incentive to sign up with the United States.

Thus, when the President sent a former Democratic chairman of the House Foreign Affairs Committee, James P. Richards, to the Middle East in the spring of 1957 to recruit supporters, only one could be found: Lebanon. Indeed, Charles Malik, the Lebanese foreign minister, had hailed the Doctrine even while it was being debated in Congress. Now, on the occasion of Ambassador Richards' visit, President Chamoun and the American issued a joint communiqué in which the United States agreed to extend economic and military aid and Lebanon agreed to ask for assistance in the event it was attacked by "international communism." The communiqué, which was hailed in Washington as a vindication of the Eisenhower Doctrine, precipitated a political crisis in Lebanon. In fact, the dissension stirred up by the proposed ideological alliance led directly to the civil war and American intervention a year later.

Three

To President Chamoun, the Eisenhower Doctrine looked like a promising way to solve some pressing domestic political problems. Lebanon, having declared its independence from France in 1943 and secured it two years later, had had a remarkably stable fifteen-year history under only two presidents, Chamoun and his predecessor, Bishara el-Khouri. It was the only Arab country in the Middle East with a Christian majority. Indeed, Lebanon was almost a model of American hopes for underdeveloped countries. It had survived as an unusually effective democratic society for the Middle East because its domestic political life was built on a series of explicit compromises. The parties, which divided along religious lines, always had agreed to share the major offices. Christians filled the top offices of president, foreign minister, and commander-in-chief of the army, and the Muslims took over as prime minister and speaker of the house.

Now the fifteen-year compromise was in danger. Chamoun's leadership was challenged from two quarters. First, the Muslims were fast turning into a majority as a result of a galloping birth rate and the immigration of refugees from Palestine. Second, Arab nationalism, which Nasser was promoting throughout the Middle East, was winning converts among most of the Muslims and even among many Christians. An Arab who had wrested the Suez Canal from the great European empires and had become a world figure aroused feelings of pride in every Arab country.

There was a small Lebanese Communist party which had on occasion been outlawed but was functioning legally in 1957. However, it had little impact on Lebanese politics or on the developing civil war. Lebanon, in many ways the most successful economy in the Middle East, was not fertile ground for a revolutionary party dedicated to radical economic change. Chamoun himself made little of the internal communist danger. "With appropriate measures," he told an interviewer rather nonchalantly in April, 1957, "its advance can be halted."[21]

Lebanon's traditional foreign policy was to avoid taking sides among the other Arab nations. While President Chamoun's sympathies were with the Western-oriented countries such as Iraq and Jordan, his government did not join the Bagdad Pact in 1954. Now, three years later, he moved quickly to line up with the West because he saw American backing as the only hope of perpetuating his own role and that of his party. Under the constitution, Chamoun was not eligible to succeed himself when his term ended in 1958. The opposition feared, correctly, as it turned out, that the president would attempt to amend the constitution to permit another term and that the United States would support that attempt. "Most politically active Lebanese believe," Manfred Halpern has written, "that the Lebanese President and Foreign Minister, though they failed to consult with other members of their government, had from the start acted in concert with the CIA."[22] It also appears that the CIA helped to elect Chamoun in 1952.[23] Whatever its clandestine activities in Lebanese politics were, however, the United States was quite openly banking on Chamoun as the most promising Lebanese politician to withstand the tide of Nasser's "positive neutralism." The State Department feared that opposition politicians would fall under Nasser's sway and end up as antagonists of the United States. The clumsy effort to prevent that result had the effect of strengthening Chamoun's opposition and turning the United States itself into a Lebanese election issue.

When Chamoun's government submitted the Eisenhower Doctrine to Parliament, a heated debate began at once. The Sunni, who were Muslim Arabs, were pro-Nasser. Their deputies argued that subscribing to the Doctrine would accomplish nothing but to antagonize Nasser and the Soviets. The country could continue to receive U.S. aid as it had for some time, whether it subscribed to the Doctrine or not. If it became necessary to fight communism, they insisted, they would be able to do that without inviting in U.S. troops in advance. In the parliamentary debates of early April, these opposition deputies asked the government not to insist upon a vote of confidence on the Eisenhower Doctrine. When Chamoun demanded the vote, six opposition deputies resigned in protest to begin a campaign against the Eisenhower Doctrine in the next election.

These opposition deputies formed a "National Union Front" in the spring of 1957, made up mostly of Muslim, but also some Christian, political leaders. At a mass rally in Beirut the Front set forth its demands: The government must return to the strict neutrality provided for in the National Pact of 1943 at the time of Lebanon's independence; Lebanon should not permit foreign bases or other limitations on its freedom and independence; the Chamoun government must not be permitted to succeed itself. (The president had proposed enlarging the chamber by fifty percent, just enough to ensure his continued control and to permit enactment of the constitutional amendment authorizing a second term.) The government accused the opposition of subservience to Nasser but did not charge, nor could it have truthfully charged, that communists were a significant force behind the campaign against the Eisenhower Doctrine.

The government won the elections of June, 1957, and several of the opposition leaders lost their seats. Chamoun had succeeded in tagging them as "Nasser's candidates." However, even among Christian politicians like Hamid Frangieh, who longed to succeed him, a coalition against the president was forming. Other leaders too saw their personal careers thwarted if Chamoun were allowed a second term. The next year, parliamentary debates grew increasingly bitter. There was a rash of bombings and riots, which the government blamed on "foreign agents" from Egypt and Syria. Personal attacks on Chamoun flared in the chamber. When, in February, 1958, Egypt and Syria joined to form the United Arab Republic, the Lebanese Muslims were thrilled. Some talked openly of being the next to join. Demonstrations and clashes with the police broke out at a number of public celebrations of the founding of the United Arab Republic. Arms and ammunition were smuggled into the country from Egypt.

On May 7, 1958, Nassib al-Matni, the editor of the sharply antigovernment newspaper *al-Talegraph,* was found murdered on a street in Beirut. The following day rioting broke out in Tripoli, followed by clashes in other parts of the country and by a newspaper strike. Barricades went up in the Muslim section of Beirut. In the next few days the situation grew more serious. The U.S. Information Service Library in Tripoli was sacked, and the remaining four U.S. libraries were closed. When the United National Opposition Front demanded the immediate resignation of Chamoun, the president promptly accused the opposition leaders of being Egyptian agents.

In the first week of what now was developing into a full-scale civil war, the United States announced that it was doubling the Marine contingent attached to the Sixth Fleet in the Mediterranean and it would consider sending troops to Lebanon if requested. Arms were immediately airlifted to Chamoun's army. But many of these soon found their way into the hands of the partisans.[24]

Although he made it clear that he did not consider Lebanon to be in danger of attack "from a country which we would consider under the control of international communism," that did not mean, Secretary Dulles warned, "that there is nothing that can be done."[25] The Eisenhower Doctrine, he explained, contained another provision which states "that the independence of these countries is vital to peace and the national interest of the United States. That is certainly a mandate to do something if we think that our peace and vital interests are endangered from any quarter."[26]

The rebels soon held the areas bordering Syria and began to receive arms, money, and men across the frontier in increasing numbers. Perhaps as many as three thousand infiltrated across the border at the height of the revolt, although the UN Observation Group was unable to identify any Syrian infiltrators among the rebels.[27] The Lebanese Communist party was never able to organize or control events. Many influential Lebanese, including former President Bishara el-Khouri and Patriarch Paul Meouchy, supported the rebels. Despite Chamoun's demands that the army promptly put down the rebellion and end the strike, General Fuad Chehab, the commander-in-chief, refused to commit the army against what he considered a mass protest rather than subversion. From May to July he used his six-thousand-man army to patrol the streets and to prevent clashes between Christians and Muslims. He wanted at all costs to keep the army, which was about two-thirds Christian and one-third Muslim, above the political fray now threatening to split the country.

Four

President Chamoun brought formal charges against the United Arab Republic before the Arab League on May 21. Six days later he brought the same charges to the United Nations Security Council. He had, he claimed, "innumerable proofs, formal and irrefutable," of the intervention of Syrians and Egyptians in the rebellion, including infiltration of armed men, shipments of arms, and violent propaganda campaigns against the Chamoun government.

The last charge was easily substantiated. Radio Cairo openly exhorted the Lebanese to violent overthrow of the government. "Arise, my brethren, on the police force and the army," the Egyptian broadcasters had urged the Iraqis on May 2. Now, as violence mounted in Lebanon, Radio Cairo tried to whip up the crowds in Beirut too. On May 9 the voice from Cairo cried, "The free people of Lebanon know very well how to bring about the overthrow of the government."[28]

The other charges were much more difficult to substantiate. The United Nations sent an Observation Group to Lebanon on June 11. Secretary-General Hammarskjöld personally conducted an investigation. In its reports during the summer the UN Group found no evidence of massive U.A.R. intervention. They could not identify any infiltrators and conceded only the possibility of some arms traffic from Syria. The UN Group was cautious in its findings, not only because they wished to promote a compromise but also because it was difficult to tell who was an infiltrator from a village a few miles across the border and who was a legitimate Lebanese rebel. U.S. officials, who had information from covert sources, which they could not expose, that Egypt was actively supplying guns and money, felt frustrated. The Chamoun government was outraged that the UN had disputed its interpretation of the events, for its credibility was seriously weakened. No doubt the Observation Group did minimize the extent of U.A.R. participation. But essentially they were correct. Nasser was trying to exploit the political turmoil in Lebanon, but he did not create it. Lebanon, which had always abounded in clandestine arsenals and arms markets, did not need foreign weapons for its domestic violence. Egyptian intervention was neither the stimulus nor the mainstay of the civil strife. Once again a government that had lost the power to rule effectively was blaming its failure on foreign agents.

In the fifteen months between the enactment of the Eisenhower Doctrine resolution in March, 1957, and the landing of the Marines in Lebanon in July, 1958, the United States had made two previous efforts to arrest political developments in the Middle East with a show of force. In April, 1957, President Eisenhower rushed the Sixth Fleet to the eastern Mediterranean when it appeared that Jordan's left-wing Prime Minister Suleiman al-Nabulsi with the encouragement of Cairo was trying to unseat King Hussein. The Eisenhower Doctrine had fanned the political dissension in Jordan. The king wanted closer ties with the United States, while the prime minister insisted on moving the country toward neutralism. When the prime minister announced that he was ready to recognize the Soviet Union and accept aid from any source, the king dismissed him, charging a "communist plot" abetted by Egypt. Violence broke out in Amman and the king declared martial law. President Eisenhower took public note that the "integrity" of Jordan was "a matter of vital

importance,"[29] deliberately using the language of the
Eisenhower Doctrine. The State Department openly invited the king to invoke the Doctrine by pointing out that
he had identified "International Communism" as the
threat to the independence of his country. But the king,
who welcomed the Sixth Fleet and an emergency cash
allotment of ten million dollars to pay his troops, would
not specifically invoke the Eisenhower Doctrine, and survived without it.

In August, 1957, a somewhat similar situation arose in
Syria. During the first week of the month a Syrian delegation went to Moscow and signed an agreement calling for
aid, military training, and increased trade. The next week
the Damascus government expelled three U.S. Embassy
officials for alleged complicity in a plot to bring down the
government. Two days later Afif al-Bizri, a radical army
officer described by *The New York Times* as a "ranking
communist,"[30] became chief of staff of the Syrian army.
Washington was seized with panic. "The suspicion was
strong that the Communists had taken control of the
government,"[31] Eisenhower recalls in his memoirs. Sherman Adams described the scene as it looked from the
White House at the time:

> In the summer of 1957 the Syrians were staging
> wild anti-American demonstrations in Damascus and
> threatening their pro-Western neighbors in Turkey,
> Iraq, and Lebanon. Obviously, the turmoil was Com-
> munist-inspired. . . .[32]

It was obvious that Syria would not invoke the Eisenhower Doctrine. The President, therefore, sent Loy Henderson, who had had experience in the Greek civil war, to
visit Syria's neighbors to see whether they would like to be
protected from "communist aggression" in Syria. Dulles
had stated publicly that "Turkey now faces growing military danger from the major buildup of arms in Syria."[33]
But no one in the Middle East took this seriously, for
Syria's poorly trained army of fifty thousand men was
outnumbered ten to one by the NATO-equipped Turkish
forces, by any count the best fighting machine in the
whole area. Henderson returned from his "fact-finding
mission" to Turkey, Jordan, Iraq, and Lebanon with an
alarming prognosis about the "serious effects" the Soviet
arms buildup in Syria could have "on the security of the

whole Free World."[34] Dulles told a news conference of the "deep concern" of officials in Turkey, Iraq, Jordan, and Lebanon "at the apparently growing Soviet Communist domination of Syria" and announced that the United States once again was sending in the Sixth Fleet to the eastern Mediterranean and was airlifting arms to Jordan and reinforcing Iraq and Saudi Arabia as well. When Syria demanded an explanation of this "deep concern," Jordan, Iraq, and Saudi Arabia promptly denied that they thought Syria was a threat. King Hussein left for a vacation in Italy as a gesture of confidence, and King Saud now accused the United States of being the primary source of tension. Only the Turks—who reportedly had a secret document containing Soviet promises to Syria to back military adventures against Iraq, Turkey, and Jordan—and Lebanon seemed to share U.S. concern over Syria. Chamoun had told Henderson that he could not maintain a pro-U.S. policy more than six months "if something were not done to remove a Soviet-dominated Syrian regime."[35]

In the end, Syrian Prime Minister al-Quwatli, the man who Dulles believed was under the thumb of Moscow, moved to destroy the communists in Syria. Almost six months after the Henderson mission, al-Quwatli, fearful that the communists might now be able to maneuver themselves into a ruling coalition, rushed to Cairo and arranged for the merger of Syria and Egypt, the immediate effect of which was the dissolution of the Syrian Communist party. For almost a year the United States had sought to bring about this result through clandestine activities. CIA agents had conspired with Syrian army officers to overthrow the government.[36] Emmet John Hughes recalls Under Secretary Herter's acid reference at this same period to "some recent clumsy clandestine American attempts to spur Turkish forces to do some vague kind of battle with Syria."[37] Now Syrian politicians in their own self-interest had reversed the trend which U.S. interventions had only promoted.

Five

By early July, 1958, it appeared to Eisenhower that the Lebanese crisis would also pass without an actual U.S. military intervention. As the revolutionary violence mounted, Chamoun finally agreed not to seek a second term and to leave office in September. The UN reports minimizing the extent of infiltration had precluded the State Department for the moment from making more alarming findings. But Chamoun was near panic and secured permission from his cabinet to call in U.S. forces under the Eisenhower Doctrine. Long before he sent the official request for U.S. troops, however, on July 14, he had been sounding out Washington on the possibility; and from the moment the civil war broke out in May the dispatch of U.S. forces was under constant consideration. John Foster Dulles had thought it sufficiently urgent to establish a U.S. military force in Lebanon to stem the revolutionary upheavals in the Middle East that he favored an immediate U.S. move in May, despite his great fears that this action would result in the retaliatory destruction of U.S. pipelines in Syria and the blockade of the Suez Canal.[38]

On the morning of July 14, word reached Washington of a coup in Iraq led by General Kassim. King Faisal and Prime Minister Nuri es-Said, who had brought Iraq into the Bagdad Pact and made his country the only Arab nation to become an official ally of the United States, were shot. The CIA director reported that Hussein had also been the target of a plot.

Chamoun had asked for intervention by U.S. and British troops within forty-eight hours. He was very bitter, Allen Dulles told the President, "because we have not sent U.S. troops to support him."[39] The President had already decided, he reports in his memoirs, that the time was at hand "to move into the Middle East, and specifically into Lebanon, to stop the trend toward chaos."[40]

Eisenhower called in congressional leaders later in the day and found that with few exceptions they were skeptical of getting involved in what Speaker Sam Rayburn termed a civil war. Senator Fulbright seriously doubted "that this crisis was Communist-inspired," not a startling conclusion, since the President and his advisers had received no evidence of communist involvement. Fulbright was also persuaded that the UN finding of "no evidence" of mass infiltration from Syria meant that this was an internal war in which the United States should not intervene. The President's only response was that "some of our observers definitely doubted the competence of the [UN] team."[41] On the other hand, the British, poised to land troops in Kuwait and Jordan, were enthusiastic about having the United States move in to stop revolutionary disorder in the Middle East. "We have had a request from the two little chaps," Harold Macmillan told Eisenhower over the transatlantic telephone—meaning Chamoun and Hussein.

The next day seventeen hundred men from the Second Marine Regiment landed in Lebanon. Soon U.S. forces armed with atomic howitzers reached a strength of seven thousand. One official reason for the intervention, just as for the Dominican intervention seven years later, was "to protect American lives."[42] The other was "to encourage the Lebanese government in defense of Lebanese sovereignty and integrity." The President explained in a television address that the situation was like the Greek civil war, the communist takeover of Czechoslovakia in 1948, the communist conquest of the Chinese mainland in 1949, and the attempts to take over Korea and Indochina beginning in 1950. All of these earlier situations, each quite different from the others, nonetheless had a common thread, the presence of political forces calling themselves communists. In Lebanon or indeed in Iraq, despite their numbers, the communists had yet to make their appearance as a significant factor.[43]

Eisenhower ordered Robert Murphy, a veteran diplomat who was then serving as deputy under secretary of state, to go to Beirut to explain that the purpose of the intervention was to demonstrate U.S. power and commitment in the Middle East. "Eisenhower believed," Murphy recalls, "that if the United States did nothing now, there would be heavy and irreparable losses in Lebanon and in the area generally. He wanted to demonstrate in a timely and practical way that the United States was capable of supporting its friends."[44] Just as in Greece and Vietnam, the principal purpose of the intervention was to keep neighboring countries from moving toward neutralism or communism. Another purpose was to show that the United States was willing to risk military action even if it meant a direct confrontation with Russia. Eisenhower, who did not think that the Soviets would risk war despite periodic truculent remarks by Khrushchev, wanted to dispel the sentiment he thought had developed in the Middle East "that Americans were capable only of words, that we were afraid of Soviet reaction if we attempted military action."[45]

Despite Dulles' calculation that the Russians would do nothing more than "make threatening gestures" because of their "respect for our power," especially overwhelming in bombers, Eisenhower concedes that he had many "anxious hours."[46] It turned out, however, that Dulles' predictions were essentially correct. Short of launching a war against the United States or Western Europe, there was little in a military way that the Russians could do. They did attack the intervention as "aggression" and began a vigorous diplomatic campaign for a summit conference to settle the conflict and to consider regulation of arms shipments in the Middle East. Eisenhower turned aside the proposals, arguing that the Security Council had jurisdiction of the matter. Khrushchev withdrew the proposal for the summit under pressure from Mao Tse-tung but warned that he would bring the matter up at the next meeting of the General Assembly. Eisenhower reassured the British, who felt that their intervention in Jordan was rather vulnerable to attack in the UN, that they had as much right to be in Jordan as the United States had in Lebanon, and that he didn't see any "real reason for embarrassment."[47]

When Murphy arrived in Beirut he found Chamoun a virtual prisoner in the presidential palace. For sixty-seven days he had been concentrating on avoiding assassination, never so much as approaching a window. As a consequence, he was almost totally out of touch with the fast-moving developments in the country. General Chehab, the commander of the army, still refused to carry

out the president's orders to crush the rebels, for he knew
that such a move would split the army in two and render
it useless. The general continued to hope that the army
could be the instrument to restore the political compromise which had been the basis of Lebanese life for fifteen
years. Chehab began to play a mediating role almost from
the moment the Americans arrived. A group of Lebanese
staff officers were outraged by the landing of the Marines
and had placed tanks in their path. A few moments before
the column of Marines rolled up to the tanks, Chehab
arrived and ordered the officers to hold fire.

A number of influential Lebanese who had not been
active supporters of the rebels protested the landings.
These included several religious leaders, both Christian
and Muslim. Former President el-Khouri sent a strong
denunciatory telegram to Eisenhower and to Secretary-
General Hammarskjöld. Adil Osseiran, the president of
the Chamber of Deputies, also sent a vigorous protest to
the Security Council. Murphy thought it so damaging that
he arranged to have Chamoun write Eisenhower that
Osseiran had "no constitutional status."

Nevertheless, Murphy quickly concluded that Chamoun
could not be saved and that it was essential for the United
States to assume a less partisan and more mediating role
in the civil war. He arranged a meeting with the rebel
leaders through the good offices of Colonel William A.
Eddy, a retired Marine colonel living in Beirut as a
consultant to the Arabian-American Oil Company. Murphy convinced the rebels that the United States was no
longer wedded to Chamoun, even though he was the most
pro-U.S. politician in the Middle East. Meanwhile various
factions were reaching agreement on General Chehab as
the successor to Chamoun. In a special election on July
31, Chehab was elected by the Lebanese Parliament forty-
eight to eight. Fighting died away. On October 25 the last
of the Marines sailed away from Beirut. The Arab countries agreed upon a compromise resolution in the General
Assembly, providing for the withdrawal of foreign troops
from Lebanon and Jordan as well as a pledge of noninterference by the Arab countries themselves.

The intervention in the Lebanese civil war was more
superficial than the intervention in Greece, Vietnam, or
the Dominican Republic, for the issue of social revolution

was not immediately at stake. The civil war flared up principally because of outside pressures—American insistence that the country declare itself a fully committed U.S. ally and Nasser's militant nationalism. When the pressures were relaxed after the war was settled, the country, which was essentially stable in its internal politics, reverted to its earlier patterns. Ironically, the landing of the Marines proved to be the instrument of American disengagement from an unsuccessful effort at direct manipulation of Lebanese politics.

NOTES—CHAPTER SEVEN

1. Albert Habib Hourani, quoted in Patrick Seale, *Struggle for Syria: A Study of Post-War Arab Politics, 1948–1958* (London, 1965), p. 283.

2. Quoted in *ibid.*, p. 53.

3. William R. Polk, *The United States and the Arab World* (Cambridge, Mass., 1965), p. 186.

4. Mention of the CIA involvement in the coup against Farouk can be found in Sanche de Gramont, *The Secret War* (New York, 1962), p. 186.

5. Gamal Abdel Nasser, quoted in Seale, *Struggle for Syria*, p. 193.

6. *Ibid.*

7. George McGhee, quoted in *ibid.*, p. 104.

8. *Ibid.*

9. Soviet policy toward the Middle East and local communist activity during the early fifties is discussed in Manfred Halpern, "The Middle East and North Africa," in C. E. Black and T. P. Thornton, eds., *Communism and Revolution* (Princeton, 1964), pp. 303–329.

10. Seale, *Struggle for Syria*, p. 230.

11. Quoted in Arslan Humbaraci, *Middle East Indictment: From the Truman Doctrine, the Soviet Penetration and Britain's Downfall to the Eisenhower Doctrine* (London, 1958), p. 172.

12. Quoted in *ibid.*, p. 235.

13. Soviet assistance to Egypt is discussed in Polk, *The United States*, pp. 260, 178.

14. Dwight D. Eisenhower, quoted in Rowland Evans and Robert Novak, *Lyndon B. Johnson: The Exercise of Power* (New York, 1966), p. 174.

15. Dwight D. Eisenhower, quoted in Polk, *The United States*, p. 280.

16. Dean Acheson, quoted in Evans and Novak, *Lyndon B. Johnson*, p. 176.

17. John Foster Dulles, quoted in Leila M. T. Meo, *Lebanon: Improbable Nation* (Bloomington, Ind., 1965), p. 109.

18. John Foster Dulles, quoted in *ibid.*, p. 111.

19. The British reaction to the Eisenhower Doctrine is discussed in *ibid.*, p. 115.

20. Quoted in *ibid.*, p. 116.

21. Camille Chamoun, quoted in *ibid.*, p. 123.

22. Manfred Halpern, "The Morality and Politics of Intervention," in James N. Rosenau, *International Aspects*, p. 257.

23. The allegation that the CIA helped elect Chamoun is in David Wise and Thomas B. Ross, *The Invisible Government* (New York, 1964), p. 316.

24. The diversion of arms to the partisans is discussed in Polk, *The United States*, p. 283.

25. John Foster Dulles, quoted in Meo, *Lebanon*, p. 195.

26. John Foster Dulles, quoted in *ibid*.

27. The findings of the UN Observation Group are discussed in *ibid.*, p. 130.

28. Quoted in *Foreign Broadcast Information Service*, May 9, 1958.

29. Dwight D. Eisenhower, *Waging Peace, 1956–1961*, vol. II of *Memoirs* (New York, 1965), p. 195.

30. *The New York Times*, April 29, 1957.

31. Eisenhower, *Memoirs*, vol. II, p. 196.

32. Sherman Adams, *Firsthand Report: The Story of the Eisenhower Administration* (New York, 1961), p. 287.

33. John Foster Dulles, quoted in Polk, *The United States*, p. 281.

34. Loy Henderson, quoted in Richard Stebbins, *The United States in World Affairs* (New York, 1957), p. 191.

35. Camille Chamoun, quoted in Eisenhower, *Memoirs*, vol. II, p. 202.

36. The CIA activity is discussed in Seale, *Struggle for Syria*, p. 295.

37. Christian Herter, quoted in Emmett Hughes, *Ordeal of Power* (New York, 1963), pp. 253–254.

38. Secretary of State Dulles's recommendations for an immediate military intervention are discussed in Eisenhower, *Memoirs*, vol. II, p. 266.

39. Allen Dulles, quoted in *ibid.*, p. 270.

40. *Ibid.*

41. *Ibid.*, p. 272.

42. *Ibid.*, p. 274.

43. President Eisenhower's TV address is discussed in *ibid.*, p. 275.

44. Robert Murphy, *Diplomat Among Warriors* (Garden City, 1964), p. 398.
45. *Ibid.*
46. Eisenhower, *Memoirs*, vol. II, p. 271.
47. *Ibid.*, p. 286.

CHAPTER 8

The Dominican Republic: To the Johnson Doctrine

One

WHEN PRESIDENT JOHNSON ordered the Marines into Santo Domingo in May, 1965, he was continuing a hundred-year American tradition of intervention in the Dominican Republic by other means. This is not to say that the Marines represented new means, for they had been there before. Indeed, direct military intervention in the Dominican Republic began in the administration of President Grant. In 1869 a U.S. commissioner, a front, in John Bartlow Martin's words, for "unscrupulous U.S. adventurers,"[1] on the pretext of capturing Dominican "pirates," arranged to annex the island. The Dominican president, who was quite prepared to sell his country for one hundred thousand dollars in cash and fifty thousand dollars in guns, signed a treaty of annexation aboard a U.S. gunboat. The treaty was blocked in the Senate, however, by Charles Sumner, who demanded that the United States extend "kindness, benevolence, help, protection, all that is implied in good neighborhood" but leave Dominican independence alone.

When the Marines returned to Santo Domingo, causing

evident embarrassment to the Johnson administration, it signified that the political and economic relationships on which the United States preferred to base its dominant influence in the economy and politics of the Dominican Republic had broken down. Unlike Greece, Vietnam, or any of the other sites of postwar American military intervention except Cuba, the Dominican Republic has been a political and economic satellite of the United States. Its proximity to the North American continent, its economic dependence, its long history of civil strife, have made it peculiarly vulnerable to U.S. domination. It is impossible to view the events of May, 1965, in proper perspective except against this background of continuous U.S. intervention in Dominican affairs.

During the last years of the nineteenth century the island, which had gained its independence in 1844, was aflame with rebellion and civil war. The more dictatorial became such petty tyrants as Ulises Heureaux, who ran the country for seventeen years by deportation, assassination, and the use of spies, the more they turned to the United States for support, both public and private. The repression assured a more or less continuous rebellion. "I cannot ask the insurgents to wait until I receive money from the United States with which to fight them,"[2] Heureaux noted as he refinanced the national debt with private U.S. companies, giving them the traditional privileges, then granted by dependent countries, of becoming the banker and customs collector of the Republic. In 1903 and 1904 Dominican politicians, facing fresh outbreaks of rebellion, called upon the United States for protectorate status. Kuhn Loeb Co. assumed all the foreign debts of the Republic and took over much of the financial responsibilities of the island. On the eve of America's entry into World War I President Wilson ordered in the Marines to restore order, which had been disrupted because of a series of political assassinations and chronic quarrels over foreign debts. In addition to keeping order, the expeditionary force was expected to forestall possible German penetration of the island and to secure the now considerable private U.S. investment. The Marines encountered guerrilla warfare in the eastern provinces and conducted a pacification campaign so brutal that it resulted in a Senate investigation and trials by court-martial of the principal officers involved. At the same time, the U.S. military governors initiated many reforms. They disbanded the army and established a Guardia Nacional in its stead. They built roads, schools, harbors, communications systems; they improved agriculture and reformed the fiscal system. But the occupation was hated and the departure of the Marines in 1924, after Sumner Welles, the U.S. commissioner, had worked to establish a constitution and the machinery for free elections, is still celebrated in some Dominican towns as a holiday. Ambassador Martin found that some of the politicians with whom he dealt in the 1960's had gotten their start in politics by opposing the Marines.[3]

The departure of the Marines was the opportunity that launched Rafael Trujillo's bloody career. Trujillo had been a young officer in the Guardia Nacional, who, having ingratiated himself with the U.S. Marine officers in charge of training the police and the army, swiftly rose to be the commander of the Guardia Nacional. He built a personal secret police and turned the Guardia into an army and himself into its commander-in-chief. The elected president, foreseeing a coup, appealed to the United States to declare that it would withhold recognition from Trujillo, but the State Department refused. The president then decided he had no choice but to run with Trujillo as vice-president, thus signifying the end of all legal opposition. Trujillo took over on August 16, 1930, and for almost thirty years subjected the island to a reign of terror.

Torture, exile, imprisonment, and assassination were the principal instruments of control. The tiny country had an army of seventeen thousand and a police force of twelve thousand, equipped with tanks and bombers. To these Trujillo added more subtle and profitable techniques for maintaining power. At the end of his career he and his family personally owned about eighty percent of the economy. He regularly sold his private businesses to the state and bought others from it, setting such prices as he liked. In the last fifteen years of his regime he began to acquire control of the sugar industry, the mainstay of the economy.[4]

Trujillo devoted great skill and energy to the cultivation of good relations with the United States. Joseph E. Davies, who later would send back glowing reports of his "mission to Moscow" as Roosevelt's ambassador to Stalin, was equally charmed with Trujillo, whom he also visited on behalf of the President. His recommendations resulted in a policy of debt forgiveness and the extension of private credit. Trujillo persuaded Secretary Hull to lift U.S. controls on Dominican customs, and the Benefactor, as he insisted upon being called, erected a statue of Hull as a token of appreciation. (Hull's statue was one of the first to be pulled down after Trujillo was overthrown.) During World War II he became a leading antifascist, offering a haven for one hundred thousand displaced Jews and encouraging domestic opposition until its actual appearance forced him to revert to mass executions. The Trujillo regime, recognizing its dependence upon the United States, invested heavily in public relations to ensure American good will. The capital city, renamed Ciudad Trujillo, became a minor showplace. A small, unsuccessful World's Fair was staged. The Generalissimo, who had made cautious overtures to the Soviet Union during the U.S.-Soviet alliance, now became the most militant anticommunist in the hemisphere and thereby earned the support of U.S. senators such as William Jenner and Strom Thurmond, who frequently spoke out in behalf of the "stability" and "progress" of his regime. Prominent citizens, including Franklin D. Roosevelt, Jr., and the civil-liberties lawyer Morris Ernst, became registered lobbyists. Trujillo succeeded in obtaining the services of other prominent Americans under less open circumstances. His former chief of military intelligence, Arturo R. Espallat, writes in his book, *Trujillo: The Last Caesar:*

> Trujillo had, for instance, price lists for the purchase of some U.S. Congressmen. An ordinary run-of-the-mill Representative would cost about $5,000 or less. A few House committee chairmen could be had for about three times that much, depending on the committee. Senators came higher, of course. A chairman of a key committee could run from $50,000 to $75,000.[5]

In the last six years of his life Trujillo began increasingly to alienate the United States government through a series of incidents, including the kidnapping (and presumed murder) in the streets of New York of an outspoken political opponent, Dr. Jesús María de Galíndez, and the attempted assassination of Venezuela's President Rómulo Betancourt. In June, 1959, Fidel Castro, persuaded by one of his Dominican associates, sponsored and trained an exile band of Dominicans, who staged an unsuccessful invasion of the island. The attempt inspired a new wave of repression so severe that Trujillo lost the support of the Catholic Church, which in January, 1960, publicly denounced him.

At the same time, the Dominican Republic was assuming a new economic importance to the United States sugar industry. Since 1934 the U.S. government has subsidized raw sugar on the grounds that it was necessary to pay more than the world-market price in order to assure a steady supply. The subsidy was administered by assigning quotas to various sugar-producing countries. Until Castro's assumption of power, the Cuban quota was by far the largest, as Cuban imports accounted for about one-third of all sugar consumed in the United States. Now, with Castro's cutback of sugar production and increasing U.S.-Cuban hostility, there were new possibilities for the Dominican Republic to sell a much larger quota of sugar at a premium. The value of sugar exports in 1959–60 doubled.[6]

After the attempted assassination of Betancourt, however, the fear grew among the Latin-American countries that the rampaging dictator was simply inviting a Dominican Castro. The Organization of American States met and imposed sanctions. The United States began to cut its military mission. Congressman Harold Cooley, an old supporter of Trujillo who as head of the House Agriculture Committee had virtually unlimited power to set the quotas, tried at the urging of Trujillo lobbyists to preserve the Dominican share of the sugar subsidy. But the Eisenhower administration, determined that Trujillo now had to go, imposed a special tariff on Dominican sugar which exactly wiped out the premium of 22.7 million dollars provided under the quota. Ambassador Joseph S. Farland began to make contact with underground opposition to Trujillo. In August, 1960, the United States broke diplomatic relations with the Trujillo government.

The following May, six weeks after the U.S.-sponsored invasion of the Cuban Bay of Pigs, Trujillo was assassinated. The shooting on a dark country road was planned and executed by army officers close to Trujillo who were convinced that the dictator's excesses had aroused such opposition in the hemisphere that their own interests were in danger. It seems clear that the CIA had foreknowledge

of the assassination plot and let the conspirators know
that the United States would have no objection if the
Benefactor were removed from the scene.[7]

Two

The Kennedy administration came to power with
some new ideas for Latin America. The familiar policy of
support for dictatorships, corrupt oligarchies, and military
coups was to be replaced by the Alliance for Progress.
"There is no place," the new U.S. President proclaimed at
Punta del Este in August, 1961, "in democratic life for
institutions which benefit the few while denying the needs
of the many, even though the elimination of such institutions may require far-reaching and difficult changes such
as land reform and tax reform and a vastly increased
emphasis on education and health and housing."[8] As
Arthur Schlesinger correctly points out, these were words
no President of the United States had ever before ad-
dressed to Latin America. "This is a revolutionary
task,"[9] Douglas Dillon, the secretary of the treasury,
declared, looking over at his fellow revolutionary, Che
Guevara, "but we are no strangers to revolution." Kennedy and his advisers for Latin America, who included liberal intellectuals like Arthur Schlesinger and
Richard Goodwin, veterans of the Puerto Rico experiment
like Teodoro Moscoso, and the New Dealer turned Latin-
American business adviser, Adolph Berle, were convinced
that the democratic left, represented by men like Betancourt, Muñoz Marín, and Figueres, was the best hope
of bringing modernization to Latin America without violence and without stirring up hatred for the *yanqui*. Muñoz summed up the new attitude toward the moderate-
progressive forces which the United States now planned to
nurture. They are "the only nontotalitarian element which
understands the depths of the revolutionary ferment in
Latin America and which can provide responsible leader-

ship to shape this revolution into constructive channels."[10]

The survival of the Trujillo regime, in Kennedy's view a
hopeless anachronism, blocked the rise of the moderate
forces on which he counted so heavily to bring stability to
Latin America. The elimination of Trujillo, accordingly,
was a major opportunity. The new administration, severely
criticized for the crude invasion attempt in Cuba, made no
effort to minimize its role in bringing down Trujillo.
Kennedy now hoped that the tiny island could become a
"showcase" to display the new U.S. model for Latin-
American development.

"There are three possibilities in descending order of
preference," Arthur Schlesinger recalls Kennedy musing
shortly after the Trujillo assassination, "a decent democratic regime, a continuation of the Trujillo regime or a
Castro regime. We ought to aim at the first, but we really
can't renounce the second until we are sure that we can
avoid the third."[11] He sent the veteran diplomat Robert
Murphy and the reporter John Bartlow Martin, a close
associate of Adlai Stevenson, to Santo Domingo to survey
the possibilities. Martin's one-hundred-and-fifteen-page analysis convinced the President that Joaquín Balaguer,
who had held the honorific title of president at the end of
the Trujillo era and, together with Trujillo's son Ramfis,
had stayed on to run the country, was "our only tool."
"The anti-communist liberals," the President concluded,
"aren't strong enough. We must use our influence to take
Balaguer along the road to democracy."[12]

So began a two-year campaign to transform a plun-
dered island into a society that would at once offer a
measure of justice to its citizens and continued economic
opportunity for American business. To prevent the emergence of the extreme right or the extreme left—a "takeover by the army which could lead straight to Castro"[13]
was the President's chief worry—Kennedy decided to encourage a coalition of the rival factions. The anti-Trujillo
groups were prepared to stomach Balaguer only if Ramfis
Trujillo left the country. "I see the situation the same as
you do,"[14] Ramfis told Martin in the fall of 1961, and a
few weeks later promised George McGhee, the State
Department counselor, that he was prepared to go into
exile, as his uncles had already done. But a few days later
the uncles returned. The army, under General Pedro
Echevarría, appeared to be preparing a coup. Once again

Marines were ordered to Santo Domingo. Kennedy sent eight ships with eighteen hundred fighting men on board to lie at anchor just off the Dominican harbor, ready to go ashore if Balaguer asked for them. As the flotilla came into view, Echevarría's loyalty to the government quickly revived and the Trujillos fled. The United States now urged the broadening of the Balaguer government. However, hostility to the old Trujillist erupted in riots, and Balaguer, who five years later would be the U.S.-favored candidate for president, was forced to seek asylum in the residence of the papal nuncio. General Echevarría attempted to lock up the rest of the government, desisting only under U.S. pressure. With the last of the Trujillos gone, the OAS sanctions were lifted and President Kennedy resumed diplomatic relations, appointing John Bartlow Martin as ambassador.

Three

For the next nine months a small group of U.S. citizens tried to remake the country. The American presence in the Dominican Republic in 1962 completely dominated the politics and the economy of the unhappy island. The anti-Trujillo forces were split among three major groups, each with its own warring factions. The Unión Cívica Nacional (UCN) represented the middle- and upper-class opposition to Trujillo. Starting as an apolitical civic movement immediately after the assassination, it developed into a political party under Viriato Fiallo, who led the fight against Balaguer. With support from the U.S. ambassador it became a major force in the seven-man Consejo (council of state) that ran the interim government.

The Fourteenth of June Movement also was split. The movement was named for the abortive Castro-sponsored invasion of June 14, 1959, but the men who organized it in Trujillo's prison did not actually participate in the invasion. The leader, Manuel Tavárez Justo, convinced

Martin that he was a nationalist whose party, as he put it, had been "born out of desperation."[15] But the movement also included Alfredo Manzano, who, Martin was certain, was "Moscow-directed," not only because "a few times he used the language of Communist dialectics" but also because "he evaded and seemed to enjoy it." The American ambassador recommended to Washington that the United States support the moderates in the movement against the "Castro/Communists."[16]

The third party was the Partido Revolucionario Dominicano (PRD), an exile party founded in Cuba in 1939, whose leader, the writer Juan Bosch, was about to return to Santo Domingo. The party was popular among the lower classes and stood somewhere between the other two in political complexion.

The American ambassador, who saw his assignment as remaking a country, rather quickly decided who could be used as "our tool" now that Balaguer was gone. The new president, Rafael Bonnelly, who once had been Trujillo's secretary of state of interior and police, struck him as "decent, sensible, patriotic, and upright,"[17] despite his long career as a Trujillo wheelhorse. Once his leader had been assassinated, he helped found the UCN, which then supported him for president. Now, he told Martin, "Our fate is linked. We will stand or fall together."[18] One of Bonnelly's protégés, Donald Reid Cabral, a member of one of the oldest oligarchical families, also became a confidant of the ambassador. So too did Antonio Imbert, a colonel who had been one of the assassins of Trujillo and liked to recall the event by sending Christmas cards with a picture of the spot where Trujillo had died.

Martin's overriding concern from the moment he stepped foot in the Dominican Republic was how to prevent a communist take-over. When he left the President's office, President Kennedy had jokingly referred to him as the Earl E. T. Smith of this administration (Eisenhower's ambassador to Cuba at the time of Castro's takeover), but it was no joke. A reading of Martin's exhaustive memoir, *Overtaken by Events,* reveals how deep and pervasive was his obsession with the communist danger. Curiously, in his analysis of the communist role in the Dominican Republic he was careful not to exaggerate their significance. Martin was informed by the CIA that there were "not more than one hundred well-trained, fully-committed, and fully-disciplined" Dominican communists. These were split be-

tween the Partido Socialista Popular (PSP—a Moscow-
oriented communist party), and a smaller pro-Peking
group, the Movimiento Popular Dominicano (MPD). Some
communists were in the Fourteenth of June Movement.
All three groups received small amounts of money and
arms from abroad. Martin was convinced that the communists, weak and divided as they were, did not constitute
a threat to the government. The real danger, he always
believed, was a rightist coup led by the army. To the
extent that they contributed to that, and only to that
extent, were the communists a threat. Yet every U.S.
program and policy was judged principally by gauging its
impact on the communist menace.

The politicians from the old oligarchical families and
the generals who ran the Council of State constantly
harped on the communist danger. So also on his arrival
did Juan Bosch. When a communist was arrested in April,
1961, in connection with an anti-U.S. demonstration and
the murder of a policeman, President Bonnelly cried that
Castro's plot to take over the island had begun. Actually,
as the CIA reported to the ambassador, the evidence was
rather that Imbert and the commanders of the air force
and police were about to mount a coup.

The military leaders kept urging a policy of mass repression. "I told the president to go away for three days
and everything will be all right,"[19] one of Trujillo's
assassins suggested. Bonnelly pleaded for a show of U.S.
support and was "ostentatiously" taken to lunch aboard a
U.S. warship. Despite the fact that there was no organized
communist or leftist guerrilla movement and that the
military continually pressed for purges, coups, reprisals,
and mass arrests, the programs which the United States
launched made the communists the exclusive target and
the military the chief beneficiaries. A Special Forces counterinsurgency team arrived to train the Dominican military in how to root guerrillas out from the hills. A Civic
Action Project was begun which gave the army training
and increasing responsibility for construction and reform
of the civilian economy. The government received a twen-
ty-five-million-dollar loan. A program of agrarian reform
was drawn up with the support and encouragement of the
Americans. An AID mission and a contingent of Peace
Corps volunteers arrived. But, in Martin's words, rioting
and political unrest "smothered" such efforts. He was sure

that the rioters who came night after night to cry "liberty" in front of the American Embassy, to honk horns and overturn cars, were there because they were paid. (The CIA reported that an ordinary riot could be arranged for one hundred and fifty dollars but one complete with window smashing might run as high as five hundred dollars.)

The U.S. Embassy pressed the Bonnelly government to greater repression. "But the Consejo did not crack down; and so I found myself urging other measures—methods once used by the police in Chicago."[20] Recalling that his wife had been a board member of the Illinois American Civil Liberties Union and he himself a crusader in print for civil liberties, Martin pondered how it happened that he now urged the harassment of suspects by repeated arrests, midnight raids on their homes, and beatings. "Such methods," the ambassador concluded with a "bad conscience," were justified in support of a "faltering Carribbean government that the Castro/Communists sought to overthrow."[21] When he returned to Washington for consultations, Martin asked President Kennedy for more antiguerrilla and coastal-patrol forces and some Mexican antiriot squads from Chief W. H. Parker's Los Angeles police force.

Between March, 1962, and September, 1963, when the Bosch government fell, the United States made foreign-aid grants to the Dominican Republic totaling eighty-four million dollars. (Five million for schools, two million for agricultural credit, one million for roads, two million for housing, and 1.7 million for an agrarian institute were the principal projects.) The implementation of the aid agreements was exceedingly slow because, as Martin explains it, "Anything used on a project that had to be bought abroad had to be bought in the United States. At least half of such purchases had to be sent to the Republic in United States ships."[22] Each expenditure required specific negotiation and approval from U.S. officials.

Two basic economic decisions faced the Dominican Republic as it prepared for the first election without the Trujillos in over thirty-eight years. One concerned the sugar quota. At the end of the Eisenhower administration, the Dominican economy and the U.S.-owned South Puerto Rico Sugar Company (which produced about thirty percent of Dominican sugar) benefited from a quota under which the U.S. government paid a premium above the

world-market price on nine hundred thousand tons a year.
In 1962 the Kennedy administration, under pressure of
domestic beet-sugar producers, balance-of-payments difficulties, and a desire for a more flexible instrument of
diplomatic pressure, decided to substitute a worldwide
quota for the country-by-country quota. In practical terms
this meant that the Dominican Republic could not count
on selling any definite amount. Since sugar accounts for
about fifty percent of their foreign exchange and the local
industry was too inefficient to compete at the lower world-
market price, this meant a monumental crisis. "To put it
bluntly," Martin later wrote, "the Dominican Republic
might go broke if it lost its U.S. sugar quota."[23] Both the
army and the communists, according to the CIA, were about
to start an insurrection. Finally, a compromise bill was
passed which restored about half of the former quota. The
Consejo was saved, but the incident dramatized the
economic hold of the United States on the island. It was a
fact that lent authority to Ambassador Martin's rejoinder
to Juan Bosch, when as a presidential candidate he exclaimed, "No one wants this government." Martin answered, " 'We do.' I said it quietly and coldly."[24]

The other basic economic decision concerned the fate
of Trujillo's personal empire, particularly the Haina sugar
properties, which produced over two-thirds of the national
crop. The Businessmen's Council on International Understanding, a private U.S. group, sent George Walker, an
executive of the Koppers Company, to lobby for the
transfer of the Trujillo properties to private investors. This
Martin opposed. "We would be accused of having sent the
fleet to throw the Trujillos out in order to get our hands
on their properties."[25] Bosch campaigned on a platform
of distribution of the Trujillo lands to landless peasants
and made a start in this direction after his election.

Martin worked frantically to assure that the election
would take place, promising "Tony" Imbert that he would
be made a general if he agreed not to launch a coup
against the duly elected president. Despite the fact that
spokesmen of the Church had denounced him as a
"Marxist-Leninist," Bosch won about sixty percent of the
vote, much to the surprise of the American Embassy. His
support came primarily from the lower classes, who were
attracted to his program of radical land reform and increased agricultural wages. The Americans—some of

whom thought he was dangerously leftist, others of whom, including Martin, distrusted his personality—looked on his election with a mixture of relief and foreboding.

Four

President Bosch lost no time in trying to establish his independence from the United States. His conversations in Washington with administration officials right after his election convinced the assistant secretary of state, Edwin Martin: "I think we have our problems."[26] A few days after his return to Santo Domingo he denounced a contract that the Consejo had made with Esso for an oil refinery, the only large new American investment in the Republic since the fall of Trujillo. Next he visited Europe and negotiated a one-hundred-and-fifty-million-dollar loan from a consortium in Zurich. "We are changing our image —the moral, political, economic image of the country," Bosch declared in his inaugural address. "We are changing it into a revolutionary democracy."[27] Ambassador Martin recorded his immediate impressions of the new leader: "Bosch is a divider, a splitter, a schemer, a destroyer."[28]

Bosch continued to challenge U.S. interests by threatening to cancel some molasses and sugar contracts negotiated the year before. The U.S. ambassador threatened to invoke the Hickenlooper Amendment, which forbids foreign aid to countries that confiscate American property. Bosch was furious about the contracts, which to him meant that foreign "sugar men will take six and a half millions out of here in profits,"[29] but under pressure he honored them. Relations with the United States became increasingly strained. Bosch was reported to have made a statement to an Argentine radio station that Latin America must work out its own problems and not rely on the Alliance for Progress. *Business Week,* the *Chicago Tribune,* and then many other U.S. periodicals began to attack the Bosch government. Some of the advisers were supposed to be Castro sympathizers. He was too slow in closing down a school for subversives. Loans and grants from the United States dwindled. Martin, who was convinced that the president was not a communist, spent much of his time lecturing Bosch on measures for dealing with the communists. Liberal use of deportation and a Dominican Smith Act to control subversives were repeatedly proposed. He also tried to persuade him to go slow in implementing the new constitution. Businessmen were "highly disturbed" about such provisions as compulsory profit sharing, the prohibition against large landholdings, and restrictions on property holdings by foreigners. It was important, Martin emphasized, for the government to keep good relations with business and he recommended that Bosch accept a speaking invitation before the American Chamber of Commerce.

Although Martin himself gave them little credit, the CIA began to report to Washington all sorts of rumors of communist plots. This had the effect of cooling still further the Kennedy administration's enthusiasm for the Bosch government. Members of the opposition parties made a point of spreading stories about Bosch's communist connections. One even made a secret trip to Washington to propose a coup. President Bosch accused the South Puerto Rican Sugar Company of trying to overthrow his government. Congressman Armistead Selden took the House floor to attack the "subversive penetration" of the Dominican Republic, referring particularly to the return of one hundred and fifty Dominican citizens who had been deported under Trujillo and the Consejo governments.

Bosch, who later wrote that his dream was to turn the island from a "dominion" into a "country," continued to assert a personal style that reflected his desperate longing for national independence and dignity. This succeeded only in infuriating both the local oligarchy and the American officials. The CIA stepped up its investigations of Bosch's associates, including Sacha Volman, director of CIDES, a research and planning center Bosch had set up to give training and advice on development. (At the moment of the investigation, Volman was himself receiving CIA funds funneled through a private U.S. foundation.) [30]

Bosch imposed what amounted to a tax on sugar profits to finance housing for workers, which cost the South Puerto Rican Sugar Company twenty-five million dollars, but he made it clear that he did not intend to confiscate

American holdings in the manner of a Castro. Nevertheless, Senator George Smathers, who was close to U.S.
business interests in Latin America and had urged sending
Marines into the island when the Trujillos fled—"Many
Americans having invested $250 million in the Dominican
Republic believe that Generalissimo Trujillo was the best
guarantee of American interests in the country . . . open
intervention must now be considered to protect their property and to prevent a communist coup. . . ."[31]—denounced him as a Castroite. As Bosch continued his
dogged but largely futile effort at reform, the proponents
of gunboat diplomacy became more vocal. Congressman
Armistead Selden of the House Foreign Affairs Committee
told Ambassador Martin that Bosch should stop making
political statements that made it impossible for a conservative American congressman to support him.

Despite its reservations, the Kennedy administration
continued to defend Bosch. In the summer of 1963 the
American Embassy helped rescue the president from an
imminent *golpe*. A few stories favorable to the regime
began to appear in the U.S. press. Martin pressed Bosch
to prohibit all travel to Cuba, arguing that such a move
would improve his public image. To save himself the
president must now try to unite the country, not continue
to split it. He must make a "lofty speech." Taking some
notes from his pocket and handing them to the president,
the ambassador recalls that he remarked somewhat apolo-
getically, "I've written speeches for other writers and it's
an unrewarding job, but here it is."[32]

Even if he could have brought himself to take all the
advice Martin offered him, it was too late for Bosch. Too
many groups were now arrayed against him. Among the
ranks of Bosch's enemies were many of the Americans
who had poured into the island to man the Embassy, the
AID Mission, the Military Assistance Mission, the CIA, the
corporations, private consulting firms, and other institutions for transforming the country that had sprung up in
the few months since the Trujillos' departure. The sympathies of the U.S. military attachés ran more to their
Dominican brothers in arms than to Bosch. The naval
attaché, Bevan Cass, for example, had "misgivings" about
Bosch's attitude toward the communists and warned the
ambassador that he didn't "know how much longer I can
go on supporting him."[33] Sam Halper, a *Time* correspondent, later reported that the military coup ousting

Bosch went into action "as soon as they got a wink from
the U.S. Pentagon."[34] Also allied against Bosch was the
AFL-CIO Latin-American trade organization, ORIT, which
had formed a federation of unions in the Dominican
Republic called CONATRAL as a counterpoise to the existing
Dominican trade unions, a strong base of Bosch's support.
CONATRAL placed an ad in *El Caribe* one week before the
coup urging the people to put their faith in the army to
defend them against communism.

On September 25, 1963, Imbert and Colonel Wessin y
Wessin, whom Bosch had tried to oust because he was
openly plotting a *golpe* in the name of anticommunism,
succeeded in driving Bosch from office. Martin inquired
about the possibility of bringing in U.S. warships, but the
State Department expressed reluctance unless there was a
danger of a "communist takeover." Martin asked Bosch
whether he wanted the Marines to land. The president,
already a prisoner in his palace, said no. The United
States then delivered a strong protest at the sudden death
of constitutional government after only seven months and
broke diplomatic relations.

Five

The officers who staged the coup set up a government by triumvirate and abolished the 1963 Bosch constitution and much of his reformist legislation. Although the
Kennedy administration had regarded Bosch as quixotic
and unreliable, and, with considerable justification, an
inefficient administrator without adequate political skills, it
was crushed that the "showcase" of the Alliance had been
so quickly smashed. "I take it we don't want Bosch
back,"[35] Kennedy asked Martin on his return to Washington. "No," the ambassador replied, "he isn't a president." But the principle of constitutional government
would be supported by cutting off all military and economic
aid to the new regime.

Two months later President Kennedy was dead. Within

three weeks his successor had resumed relations with the regime dominated by Donald Reid Cabral, who now ruled in collaboration with the military. One of Reid Cabral's first acts was to invite an American businessman, Peter Nehemkis, to come down to advise them on a timetable for elections, trusting that he would report a favorable impression of the new regime to the White House. Nehemkis's report, coupled with the equivocal State Department recommendations, strengthened Johnson's own inclinations. On the same day the President announced the resumption of relations, he appointed Thomas Mann as assistant secretary of state for Latin-American affairs. Mann, who had been in charge of Latin-American policy in the Eisenhower administration, was more convinced than the men of the New Frontier that private investment rather than U.S.-backed government planning was the key to stability in Latin America. He pointed out that Diego Bordas, the economic "czar" of the brief Bosch regime, had infuriated local businessmen as well as U.S. investors by his handling of the economy, notably the sugar properties. His appointment sparked renewed interest of U.S. businessmen in Caribbean investment. Mann also announced a new policy toward military dictatorships and military takeovers. The United States could not put itself in a "doctrinaire strait jacket of automatic application of sanctions to every unconstitutional regime in the hemisphere." This policy he defended privately as a dose of "realism" to replace the Kennedy "idealism" that had failed. During the nineteen months of the Reid Cabral government private U.S. investment increased sharply. In the first nine months of the junta, one hundred and seventy-five million dollars was invested. (Only sixty-four million dollars in U.S. private funds had flowed into the island during the seven months of the Bosch government.) The Midland Cooperatives of Minneapolis negotiated an oil-refinery contract. Another U.S.-Canadian firm announced that it would build a seventy-eight-million-dollar refinery. The World Bank made a 1.7-million-dollar loan for a hydroelectric study. Six private U.S. banks lent thirty million dollars. The military missions, the AID missions, and the rest of the American presence returned.[36]

Meanwhile the endless cycle of plotting continued. Bosch in exile made a pact at Río Piedras, Puerto Rico, with the Social Christian party to collaborate on a coup to restore the constitution. Inside the Dominican Republic, the Fourteenth of June Movement, which by 1963 claimed two hundred and fifty thousand sympathizers, and the MPD (the Maoist faction) went to the hills.[37] They were not brought into the pact and there is no evidence, according to Martin, that Bosch ever talked with the leaders of the communist parties. The Fourteenth of June Movement and the two communist parties decided independently to support the Bosch coup, the plan for which was an open secret.[38] Dissatisfaction with the Reid Cabral government was spreading to other groups as well. Sugar prices had fallen. There was mass unemployment (in Santo Domingo about forty percent). At the urging of the U.S. government and the International Monetary Fund, Reid Cabral had continued the financial austerity program of his predecessor. There were many splits in the military. Many of the younger officers, who unlike their superiors were not sharing the personal fringe benefits of foreign aid, became converts to constitutionalism. Under U.S. prodding for "reforms," Reid Cabral decided to cut the funds of the armed forces, which took thirty-eight percent of the national budget. With this decision, the last source of support for his regime collapsed.

The rebellion broke out on April 24, 1965. Although the exact sequence of the earliest moments of the rebellion is still difficult to verify, it appears that the initiative was taken by younger army officers (many of them sons of Trujillo generals) working with civilians from Bosch's party. According to Bosch, the constitutionalist officers led by Colonel Rafael Fernández Domínguez and Colonel Miguel Angel Hernando began to revolt two days before the agreed date because Reid Cabral, having discovered the plot, was moving to arrest the conspirators. For the first thirty-six hours the rebels had the military initiative. They captured two major army camps. The next day the PRD forces seized the radio station and announced that the government had been overthrown. The CIA, which had known for two weeks that a plot was impending, reported that it had identified several members of the PSP and the Fourteenth of June Movement among the rebels. The air force, under General Wessin y Wessin, was preparing to launch a countercoup. In the early hours of the revolt it appears that there were several more or less independent military factions seeking power. On Sunday, April 25, after failing to get either his own army to fight for him or a promise of U.S. Marines, Reid Cabral resigned and one of Bosch's associates, José Rafael Molina Urena, was sworn in by the rebel officers as provisional president. In the group surrounding the new president, the CIA reported, were members of the PSP and other communists.

The U.S. Embassy, which had sent an assessment on Saturday that this was "just another revolution," a day later sounded the alarm. The chargé d'affaires, William Connett, cabled Washington that there was a "serious threat of communist takeover"[39] and that a "U.S. show of force might be needed." Philip Geyelin of the *Wall Street Journal*, who studied official records and had access to cables, concludes that within the first twenty-four hours of the revolt, "the Santo Domingo embassy had clearly cast its lot with the 'loyalist' military cabal and against the rebellion's original aim: The return of Juan Bosch. . . . Restoration of the Bosch regime would be 'against U.S. interests,' the embassy counseled."[40]

The Embassy also advised Washington, according to Geyelin, that U.S. military attachés had given Wessin's forces "a go-ahead to do 'everything possible' to prevent what was described as the danger of a 'Communist take-over.' " Bosch has stated on several occasions that U.S. air and naval attachés began to order Wessin's forces to bomb Santo Domingo. Tad Szulc of *The New York Times*, who also saw the Embassy cables, confirms the early role of the U.S. attachés in supporting the anti-Bosch forces:

> Messages between the embassy in Santo Domingo and the State Department in Washington Sunday and Monday had disclosed growing concern over the navy's role and one of the principal functions of the embassy naval attachés had become to persuade Captain Rivero Caminera to cast his lot with the loyalist troops or at least remain neutral. To judge from the lobbing of shells into the Presidential Palace area Tuesday morning, the attachés' efforts had proved successful.[41]

When Ambassador Bennett returned on Tuesday from an ill-timed visit to his mother in Georgia, he told the rebel leaders that they must put a stop to "this senseless slaughter" and, besides, they were not "governing effectively."[42] The rebel leaders came to Bennett on Tuesday afternoon asking him, together with the papal nuncio, to negotiate with Wessin for a cease-fire. Bennett, who thought that the rebel broadcasts had a "Castro flavor," refused. The rebels clearly had the upper hand at this point on the battlefield.

The following day Bennett requested and received authorization from Washington to provide Wessin's forces with fifty walkie-talkie radios. The CIA officials in the Embassy received a steady stream of informers in their cubicles and began to amass a file on supposed communist subversion in the Dominican Republic. As early as Monday the Embassy had cabled Washington that Bosch must be stopped at all costs or else there would be "extremism in six months" in the Dominican Republic. Now Ambassador Bennett sent the telegram marked "critic," which President Johnson has said was the basis of his decision to intervene. "You can imagine what would have happened," he is reported to have said privately on May 3, 1965, "if I had not done so and there was an investigation and the press got hold of that cable."[43]

Six

Bennett's hysterical cable arrived at five-thirty P.M., Wednesday, April 28. In sum, the situation in Santo Domingo had collapsed. The police could not keep order. American lives were in danger. "The Generals at San Isidro were dejected, several were weeping, and one was hysterically urging 'retreat.'" The Embassy recommended a platoon of U.S. Marines to take control of the Embassy grounds and the evacuation center. A few minutes later another cable came in for the President. Bennett urged "armed intervention which goes beyond the mere protection of Americans" to "prevent another Cuba."[44] Admiral Raborn, sworn in earlier that day as director of the CIA, said that three communists were among the rebel leadership although he didn't yet have their names. Exactly sixty-seven minutes later President Johnson gave the orders that sent the Marines ashore. He asked for a written request from the military junta for U.S. military intervention, citing the danger to lives and property in order to provide the "juridical basis"[45] of the action. (The leader of the military junta, Colonel Benoit, had first asked for Marines because of the threat of "a communist takeover.") In President Johnson's speech later that night, the landing was explained purely as a rescue operation.

In Santo Domingo, the Embassy began to pour forth a rising stream of hysterical rumors, atrocity stories, and alarmist reports for the benefit of the American correspondents on the scene as well as the anxious officials in Washington. Bennett cabled the secretary of state that Colonel Caamano had "personally killed" the former president's aide-de-camp and had "gone berserk," committing many atrocities. The rebels were parading with severed heads of their victims. Mass executions were taking place to the Castroite cry, "Paredón!" ("To the Wall!") A list was passed out to the correspondents containing the names of fifty-three Dominican communists who were supposed to be the driving force behind the rebellion. Embassies were being ransacked, the ambassador declared, and some fifteen hundred innocent people were murdered and shot and their heads cut off. President Johnson himself later repeated many of these statements in his speeches. U.S. correspondents on the scene have demonstrated that none of these stories was true and officials later denounced the press for reporting such unverified rumors.[46] The list of communists, which later became a political cause célèbre, was highly inaccurate, since it contained a number of individuals who were not in the Dominican Republic at the time or who were in jail. The real point about the list, however, is that the individuals named had nothing to do with starting the revolt and had very little prospect of "taking it over," as the Embassy had tried to argue (although no doubt they would have liked to).

The communist issue was "surfaced" the same day that Ambassador Bennett was recommending to Washington a full-scale landing to crush the revolt. "Now that we are in this," Martin quotes him as advising the secretary of state, "we must do the full job as needed."[47] The tenor of Bennett's messages makes clear that his concerns were political, not humanitarian:

While I regret reliance on a military solution for a political crisis engendered by a confused, democratic left, all valid elements of which are either in hiding or in asylum as much from extremists in their own camp as from the military forces, the plain fact is that while leftist propaganda may fuzz the issue, the issue here now is a fight between Castro-type elements and those who oppose.[48]

Theodore Draper has made a careful analysis of the reports and messages surrounding the decision to send in Marines and confirms the impression of correspondents on the scene such as Tad Szulc, Bernard Collier, Dan Kurzman, and Philip Geyelin that the Embassy's analysis which prompted the decision rested on the undesirability of a rebel victory rather than the fact, as the President later described it, that "American blood will run in the streets." On May 2 the President publicly declared that the revolution had taken a "tragic turn." "What began as a popular democratic revolution that was committed to democracy and social justice moved into the hands of a band of Communist conspirators."[49]

It is quite clear that the President never had the warm feelings toward the early stages of the revolution that his words implied. He was confirmed in his anxiety about a possible communist outcome, his dominant concern from the first, by the agitated report of John Bartlow Martin, who had been sent down to the island to open up contact with the rebels. Martin went to Colonel Caamano's headquarters and spoke with him and a civilian associate, Hector Aristy, whom he described as "a smooth operator in both business and politics, intelligent, ambitious, joining party after party."[50] Caamano declared his loyalty to Bosch and complained that the U.S. Marines had disarmed members of the rebel forces and turned them over to the police. (From the first, the presence of the Marines had helped the military junta, since the Marines took up positions that split the rebel sector and allowed the retreating forces of the generals to regroup and then invade the rebel strongholds.) Martin was convinced that Caamano was under the domination of Aristy because the latter did a great deal of the talking and occasionally corrected him. The CIA had told Martin that several communists had been seen at the rebel headquarters. There was no evidence that Aristy was a communist, but "he was astonishingly well informed about military matters."[51] Perhaps, Martin wondered, he had received training in military tactics in a Soviet-bloc country, although there was no evidence that he had ever been to one. Then a young demonstrator outside the Caamano headquarters shouted, "Yankee, go home!" and, Martin reports, "immediately a powerful hand gripped his shoulder from behind and jerked him out of sight. He had used the wrong script." Martin has published the story twice to convey the process of political paranoia in which he came to the conclusion that Caamano was likely to become a Dominican Castro and that he was under the control of communists. He telephoned his impressions to Johnson shortly before the President announced that the revolution had taken a "tragic turn." Since Martin had expressed doubts about the communist takeover while being briefed in Washington just prior to his emergency visit to the island, his report carried great weight.

Martin then went to Puerto Rico to see Bosch. It was the first time an American official of the Johnson administration had contacted him with the exception of Abe Fortas, an unofficial emissary of the President who had been there the day before, and some FBI agents looking for information on Dominican communists. Martin, according to his own account, discouraged the deposed president from returning to the island. "Mr. President, you'd be killed," he warned.[52]

Once the full complement of Marines had landed, the communist takeover that had been proclaimed by President Johnson as the justification for the landing of an invasion force receded into a mere "possibility" or, at worst, a "very serious threat." Such terms, it appears, reflect more accurately the actual thinking of the Johnson administration at the time the intervention was ordered. The threat was not that the communists had taken over but that events were out of control and might lead to a nationalist, anti-U.S. regime that could look to Castro or to Moscow for help. As the President remarked a few days later, he did not intend to "sit in a rocking chair" and let that happen.

To justify the intervention, which had aroused violent opposition from traditional friends of the United States because of its crudeness and the swathe of lies in which it was wrapped, the State Department began a direct assault on the concept of nonintervention, the rhetorical foundation stone of Latin-American policy enshrined in numerous treaties, declarations, and Pan-American Day speeches. In the early weeks of the crisis, Under Secretary Thomas Mann told newspaper correspondents that the OAS and UN charters were drawn up in "19th century terms." Five days after the President announced that the real mission of the Marines was to prevent a communist takeover, Averell Harriman remarked in Montevideo that the principle of nonintervention was becoming "obsolete."[53] By a vote of 315 to 52 the House of Representatives passed a resolution proposed by Congressman Selden justifying the unilateral use of force on foreign territory by any nation which considers itself threatened by "international communism, directly or indirectly." The State Department offered no objections. The President tried to depict the landing of the Marines as a new conceptual breakthrough in international relations rather than as the *déjà vu* from the Wilson era that it actually was. Three weeks after the landing of the twenty-three-thousand-man expeditionary force, the President, wearing the robes of the honorary doctorate of laws just awarded him, assessed the juridical significance of the events:

> The first reality is that old concepts and old labels are largely obsolete. In today's world, with enemies of freedom talking about "Wars of national liberation," the old distinction between "Civil War" and "International War" has already lost much of its meaning. . . . The moment of decision must become the moment of action.[54]

This is the essence of the Johnson Doctrine—a virtually unlimited claim of legitimacy for armed intervention in civil strife.

The military outcome was a foregone conclusion once the Marines landed, for it was clear from the start which side they were supporting. Despite their official neutrality, the Marines invaded the rebel strongholds and permitted General Imbert's forces safe conduct through the U.S. Security Zone. The U.S. forces continued to supply weapons, food, and advice and actually attacked rebel positions. (The claim was self-defense, which in a few cases was a justifiable one.)

When the rebels were clearly defeated and the provisional president, Molina Urena, sought asylum, an inter-

American force under the Organization of American States, designed to replace the U.S. force, began to land. All military operations continued, however, to be coordinated by the U.S. commander, General Bruce Palmer, and the U.S. troops remained for many months. On September 3 an uneasy settlement following a series of broken truces was concluded. Peace returned. The Marines were slowly withdrawn.

Seven

At least as crucial in determining the outcome of the Dominican revolution as the activity of the Marines was the role of U.S. diplomats. When Martin returned to Santo Domingo in the midst of the crisis, the first major Dominican figure he went to see was General Imbert, with whom he had established good working relations during his ambassadorial tour. The CIA and the military had originally favored full-scale support for General Wessin y Wessin, who appeared on the cover of *Time* magazine the first week of the revolt as a Dominican national hero. But he had acted imprudently, demonstrating enough force to reveal himself as a brutal figure but not enough to defeat the rebels. His end was ignominious. A visit in the night by a CIA agent and a U.S.-army attaché with an offer of a military-attaché post in Madrid or Paris and fifty thousand dollars cash was followed by a visit from General Palmer and the Brazilian general in charge of the Inter-American Force telling him that "he had to go." "Never would I have imagined," he later wrote, "that an army officer of my rank would have been taken to the airport in full uniform and tossed out of the country with a bayonet at his back."[55] Now Martin attempted to secure U.S. backing for Imbert, who had held himself aloof from Wessin and the other generals. When Martin asked him whether he wanted to form a new government, he replied with characteristic candor, "I do it. For my country. Not for myself. What the hell I want to get into this mess for."

During May and June the United States supported Imbert's sacrifice with the sum of twenty-one million dollars. But already, in late May, McGeorge Bundy, the special assistant to the President for national security, arrived in Santo Domingo to try to establish a civilian government. When Imbert heard that the United States was now trying to build a government around Silvestre Antonio Guzmán, Bosch's former minister of agriculture, he shouted, "First the Americans talk me into putting together a government and now they tell me to quit. What the hell is the matter with you people."[56] (Martin later mused about the irony of the situation, that he, a liberal, was treating with Imbert while Thomas Mann, known for his conservative views, was working with Bundy to reinstate a member of Bosch's cabinet.)

Imbert refused to give way to Guzmán. After spreading stories of his alleged financial irregularities and accusing the U.S. of betraying the country to communism, he finally launched a murderous offensive against the rebels which the United States, despite the recommendations of Bundy, did nothing to oppose. Indeed, as the offensive gained momentum, U.S. Marines fired on the rebels, killing Colonel Hernando, one of the leaders. At the same time, Bundy continued his negotiations with Guzmán, whom the rebel chief, Colonel Caamano, had said that he would support.

It was becoming increasingly clear, however, that the supporters of Guzmán in the U.S. government were losing. Ellsworth Bunker, appointed U.S. ambassador to the OAS, took over the negotiations in early June along with Jack Hood Vaughn, the assistant secretary of state for Latin-American affairs, and Mann, who as under secretary still retained primary interest in Latin America. During the first week of June, Tad Szulc, *New York Times* correspondent, learned that Vaughn favored a plan for a provisional government and election and that the "State Department was hoping for a victory at the polls by Joaquín Balaguer."[57] Mann rejected Guzmán as part of the "unclean Bosch crowd."[58]

All through June the administration struggled with alternative approaches for the reestablishment of control and stability. One was symbolized by "Operation Tiger," a plan to use the Inter-American Force to crush the rebels. Another, totally contradictory, was "Operation Puma," a scheme for disarming Imbert's troops. From June to September Bunker, who knew something of the Dominican scene from a long and intimate connection with the U.S. sugar industry, worked to build a provisional government under Hector García-Godoy, a career diplomat who had been Bosch's foreign minister. Finally in September the United States cut off financial support to Imbert and succeeded in ending his four-month reign, a regime which had been characterized by beatings, arrests, and executions. The United States now felt strong enough in the Dominican Republic to challenge the government it had done so much to create. U.S. funds had poured into the island beginning in July. "In all, we spent about $150 million in the Dominican Republic in 1965," Martin writes, "a tragic irony if one recalls the difficulty both Ambassador Bennett and I had in getting far less money for peaceful works."[59] In the year following the revolution the Dominican Republic received the highest per-capita aid of any country in Latin America—32.1 dollars compared to 13.4 dollars for Chile, the nearest rival. The administration established an enormous embassy in Santo Domingo, rivaling only the one in Saigon for size and multiplicity of operations. As in Vietnam of the Diem era, a U.S. counterpart was appointed for every major Dominican government official.

Private U.S. investment in housing and tourism began to flow into the island once more. The shooting had scarcely stopped before new Hilton Hotels, Holiday Inns, and housing projects sponsored by IBEC, a Rockefeller-family company, were being planned. The South Puerto Rican Sugar Company, now merged with Gulf and Western Industries, decided to diversify and use some of its beach-front property for a new tourist center.

Once again U.S. business sensed that "stability" was returning to the island and the danger of a Dominican Castro was receding into the shadows. With the evidence at hand that the United States was prepared to occupy the island to prevent a revolution, U.S. business took increased confidence, and private investment, supported in many cases by low-interest AID development loans, increased dramatically.

On June 1, 1966, the second presidential election in over forty years was held in the Dominican Republic. Bosch, who had returned several months earlier, agreed to run but was so fearful for his personal safety that he never left his residence during the campaign. Joaquín Balaguer, the former Trujillist president whom the United States had supported in the Kennedy administration before he was forced into exile, again had the backing of the local oligarchy and the now enormous U.S. Embassy. During the months preceding the campaign the army continued to intimidate the opposition. On December 19, 1965, army tanks attacked Colonel Caamano and other leaders of the April 24 revolution while they were sitting at the Hotel Matum attending a requiem mass for one of the colonels killed in the revolt. The offices of the proconstitutionalist magazine *Ahora* were bombed, along with radio and television stations that had supported the constitutionalist side. The election itself seemed to be reasonably free, according to a U.S. Observation Team made up of Norman Thomas and other American liberals—although not without evidence of irregularities. But the context of continued intimidation by the military and strong U.S. support for Balaguer (behind declarations of neutrality) strongly influenced the outcome against Bosch.

For the United States, Balaguer's election was a victory, for it signified a return to the forms of constitutionalism without the dangers to U.S. interests which, in the State Department view, Bosch had represented. Though Balaguer was prepared to repress opposition which he considered dangerous and to staff his government with former colleagues from the Trujillo days, he was no Trujillo. He was not a bloody tyrant, but a cautious caretaker ready to move his country along the path of stability which the United States had prescribed as the only mechanism of change in this hemisphere it will tolerate.

NOTES—CHAPTER EIGHT

1. John Bartlow Martin, *Overtaken by Events: The Dominican Crisis from the Fall of Trujillo to Civil War* (New York, 1966), p. 22.

2. Ulises Heureaux, quoted in *ibid.*, p. 25.

3. The best account of the early history of U.S. relations with the Dominican Republic is to be found in Sumner Welles, *Naboth's Vineyard; The Dominican Republic, 1844–1924* (2 vols.; New York, 1928).

4. For a description of Trujillo's techniques of control, see Edwin Lieuwen, *Generals vs. Presidents: Neo-Militarism in Latin America* (New York, 1964), p. 55. See also Robert D. Crassweller, *Trujillo: The Life and Times of a Caribbean Dictator* (New York, 1966).

5. Espallat's book was published in Chicago in 1963. The quotation in the text is on p. 81.

6. Martin describes the operation and significance of the sugar quotas in *Overtaken by Events*, pp. 161–177. See also, for a description of U.S. sugar lobbyists, Daniel M. Berman and Robert A. Heineman, "Lobbying by Foreign Governments on the Sugar Act Amendments of 1962," in *Law and Contemporary Problems*, September 1963, pp. 416–427. I am grateful to Fred Goff and Michael Locker for their privately circulated paper, *The Violence of Domination: U.S. Power and the Dominican Republic*, in which my attention was called to this and several other important references. This paper is available from the North American Congress on Latin America, Box 57, Cathedral Station, New York City, N.Y.

7. That the CIA had foreknowledge of the plot against Trujillo and gave assistance to it has been confirmed to me privately by individuals in the U.S. government in a position to know and in whose judgment and veracity I have confidence. See also Norman Gall, "How Trujillo Died," in *The New Republic*, April 13, 1961, for an account of CIA arms shipments to the Trujillo assassins.

8. John F. Kennedy, quoted in Arthur Schlesinger, Jr., *A Thousand Days: John F. Kennedy in the White House* (Boston, 1965), p. 761.

9. Douglas Dillon, quoted in *ibid.*, pp. 761–762.

10. Muñoz Marín, quoted in *ibid.*, p. 765.

11. John F. Kennedy, quoted in *ibid.*, p. 769.

12. John F. Kennedy, quoted in *ibid.*, p. 770.

13. John F. Kennedy, quoted in *ibid.*, p. 771.

14. Ramfis Trujillo, quoted in Martin, *Overtaken by Events*, p. 80.

15. Manuel Travarez Justo, quoted in *ibid.*, p. 72.

16. *Ibid.*

17. *Ibid.*, p. 89.

18. Rafael Bonnelly, quoted in *ibid.*, p. 88.

19. Quoted in *ibid.*, p. 97.

20. *Ibid.*, p.100.

21. *Ibid.*

22. *Ibid.*, p. 146.

23. *Ibid.*, p. 162.

24. *Ibid.*, p. 180.
25. *Ibid.*, p. 116.
26. Edwin Martin, quoted in *ibid.*, p. 309.
27. Juan Bosch, quoted in *ibid.*, p. 325.
28. *Ibid.*, p. 329.
29. Juan Bosch, quoted in *ibid.*, p. 356.
30. For a critical account of Volman's activities, see Ruth Sheriff, "How The CIA Makes Friends and Influences Countries," in *Viet-Report*, January-February 1967, p. 15.
31. George Smathers, quoted in *The Congressional Record*, May 31, 1966.
32. Martin, *Overtaken by Events*, p. 504.
33. Bevan Cass, quoted in *ibid.*, p. 504.
34. Sam Halper, "The Dominican Upheaval," in *The New Leader*, May 10, 1965.
35. John F. Kennedy, quoted in Martin, *Overtaken by Events*, p. 601.
36. For an account of foreign investment in the Dominican Republic immediately following the overthrow of President Bosch, see Goff and Locker, *The Violence of Domination*.
37. For a description of prerevolutionary plotting, see Martin Niederlang, *La Révolution de Santo-Domingue* (Paris, 1966).
38. Martin reports that the CIA had known about the coup for two weeks. See Martin, *Overtaken by Events*, p. 645.
39. William Connett, quoted in *ibid.*, p. 650.
40. Philip Geyelin, quoted in Theodore Draper, "The Dominican Crisis," in *Commentary*, December 1965, p. 39.
41. See Tad Szulc, *Dominican Diary* (New York, 1965).
42. W. Tapley Bennett, quoted in Martin, *Overtaken by Events*, p. 653.
43. Lyndon B. Johnson, quoted in Rowland Evans and Robert Novak, *Lyndon B. Johnson: The Exercise of Power* (New York, 1966), p. 511.
44. W. Tapley Bennett, quoted in Martin, *Overtaken by Events*, pp. 656–657.
45. *Ibid.*, p. 657.
46. For an account of the atrocity stories and their falsity, see Szulc, *Dominican Diary*.
47. W. Tapley Bennett, quoted in Martin, *Overtaken by Events*, p. 659.
48. Evans and Novak, *Lyndon B. Johnson*, p. 514.
49. Lyndon B. Johnson, quoted in Draper, "The Dominican Crisis," p. 42.
50. Martin, *Overtaken by Events*, p. 669.
51. *Ibid.*
52. *Ibid.*, p. 677.
53. Draper, "The Dominican Crisis," p. 66.
54. Lyndon B. Johnson, Speech at Baylor University, May 28, 1965.

55. General Wessin's account is quoted in Draper, "The Dominican Crisis," p. 65.

56. Silvestre Antonio Guzmán, quoted in Szulc, *Dominican Diary*, p. 241.

57. *Ibid.*, p. 313.

58. *Ibid.*

59. Martin, *Overtaken by Events*, p. 700.

CHAPTER **9**

America in Vietnam:
The Four Interventions

One

THE SAME CONSIDERATIONS that impelled the U.S.
intervention in the Greek and Lebanese civil wars also
prompted the American decision to suppress the insurgency in Vietnam. In each case the real estate in question was
of little concern. Nor was the fate of the Greek, Lebanese, or Vietnamese people more than a secondary
consideration. There were no powerful ethnic minorities in
the United States to campaign for a U.S. commitment to
their brothers in the homeland. U.S. commercial interests
in Greece at the time of the intervention were insignificant. Lebanon, unlike its neighbors, was not a vital source
of oil or anything else for the United States. Despite
occasional remarks of President Eisenhower and others
about the "importance to the Free World" of the tungsten
and rubber of Indochina, that region, too, had little role in
the U.S. economy.

In each case the United States committed its power
because of events that occurred elsewhere. Greece became
a rampart of the West as a consequence of the Soviet
efforts to transform Eastern Europe into an empire and
her abortive claim to a share of power in the Mediter-

ranean. The landing in Lebanon during the civil war was a spasm response to a revolution that had just occurred in Iraq. Vietnam acquired central importance for America as a result of the collapse of noncommunist China. In Vietnam, as in Greece, the United States, alarmed by the decline of her allies England and France and the rise of new challengers, reached out for the imperial responsibilities now dropping from failing hands.

The first U.S. troops to arrive in Vietnam were a small contingent of Marines, from the U.S.S. *Constitution*, who landed on May 10, 1845, in an unsuccessful attempt to rescue a French bishop. They sailed away promptly[1] and U.S. forces did not return to Indochina until the end of World War II. By 1941, however, the peninsula had begun to assume importance in U.S. foreign policy.

In July, 1941, shortly after the Japanese had invaded Indochina, President Roosevelt proposed to the Japanese ambassador that the United States, Britain, China, Japan, and the Netherlands agree to the neutralization of the Indochinese peninsula and Thailand.[2] The final U.S. negotiating position on the eve of the war included a demand that Japan withdraw from Indochina. Throughout the war, Roosevelt remained conscious of the fact that conflict over Indochina was one of the principal occasions for the outbreak of war. Secretary of State Hull recalls: "That French dependency stuck in his mind as having been the springboard for the Japanese attack on the Philippines, Malaya, and the Dutch East Indies."[3]

Frequently in the war years FDR would express his own views on the future of Indochina. He told Hull and Admiral Leahy in October, 1943, that he favored an "international trusteeship" for the region. A few months later he expanded on these views in a memorandum to Hull:

> I saw Halifax last week and told him quite frankly that it was perfectly true that I had for over a year expressed the opinion that Indo-China should not go back to France but that it should be administered by an international trusteeship. France has had the country—thirty million inhabitants—for nearly one hundred years, and the people are worse off than they were at the beginning.[4]

His interest in ending colonialism in Indochina stemmed not only from his sympathy for the vic-

tims of exploitation—Chiang Kai-shek told him that
"for every dollar they have put in, they have taken out
ten"[5]—but also from his concern that a feeble imperial
outpost could once again become a springboard for attacking U.S. interests in the Pacific. His annoyance with
both the collaborationist Vichy regime and the obstreperous De Gaulle did not increase his sympathy for French
imperial claims. By early 1945, however, he was encoun-
tering considerable resistance to the trusteeship idea. Some
of it came from Hull and others in the State Department,
who favored leaving colonies in the hands of the imperial
powers, provided they pledged themselves to offer eventu-
al independence, as the United States had done with the
Philippines. The principal opposition, however, came from
the British. As Roosevelt remarked to a group of reporters
on board the U.S.S. *Quincy* as she was steaming toward
Yalta, "Stalin liked the idea. China liked the idea. The
British didn't like it. It might bust up their empire, because if the Indo-Chinese were to work together and
eventually get their independence, the Burmese might do
the same thing to England."[6]

The President had decided that French troops should
not participate in the liberation of Indochina, as the State
and War departments had recommended. Indeed, he personally instructed the War Department not to give accred-
itation to any French military mission in the Southeast
Asia Command. At the same time, he rejected a proposal
by the Office of Strategic Services that the United States
aid resistance forces in Indochina then organizing under
Ho Chi Minh. "You might bring it up to me a little later
when things are a little clearer," the President noted on
the oss memorandum.[7]

American military officers had met Ho Chi Minh and
his future military commander, Vo Nguyen Giap, in Kun-
ming, China, in 1944. At that time the Vietnamese resistance leaders were planning the strategy which, they
hoped, would sweep out the Japanese and set up an
independent government run by the Vietminh, a coalition
of left and moderate organized by Ho and other communists in 1939. U.S. officers of the China-Burma-India
theater began to supply Ho with arms. In early 1945 Ho
Chi Minh established uncertain control over the northern
regions of Vietnam. As the Chinese, British, and U.S.
troops poured back into Vietnam in the wake of the
Japanese collapse, the Vietminh extended its claims to all

Vietnam. On September 2, 1945, Ho proclaimed the establishment of the Democratic Republic of Vietnam.

The same month, General Philip E. Gallagher arrived to head a U.S. military mission. An office of the OSS was set up in Hanoi under Major Patti. Both U.S. officers supported Vietnamese independence under Ho and opposed the restoration of French colonial rule. On September 20, 1945, General Gallagher wrote his superior:

> The Annamite party, Viet Minh, led by Ho Chi Minh, who is the Prime Minister, is definitely in the saddle. This Ho Chi Minh is an old revolutionist and a political prisoner many times, a product of Moscow, a communist. He called upon me and welcomed us most profusely, gave me a very beautiful red banner with my name on it and some remark about the "Great American Nation," etc. His political party is an amalgamation of all lesser parties. There may be some smaller bandit groups, but they are negligible, and he has told me that, regardless of the decision of the big powers regarding whether France would or would not be permitted to come back in, his party expected to fight, that they are armed, well supplied, and will resist all French efforts to take over FIC. In this regard, it is well to remember that he is a revolutionist whose motto is "Independence or Death."[8]

General Gallagher broadcast over Ho's radio in 1946. Major Patti introduced General Giap to Jean Sainteny, the leading French official in Hanoi. The Americans flew a guard of honor of two fighter planes over a parade in Hanoi celebrating the newly proclaimed independence. In the United States, *Newsweek* magazine compared Ho Chi Minh to George Washington. While General Giap publicly celebrated the "particularly intimate relations" which the Vietminh enjoyed with the United States and Ho told a State Department official that he regarded the United States as the "one nation most likely to be sympathetic to our cause," the returning French did not conceal their annoyance at "the infantile anticolonialism" of the Americans. (The following year *Le Monde* gave circulation to reports that the OSS was actually attempting to negotiate personal economic concessions with Ho on behalf of General William Donovan, the Wall Street figure who was chief of the OSS.)

On March 6, 1946, Ho and Sainteny signed an agreement recognizing the Democratic Republic of Vietnam as "a free state with its own government, parliament, army and finances, forming a part of the Indochinese Federation and the French Union."[9] In exchange for the recognition of autonomy, Ho agreed to the return of fifteen thousand French troops. "I am not happy about it, for basically it is you who have won," Ho remarked at the signing. "But I understand that you cannot have everything in one day."[10]

Two

The French troops returned and Paris' negotiating position toughened. When Ho Chi Minh arrived in the French capital in the summer of 1946 to discuss the practical details of the new relationship with France, he was greeted as a chief of state by the Paris City Council. He laid a wreath on the Tomb of the Unknown Soldier. The Vietnamese flag flew in the streets. But the French made no concessions. The only result of the long negotiations between Ho and the French delegation, composed mainly of conservative military officers (including General Salan, who ten years later led the generals' revolt against De Gaulle in Algeria), was a vaguely worded "modus vivendi" which avoided the real issues of independence. To hedge against the results of the referendum which they had pledged to give, the French set up a puppet Republic of Cochin China and recognized it while Ho was in France. This tactic was frustrated shortly afterward, however, when the leader they had installed committed suicide.

As it became clearer that the French and Vietnamese nationalists of every political view had sharply divergent views on the process of independence, violent clashes began to break out. The French accused the Vietnamese of terrorism. On November 23, 1946, they turned the full force of their artillery on the city of Haiphong and killed more than six thousand Vietnamese.[11] Less than a month later the Vietnamese cut off the water and electricity supply for Hanoi and launched an attack. The war for Indochina had begun. Although it mounted in savagery, it could not claim world attention. The colonial issue of the moment was Indonesia. The Soviet Union's delegate to the United Nations told Vietnamese nationalists who came to see him that Russia was not interested in Vietnam. Ernest Bevin announced in Parliament that Indochina was a problem for the French alone.[12] In France the communists, still hopeful of taking power, played the role of French nationalist, not revolutionary partisan. "Are we, after having lost Syria and Lebanon yesterday, to lose Indochina tomorrow, North Africa the day after?" *L'Humanité* asked its readers.[13]

In the United States, Secretary of State George Marshall issued a statement on February 7, 1947, expressing the hope that "a pacific basis of adjustment of difficulties could be found."[14] The French took this to mean that the Truman administration favored a prompt negotiated settlement.

The French, however, were pursuing another course. In early 1947 they began negotiations with Bao Dai, the Vietnamese nationalist who had served as emperor under the Japanese and, for a short period, as supreme political adviser to Ho's Democratic Republic. During the year the role of the left in France weakened and support for a more militant anti-Vietminh policy gathered. Meanwhile, William C. Bullitt, who had been U.S. ambassador to France, became a leading salesman for the policy of installing Bao Dai as a rival nationalist leader to win the Vietnamese "independence" movement away from the communists. After visiting Indochina in late 1947 he carried on private negotiations with both Bao Dai and the French government, returning to the United States at the end of the year to write an article endorsing Bao Dai for *Life* magazine. The French interpreted these activities as an official U.S. initiative.

During the next two years the French installed the Bao Dai regime and in March, 1949, concluded the Elysée Agreements, which provided that "the government of Vietnam should exercise fully all of the attributes and prerogatives implied by internal sovereignty."[15] The French economic regime, however, was unchanged and France

reserved broad powers of intervention in the Vietnamese
economy and politics.

The United States first began to take a serious interest
in Indochina in the summer of 1949. From the first
moment Vietnam and its Southeast Asian neighbors
caught the attention of the National-Security Managers it
was seen not as a web of political conflict in desperate
need of settlement or, indeed, as an area of intrinsic
importance at all, but as a rampart to contain China, now
transformed into the world's most populous communist
state. Thus Indochina became an object of commitment in
the backwash of Mao's triumph. The Kuomintang government had fled to Formosa, and communist troops were
now only miles from the Indochinese border. In August,
1949, Dean Acheson, who was already under heavy attack
for a "sorry record of well-meaning mistakes"[16] in "losing"
China, warned, "Should the Communist regime lend itself
to the aims of Soviet Russian imperialism and attempt to
engage in aggression against China's neighbors, we and the
other members of the United Nations would be confronted by a situation violative of the principles of the
United Nations Charter and threatening international
peace and security."[17] The Vietnamese foreign minister
was "happy to note the good disposition of the American
State Department" and predicted that it could not fail to
bring his people "effective guarantees of liberty and security."[18] A committee to review U.S. policy toward Indochina, headed by Philip C. Jessup, had visited the area
and had recommended increased commitment.

In his instructions to Jessup, Acheson set out the new
premise of U.S. policy in Asia:

> You will please take as your assumption that it is
> a fundamental decision of American policy that the
> United States does not intend to permit further ex-
> tension of Communist domination on the continent of
> Asia or in the southeast Asia area. . . .[19]

The Americans now began to press the French to ratify
the agreements giving Vietnam independence. While the
French parliament was debating the issue in early 1950,
Ambassador Philip C. Jessup publicly offered premature
congratulations to Bao Dai on the establishment of the
state of Vietnam and expressed Secretary Acheson's

"confident best wishes" for a closer relationship. The State Department recognized the Bao Dai government within one week of ratification. Three weeks later France had delivered an official request to the United States for military and economic aid. The State Department, worried by both the spread of revolution in Asia and the effect that the colonial war was having on France's contribution to NATO, was more than happy to comply.

In signing the agreement to provide aid to the French in Indochina on May 8, 1950, Dean Acheson identified the problem as "Soviet imperialism" and the solution as "the promotion of genuine nationalism . . . within the French Union."[20] With the outbreak of the Korean War the following month, Indochina assumed much greater importance in American planning. The French convinced President Truman that their campaign in Indochina directly supported the effort in Korea. When he announced the decision to send U.S. ground forces to Korea, the President at the same time revealed the new policy of accelerated military aid for French operations against the Vietminh.

Three

The French-American partnership in support of Bao Dai was an ambivalent relationship from the first. The French military distrusted the Americans. They suspected that behind anti-colonial rhetoric plans were hatching to supplant French economic concessions with American. They resented direct American overtures to Bao Dai and feared, correctly, as it turned out, that they might become the superfluous man in Indochina. Yet they needed American aid desperately if they had any hope of holding on to the area. They insisted that the aid should not go directly to the Vietnamese, lest they establish a direct client relationship with the Americans. "I will never agree to equipment being given directly to the Vietnamese," the French commander-in-chief in Indochina declared. "If this should be done I would resign within twenty-four hours."[21] But when Acheson announced the decision to support "genuine nationalism" in Asia by aiding Bao Dai, he made a point of declaring that the aid would go directly to Vietnam and the other associated states of Indochina, Laos, and Cambodia.[22] After the attack on South Korea in June, 1950, the United States sent a military mission to Vietnam and stepped up its aid. As U.S. aid increased, more and more of it went directly to the Vietnamese, avoiding French intermediaries entirely. The outraged French colonial administrators referred to the chief of the U.S. aid mission as "the most dangerous man in Indochina," but they were powerless to object, for by 1954 the United States was paying about eighty percent of the cost of the war. The Vietnamese played on the French-American rivalry. One prime minister appealed openly for direct American aid so that he could build a Vietnamese army and take over the struggle from the French. Bao Dai dismissed him under French pressure. Another appealed publicly to the United States "to bring pressure on France in order to achieve democratic freedom. We want the right to decide our own affairs for ourselves."[23]

Nevertheless, as the military situation deteriorated, the French kept asking for vast increases in aid. The State Department had come to the conclusion, as Ambassador Bruce told the Senate Foreign Relations Committee, "that if Indochina went, the fall of Burma and the fall of Thailand would be absolutely inevitable."[24] So convinced were they of the reality of the falling dominoes that Bruce made it clear that it would be a long time before "it will be safe to withdraw" foreign troops from Vietnam. Washington had promised an extra three hundred and eighty-five million dollars to help finance the "Navarre Plan," an ambitious scheme for a reinforced effort to subdue the Vietminh. In January, 1954, Paris had asked for four hundred American mechanics and maintenance men, but the National Security Council decided to send only two hundred. President Eisenhower denied that this was the beginning of a U.S. military intervention, for as he told his press conference, there could be "no greater tragedy."[25]

But the moment for a major U.S. involvement in Vietnam was at hand. The French were coming to the end of their strength. On January 14, 1954, the Central Intelligence Agency reported to President Eisenhower that the French garrison at Dien Bien Phu, totaling about eleven thousand troops, was down to six days' supply of rations.[26] President Eisenhower began to consider seriously the possibility of a large-scale U.S. military intervention. He appointed a committee of the joint chiefs of staff, Allen Dulles, and Roger Kyes, the deputy secretary of defense, to develop a plan for aiding the French. Meanwhile the President, as he himself described it, "carefully examined methods and procedures calculated to win the approbation of most of the Free World" for a military intervention.[27] One approach considered was to have the French Union request the United Nations to authorize a military expedition. Another was to put together a joint expeditionary force including "token forces" from Britain, Australia, and New Zealand, which would, as Eisenhower has expressed it, "lend real moral standing to a venture that otherwise would be made to appear as a brutal example of imperialism."[28] The President was dubious about putting U.S. ground forces in Asia and thought that the air strikes around Dien Bien Phu, which some military advisers were recommending, would "comprise an act of war" without being "decisively effective."[29]

The problem of U.S. military planning was complicated by the indecision of the Laniel government. As the Berlin Foreign Ministers' Conference opened on January 25 to discuss Germany, Austria, and the Far East, it was apparent that Bidault, the French foreign minister, wanted to arrange a negotiation of the Indochinese war. Soon Dulles cabled the President that he was unable to withstand the pressure for a conference without bringing about the fall of the Laniel government. Saving the government was considered urgent. "We were convinced," Eisenhower has written, "that no succeeding government would take a stronger position than his on the defense of Indo-China or in support of the European Defense Community."[30] The latter was Eisenhower's dream. When the Chamber of Deputies six months later voted to reject EDC, Eisenhower was moved to make a rare extemporaneous speech calling the defeat of EDC "a major setback for the United States."[31] In Washington Dulles pronounced it a "tragedy."

The Berlin Conference set April 26 as the date for the convening of the Geneva Conference on Indochina. In mid-March the French position in Dien Bien Phu started to collapse. The CIA estimated that the French had only a fifty-fifty chance of holding out.[32] The French themselves were even more pessimistic. The possibility of sending ground troops was discussed with greater frequency. French military commanders were sounding out Admiral Radford on the possibility of U.S. reinforcement. Eisenhower made it clear, however, that if American troops were committed, the United States would insist on taking over the management of the war. "Some of my advisers," Eisenhower writes, "felt that the French . . . would rather abandon Indo-China, or lose it as a result of a military defeat, than save it through international intervention."[33] French-U.S. relations were extremely touchy. When the French defense minister suggested that any settlement would have to involve China and require concessions to China from the United States, Under Secretary of State Smith bridled. "It seems to me," he told the President later, "that he has been extremely free with our negotiating position."[34] As the final moments of the French Empire in Southeast Asia were being played out, it was not altogether clear whether the Americans were going to save the French or the French were going to become the advance guard for a new American presence in Asia.

Four

When General Paul Ely, the French chief of staff, had flown to Washington on March 20 to inform the Americans of the desperate turn which the situation at Dien Bien Phu had taken, he was rather surprised to hear Admiral Radford, the chairman of the U.S. joint chiefs of staff, propose military intervention. Foreign Minister Bidault has stated his firm recollection that on at least two subsequent occasions Dulles offered to use low-yield nuclear weapons against the Vietminh at Dien Bien Phu.[35] Since Radford was the principal military exponent of their use in "hot spots," as he called them, it is likely that the

question was broached to Ely. The French general returned to Paris convinced that a French request for direct
use of American planes and troops would be granted. Less
than three weeks later the administration was seeking
congressional support for this course. The National Security Council in late March decided to risk U.S. intervention
provided Britain offered at least token cooperation and the
French promised to end colonialism in Indochina in terms
clear enough to relieve the Eisenhower administration of
the embarrassment of aiding imperialism.

On April 3, a Saturday morning, Dulles and Admiral
Radford called in eight congressional leaders to a meeting
in the State Department and tried to enlist their support
for Operation Vulture, a proposed unilateral U.S. intervention to save Dien Bien Phu. What Admiral Radford
had in mind was a single two-hundred-plane air strike
launched from aircraft carriers against the perimeter of
Dien Bien Phu. Admitting under questioning that the other
joint chiefs had not given their approval, Radford defended his judgment: "I have spent more time in the Far East
than any of them and I understand the situation better."[36]

The congressional delegation included Senate Majority
Leader William Knowland, Senate Minority Leader Lyndon B. Johnson, Speaker of the House Joseph Martin, and
Minority Leader John McCormack and four others including Senator Richard Russell. Early in February Russell had gone to Eisenhower with his Mississippi colleague,
Senator Stennis, to warn against committing any American troops to Indochina. Now the leadership was being
asked by the secretary of state to support a joint resolution authorizing the immediate use of air and naval power
in Indochina. Lyndon Johnson demanded to know what
help could be expected from allies if the United States
made the commitment that was being asked. McCormack,
still smarting under the indictment Senator Joseph McCar-
thy had delivered at the Lincoln Day dinner six weeks
earlier, expressed surprise that the secretary would look to
"the party of treason" for support. After a tense two-hour
discussion it became clear that Dulles could not get any of
the congressional leaders to commit himself in favor of
U.S. intervention until other nations agreed to join in and
the French agreed not to pull out.

The campaign to meet those other conditions began the
next day. On Sunday night Eisenhower met in the upstairs
study of the White House with Dulles and Radford. As

Sherman Adams, his closest assistant, recalls it, the President "agreed with Dulles and Radford on a plan to send American forces to Indo-China,"[37] if the conditions demanded by congressional leaders could be met. A tentative date for the operation—April 28—was set. Eisenhower sent a letter to Churchill proposing a coalition "to bring greater moral and material resources to the support of the French effort." If Indochina should "pass into the hands of the Communists," the President warned, "the ultimate effect on our and your global strategic position with the consequent shift in the power ratios throughout Asia and the Pacific could be disastrous and, I know, unacceptable to you and me."[38] The President attempted a Churchillian closing:

> If I may refer again to history; we failed to halt Hirohito, Mussolini and Hitler by not acting in unity and in time. That marked the beginning of many years of stark tragedy and desperate peril. May it not be that our nations have learned something from that lesson. . . .[39]

The administration now began a series of public statements to emphasize the gravity of the impending French collapse and to prepare public opinion for intervention. As early as March 29 Dulles had spoken publicly about the need to take "united action" that might "involve serious risks." On April 7 the President told a press conference that the loss of Indochina, under the "falling-domino" principle, would threaten India, Japan, Indonesia, and the Philippines, to say nothing of the territories that bordered Indochina. The next week Vice-President Nixon delivered far stronger remarks in an "off-the-record" talk to newspaper editors:

> The United States as a leader of the Free World cannot afford further retreat in Asia . . . if this government cannot avoid it, the Administration must face up to the situation and dispatch forces.[40]

Accused in Congress of "whooping up for war,"[41] Nixon was commended by the President for awakening the country to the seriousness of the situation. "One of the boldest campaigns of political suasion ever undertaken by an

American statesman"[42] was Richard Rovere's judgment in his *Washington Letter* of April 8, 1954. "Congressmen, political leaders of all shadings of opinion, newspapermen, and radio and television personalities have been rounded up in droves and escorted to lectures and briefings on what the State Department regards as the American stake in Indo-China,"[43] he reported. The dominoes were falling so fast in these briefings that Rovere wondered whether Dulles thought that the United States could survive a communist victory in Indochina. (The secretary a few days later said he thought it could.)

The cause of all this desperate talk was China. While there was, according to Eisenhower, "no incontrovertible evidence of overt participation by Chinese troops in the Indo-China conflict,"[44] the vision of yellow hordes pouring over the rice paddies of Asia obsessed official thinking. In 1952 Acheson had discussed the possibility of a Chinese invasion with British Foreign Minister Eden and proposed a blockade of the Chinese coast in the event that should happen. "I personally thought it unlikely that China would enter the war and said so,"[45] Eden recalls. But the Eisenhower administration, having taken political risks to make an uneasy peace in Korea, was even more concerned than its predecessor with the Chinese threat. Dulles' "massive-retaliation" doctrine was intended to apply to China. If the Chinese intervened in Vietnam, there would be "grave consequences which might not be confined to Indo-China."[46]

The campaign to enlist domestic support was meeting with some success. In a Senate debate early in April only Senator Everett Dirksen took an unequivocal stand against American intervention. Most of the others stated a willingness to intervene if America's allies could be persuaded to participate. The effort to enlist the allies, however, was going less well. In February, before the situation at Dien Bien Phu had deteriorated, Under Secretary Smith had told the British ambassador that "there was no intention of sending American troops into Indo-China."[47] Now, in April, with the Geneva Conference only three weeks away, the Americans were proposing, according to Eden, "concerted action under Article 51 of the United Nations Charter against China."[48] Eden recalls: "We were informed that the proposed warning would carry with it the threat of naval and air action against the Chinese coast and of active intervention in Indo-China itself."[49] The French, who now wanted only to make a brave enough military show to forestall a capitulation, were concentrating their thoughts on the problem of how to negotiate their way home.

Eden thought the U.S. plan made no sense. The threat to bomb China for doing some unspecified future acts of aggression would not cause them to stop their present flow of military supplies to the Vietminh, and it might provoke a world war. A week later Dulles again urged Eden to support military intervention in Indochina and agreed to drop the ultimatum to China. Indochina was Manchuria and the Rhineland in one, and the place to stand. Still Eden resisted, arguing that British public opinion would not favor expanding a war a week before the opening of the conference that had been called to settle it. Dulles turned on the French. They had collapsed as a great power and thereby had left a "vacuum" which must be filled.[50] Three days before the conference, Dulles made his final appeal for British support for an air strike at Dien Bien Phu. General Gruenther argued that it was needed to save the morale of the French garrison even if it did no more. Admiral Radford attempted to reassure the British about China. "He had never thought that the Chinese would intervene in Indo-China, nor had they the necessary resources available. If they attempted air action, we could eliminate this by bombing the Chinese airfields, which were very vulnerable."[51] Dulles turned to French Foreign Minister Bidault, who was also present, and handed him a draft proposal which he had first shown briefly to the British. As Eden understood the proposal, the United States was prepared "to move armed forces into Indo-China and thus internationalize the struggle and protect Southeast Asia as a whole."[52] Bidault hesitated for several minutes, then accepted the proposal. The French urged Eden to go along with Dulles' plans, but later in the evening they changed their mind. Bidault sent word to London that he was against American intervention.

As the conference opened on April 26, French statesmen in Paris and Geneva had abandoned hope of military resistance and were looking for the least disastrous path of diplomatic extrication. "Bidault gives the impression of a man close to the breaking point,"[53] Dulles cabled the President from Geneva. The French generals, however, were still urging an air strike. Churchill and Eden had concluded that the Americans were asking them "to assist in misleading Congress into approving a military operation" that was both ineffective and provocative of a major war. Finally, Congress began to reflect increased nervousness about the still-rumored U.S. intervention. A rider was introduced in the House designed to limit the President's authority to send troops anywhere in the world. Eisenhower called in the congressional leadership, told them of the failure to get British support. We are not going to "carry the rest of the world on our back," he told them. "The French have asked us to send planes to Dien Bien Phu but we are not going to be involved alone in a power move against the Russians."[54]

The beginning of the conference did not end serious U.S. consideration of intervention, however. Convinced that the British were unreliable, Dulles and Smith talked privately with the French about supporting an enclave of resistance backed up by a vast training program for native Vietnamese forces. At the end of May the United States promised Bidault three divisions, should the conference fail. Indeed, it soon became clear that the Americans were hoping for a breakdown of the Geneva talks, since Dulles was convinced that a cease-fire would lead to the surrender of Indochina. Eisenhower told Smith to do "everything in his power to bring the conference to an end as rapidly as possible."[55] When it became clear, however, that the British and French were determined to reach a settlement, especially after Mendès-France became premier and pledged to bring peace to Indochina in thirty days, Dulles decided to disengage from the conference but to let it proceed. He obtained an agreement from the British that the acceptable cease-fire should preserve "at least the southern half of Vietnam" and "not contain political provisions which would risk loss of the retained area to communist control."[56] He then recalled Smith, the senior U.S. delegate, sending him back only after the terms of the settlement had been drafted. At the final session Smith declared that the United States would not "join in" the agreements but would "refrain from the threat or use of force to disturb them."[57] The very partition, which Smith had told the British months earlier would lead to communist domination of Southeast Asia, was now a reality.

The Geneva accords represented a genuine compromise, for they satisfied neither side. "Only the Viet Minh,

the winners, lost or were sold out,"[58] U.S. foreign-service
officer Douglas Pike puts it in his book *Viet Cong*. "Ho
Minh somehow was persuaded—apparently by a joint
Sino-Soviet effort—to settle for half the country." Ho was
undoubtedly willing to postpone the victory of his independence movement over the entire country because he
believed that he would win "the general elections which
will bring about the unification of Vietnam," provided for
in Article 14 of the armistice agreement, which were
scheduled to be held no later than July 20, 1956. The
United States was not entirely happy with the results
either. According to Lieutenant General Andrew Good-
paster, then assistant to President Eisenhower, "Mr. Dulles
thought that it [noncommunist Vietnam] was not quite
down the drain. Everyone else, I think, felt that it was."
Even Dulles told General Collins, former army chief of
staff, in November, 1954, "Frankly, Collins, I think our
chances of saving the situation there are not more than 1
in 10."[59]

Five

In the decade following the Geneva accords Vietnam became a personal mission for a coalition of military
officers, professors, clerics, bureaucrats, and publicists,
who joined forces in the effort to convert the provisional
zone south of the cease-fire line at the 17th parallel into a
"viable" noncommunist state. In the intellectually arid
fifties, Vietnam was a unique challenge. A testing ground
for a wide variety of ideas on modernization, guerrilla
warfare, police administration, rural reform, and foreign
aid, the fledgling Asiatic country became the new frontier
of the Eisenhower administration.

Those who joined the campaign to establish and defend
South Vietnam acted from a variety of motives. Dulles
had reluctantly agreed to partition only after securing the
agreement of Britain and France to establish SEATO, a

regional collective-security organization designed to stem any further communist advances in Asia. "The problem," Dulles had explained to Senator Knowland as the Geneva talks were dragging to a close, "is where to draw the line . . . we are confronted by an unfortunate fact—most of the countries of the world do not share our view that Communist control of any government anywhere is in itself a danger and a threat."[60] He now saw the problem of South Vietnam as the need to build a new defense line. A U.S.-sponsored military buildup was the only way to make the one-in-ten gamble pay off.

General Collins, who was sent to Saigon as special envoy, promptly announced that the United States intended to supply the South Vietnamese armed forces with two billion dollars in military supplies in order to build it up to a strength of two hundred and fifty thousand. Despite the prohibitions of the Geneva accords against "the introduction into Vietnam of foreign troops and military personnel as well as all kinds of arms and munitions," and against entering foreign military alliances, the United States was soon paying most of the cost of running the country and virtually the entire bill for outfitting the army and the police.

The U.S. military mission under General James A. Van Fleet, fresh from his service in Greece, had arrived in 1950 to supervise American aid and, occasionally, to lecture resentful French generals on how to win the war. The mission now took over the responsibility for training the Vietnamese army. By the end of 1956 all French troops were gone, and by 1960 the U.S. Military Aid and Advisory Group already exceeded the limit of six hundred and eighty-five set by the Geneva accords.

The role of the American military in Vietnam did not become central, however, until two years later. In the Eisenhower years the primary emphasis was on "nation-building," a euphemism for the campaign to persuade the premier, Ngo Dinh Diem, to govern in a less quixotic and destructive way. Diem had been the candidate of an unlikely group that included a Supreme Court justice, a cardinal, a CIA specialist in guerrilla warfare, a professor of political science, and the editor of a socialist magazine. This mandarin mystic, who had faithfully served in the French civil service in the 1930's but had refused to work for either Ho or the Japanese, had a reputation as a strong nationalist. By 1954 he had aroused the interest of a number of influential Americans, who were looking for an instrument to discharge the responsibilities the United States had picked up as a result of the French collapse. To William O. Douglas, who met Diem in Washington in 1951, this self-exiled politician looked like the man to back, "because he is honest and independent and stood against the French influence."[61] He introduced him at a breakfast meeting to Senator Mike Mansfield and Senator John F. Kennedy, who also enlisted as backers. Diem possessed the rare asset of being both anticommunist and anti-French. He was a devout Catholic, abstemious in his personal habits, and a member of a prominent family that boasted a number of bishops. Thus, when he came to the United States to take up residence at the Maryknoll Seminary in Lakewood, New Jersey, it was not altogether surprising that he became acquainted with the archbishop of New York, Cardinal Spellman. When the French, at American urging, accepted Diem as premier in June, 1954, in the midst of the Geneva conference, the cardinal soon became an enthusiastic booster of an independent South Vietnam, which he saw as a hopeful alternative to the "surrender" of Geneva. "If Geneva and what was agreed upon there means anything at all, it means . . . 'taps for the buried hopes of freedom in Southeast Asia,' "[62] he told the American Legion. Vietnam was a victim of the communist "world plan," and Diem was a virtuous instrument for fighting the Cold War in Asia.

Other Americans saw Diem's role as slightly different from militant nationalist or Cold War fighter. Vietnam became the passionate concern of various liberals, who, while strongly anticommunist, were troubled that the United States could not provide a decent alternative. Many of them were college professors or younger officers in the Central Intelligence Agency or the foreign-assistance bureaucracy, who believed that the competition with Russia and China for the control of the underdeveloped world would ultimately be decided by the "battle for men's hearts and minds." Military aid and massive retaliation in themselves were sterile instruments. The new diplomacy demanded a conscientious effort to construct welfare-state institutions in primitive economies; in short, to stimulate a controlled revolution from the top to forestall an uncontrolled one from the bottom. The most celebrated exponent of that view was Colonel Edward

Lansdale, who had worked for the CIA in helping Ramón Magsaysay put down the Huk insurgency in the Philippines. Dulles, who had been impressed with Lansdale's success, sent him to Vietnam, just as Dien Bien Phu was falling, to look for a Vietnamese Magsaysay. The colonel also decided that Diem was the man and became a passionate partisan of the premier in his subsequent fights with the U.S. army.

But the most vocal private supporters were the International Rescue Committee and later the American Friends of Vietnam. This Vietnam lobby, unlike the China lobby of the 1940's, was made up not of old Asia hands and conservatives but of liberals for whom the Cold War overshadowed all else. The International Rescue Committee, which had been set up to handle the flow of refugees from Hitler's Europe, now concentrated on resettling refugees from communist countries. The president of the Committee, Leo Cherne, went to Vietnam in late 1954 and wrote the subscribers to the Research Institute of America service, an organization he also headed, that the effort to keep Vietnam noncommunist depended upon unstinting support for Diem. Cherne, who had also met Diem when he was at the Maryknoll Seminary, became a principal propagandist for the South Vietnamese government. He sent his associate in the International Rescue Committee, Joseph Buttinger, an editor of *Dissent* magazine and a former socialist politician in Austria, to Vietnam to help relocate the flood of refugees from the North, mostly Catholics, who took advantage of the Geneva accords to resettle in the South. But he also had the job of staging a public-relations effort on behalf of Diem. By 1955 such a campaign was badly needed.

Six

The new premier had shown in the first months in office that he would tolerate no organized groups in South Vietnam not firmly under his control. He quickly attacked various religious sects which had had political autonomy supported with private armies. He was openly contemptuous of the French, thus adding to their humiliation entailed in dismantling an empire. Bent on extending his rule to the countryside, where the central government had never before penetrated, Diem ruthlessly opposed any forces that stood in the way. He suspected that while General Ely, the French commander, was attempting a correct attitude toward his regime, French businessmen and imperial bureaucrats were opposing him. "Children leading children,"[63] was a typical French comment on the spectacle of Diem and the Americans trying to run the country. Some of these French military and buinessmen, annoyed at Diem's antagonism, secretly connived with the Binh Xuyen, a private gangster army, to get rid of him. Diem moved swiftly to crush Binh Xuyen and came into open conflict with the French army.

General Collins, who had backed Diem against an earlier attempt at a coup, now decided that Diem was too unstable to support. At this point Diem needed extraordinary backing in order to survive. Colonel Lansdale, in what Collins termed a "mutiny," persuaded Dulles to continue backing Diem. But at the same time, Buttinger launched a public-relations campaign. Cardinal Spellman, with the aid of Joseph P. Kennedy, arranged to have Buttinger present the Diem story to Kenneth Young, head of the Southeast Asia Office in the State Department, and to Senator Mansfield. The cardinal met with the editorial boards of *Life, Time,* and the *New York Herald Tribune.* Buttinger wrote in *The Reporter* and *The New Republic* in early 1955 attempting to persuade their liberal readers that Diem was a good democrat. These feverish efforts helped save the premier.

In the fall of 1955 these modern missionaries formed the American Friends of Vietnam. In addition to Buttinger, Spellman, Cherne, and Harold Oram, the public-relations counsel who had given professional assistance to these efforts, the Friends also included Wesley Fishel, a Michigan State University political-science professor who claimed credit for having "discovered" Diem while working for U.S. intelligence in the Pacific in 1950. (It was Fishel who arranged to have his university finance Diem's politically profitable trip to the United States the following year.) The Friends wrote a series of laudatory articles about Diem and placed them in the nation's popular magazines. "The Biggest Little Man in Asia" appeared in the February, 1956, *Reader's Digest*. Fishel, who spent from 1956 to 1958 in Vietnam as head of the Michigan State University project and adviser to Diem, wrote glowingly about "Vietnam's Democratic One-Man Rule." In 1958 the Friends held a conference to encourage American investment in Vietnam—a campaign that never succeeded until the escalation of the war years later. Month after month the leading periodicals of the United States published optimistic and friendly accounts of the great experiment the United States was undertaking in the far Pacific. Much of the publicity concerned the relocation of refugees. Tom Dooley, a young navy physician who had taken part in the program, wrote a best-selling account, *Deliver Us from Evil*, and became a leading propagandist for the Diem regime. He and Cherne, who also wrote about the refugees for *Look*, combined humanitarian concern and a militant anticommunism. Warning that "if the elections were held today the overwhelming majority of Vietnamese would vote Communist,"[64] Cherne declared that American prestige in Asia was dependent upon preventing that result. The answer was to strengthen the Catholic faction in South Vietnam, who alone among Vietnamese had ideological reasons to be against the communists. The British Catholic writer Graham Greene has described the American use of the Catholic Church in fighting the Cold War in Vietnam:

> It is a Catholicism which has helped to ruin the government of Mr. Diem, for his genuine piety . . . has been exploited by his American advisors until the Church is in danger of sharing the unpopularity of the United States. . . . Great sums are spent on organized demonstrations for the visitors, and an impression is given that the Catholic Church is occidental and an ally of the United States in the cold war. On the rare occasions when Mr. Diem has visited the areas formerly held by the Viet Minh, there has been a priest at his side, and usually an American one.[65]

While the Friends of Vietnam and the administration were extolling the Diem regime for American ears, a small army of U.S. bureaucrats had moved into Saigon to try to make the reality approach the rhetoric. Besides the

military-assistance mission, which had by far the most
money to spend, were smaller bureaucracies specializing in
land reform, currency control, police administration, and
construction. When Wolf Ladejinsky, an American agricultural expert, arrived in Saigon to devise a land-reform
plan for Diem, forty-five percent of the land was in the
hands of owners of thirty acres or more. Under an impressive presidential ordinance passed in late 1956, a
sweeping land-reform program was ordered. But the government could not get the landlords to agree upon a
compensation figure, and the program was largely stalled.
Even the model project at Cai-San, on which the United
States spent ten million dollars and contributed one hundred tractors in order to provide land for forty thousand
settlers, became the scene of rioting rather than the "symbol of the new country's determination to shelter people,"[66] as the aid mission's press release had called it.
When the refugees took possession, the provincial governor backed by a contingent of police denied that the plan
had called for free distribution and demanded payment
from the destitute refugees. U.S. officials kept pressing for
land reform, but the Diem regime had neither the will nor
the strength to carry out more than a token effort. By
mid-1957 *Time* magazine was pointing out: "Put simply,
Diem is still taking U.S. money by the millions, but less
and less U.S. advice."

The major interest of the Diem government was its own
security. It feared that the elections scheduled for July,
1956, would spell a victory for Ho Chi Minh and the end
of power for noncommunist politicians. The South Vietnamese attitude toward the Geneva accords is reflected in
the telegram their delegate at Geneva, Tran Van Don, sent
to Diem on July 22, 1954: "We fought desperately against
partition and for a neutral zone in the Catholic area of
North Vietnam. Absolutely impossible to surmount the
hostility of our enemies and the perfidy of false friends.
. . . We express our deepest sorrows in this total failure of
our mission."[67]

Diem soon received encouragement, however, in his plan
for permanent postponement of the elections. Cherne and
other publicists dismissed the idea of elections as a fraud.
Senator Mansfield and Secretary Dulles declared publicly
that since "free" elections were "impossible," they should
not be held.[68]

Having decided to reject the consultations with the North called for in the Geneva accords and the election—in short, any attempt at coalition politics—the Diem regime was now faced with the priority task of defending itself against mounting opposition. In this the Americans were in a highly ambiguous position. By this time they were financing the entire cost of the army and about eighty percent of the rest of the bureaucracy. Under a one-million-dollar-a-year contract, Professor Fishel and Michigan State University were running a training school for the police. They recommended that the national police "be so trained and distributed that they will very soon popularize themselves with the populace through extra services and courtesies."[69] Rather than the auxiliary army of seventy thousand men that Diem had wanted, the Michigan State planners proposed a much smaller contingent that would live in villages "and work themselves into the confidence of the citizens they serve."[70] But Diem, who was beginning to fear the resumption of insurgency, once the date for the elections had passed, was in no mood to support the professors' liberal vision of the police. On January 11, 1956, he had passed Presidential Ordinance No. 6, providing that "all persons considered dangerous to national defense or collective security . . . may be sent to concentration camps by decision of the president of the Republic."[71] By 1958 about forty thousand Vietnamese were in concentration camps. The CIA national intelligence estimates prepared in February, 1957, described the Diem regime in these words:

Diem's regime reflects his ideas. A facade of representative government is maintained, but the government is in fact essentially authoritarian. The legislative powers of the National Assembly are strictly circumscribed; the judiciary is undeveloped and subordinate to the executive; and the members of the executive branch are little more than the personal agents of Diem. No organized opposition, loyal or otherwise, is tolerated, and critics of the regime are often repressed. . . . The exercise of power and responsibility is limited to Diem and a very small circle mainly composed of his relatives, the most important being Nhu and Can.

The idea of a decentralized police administration winning the loyalty of the villagers through constructive projects was precisely what Diem didn't want.

In 1962 with the encouragement of the CIA station chief John H. Richardson, Diem's brother, Ngo Dinh Nhu, launched the strategic-hamlet program. Based on a model that had worked against insurgents in Malaya, the hamlets were lightly fortified communities in which loyal peasants were to be herded so as to set them off from the insurgents. Peasants resented the relocation campaign, and the scheme never succeeded.

The tension that developed between the mercurial and ultimately self-destructive Nhu and Richardson, the U.S. intelligence operative, was typical of the general problem facing the new missionaries. The nature of the relationship between the Americans and the Vietnamese was complicated by the fact that it was never clear which country needed the other more. Some Americans, like General Maxwell Taylor, for example, were prepared to cut short a brilliant career in Washington and jeopardize the reputation of a lifetime to try to create a new civilization in an ancient land. While there were the mundane rewards attached to service in Saigon—officers' clubs, thirty-five-cent martinis, free houses, a cook for thirty-five dollars a month, and other traditional accoutrements of the imperial outpost—many of those who elected to go to Vietnam were looking for more. They were answering the call of duty. As John Mecklin, chief of the United States Information Service in Saigon during the Kennedy administration, described his own feelings, "This was a new undertaking for Americans, and it was indigestible. It was a brave commitment of American power and prestige, and a privilege to be one of the Americans entrusted to help make it work."[72]

To the Vietnamese elite, who considered that they had had a nation since A.D. 939, when their ancestors threw out the Chinese, much of the confused and condescending talk about the "nation-building" which they heard from their American advisers was infuriating. Couldn't you continue the aid but forget the advice "the same way you help Tito without interfering in his affairs?"[73] Nhu once proposed to a U.S. official. But to the Americans such an approach was, of course, impossible. National pride was not a substitute for the ability to govern. What the United

States was interested in was developing a Saigon government efficient and strong enough to extend its rule to the countryside and to hold back communist insurgents. If the Americans often appeared to the Vietnamese rulers as clumsy and naïve imperialists who had to be tolerated because they were paying the bills, the Vietnamese exasperated the U.S. officials by continually showing how weak a reed they were on which to base U.S. national-security policy. Diem and his successors had their own interests to serve, particularly the liquidation of political enemies such as the Buddhists or obstreperous local officials. The United States National-Security Managers had their primary interest, which was to contain China and maintain a worldwide reputation for the United States as a nation willing and able to put a stop to insurgent movements.

Since these interests often conflicted, the United States made it clear on more than one occasion that its interests were paramount. Ambassador Henry Cabot Lodge told reporters that the United States would be justified in staying in Vietnam even if the government asked the Americans to withdraw, since a pullout "would certainly shake our position in Berlin."[74] When some of the governments that succeeded Diem after his assassination in November, 1963, attempted to explore a political coalition with the insurgents, U.S. officials moved decisively to block the possibility and to continue the war. America's interest, whatever the Saigon government of the moment might prefer, was to prosecute the war to a point where the communist insurgents ceased to pose a political challenge. A Vietnamese government would keep American support only so long as it appeared able to continue an effective fight against the communists.

The history of the U.S.-Vietnamese "partnership" is a story of the progressive takeover by American bureaucrats of the essential functions of government. "In effect, what the U.S. did in Viet Nam," John Mecklin wrote, describing the situation as of the early sixties, "was to set up a shadow government—though it would have been heresy to describe it that way publicly because of Vietnamese sensibilities. The shadow's function was to try to figure out what needed to be done and then try to persuade the government of Viet Nam to do it."[75]

Each U.S. official had a Vietnamese "counterpart."

Nhu, for example, was Richardson's. (One reason why the U.S. missions were so heavy in rank was that the adviser had to have a status appropriate to his "counterpart.") Much discussion in the U.S. Embassy was devoted to the techniques of manipulating Vietnamese officials. "If you do not first-name your counterpart," so an official slogan went, "you are not doing your job."[76]

The Americans in Saigon thought they were playing a part that for all of its frustrations was exciting and truly unique. Actually the role of the well-financed imperial adviser among backward peoples was hardly a new one. In 1885, two years after he had gone to Egypt to become the British consul-general, Lord Cromer wrote of his uneasiness about this "hybrid form of government to which no name can be given and for which there is no precedent."[77] It was based not upon "annexation" but rather upon "personal influence" of bureaucrats charged with maintaining "sufficiently effective supervision over public affairs." Cromer's own pride was "to remain more or less hidden and to pull the strings." The colonial bureaucrat, Cromer advised, must resist the surveillance of the press and politicians from the home country. One people cannot rule another people. Only bureaucrats can.

The U.S. bureaucracy in Vietnam seventy-five years later instinctively reached for these ideas. The effort to mislead newsmen and through them the whole U.S. population achieved such mammoth proportions that it eventually became news itself. But the proof of a "credibility gap" did not lead to any greater surveillance of the American administration of Vietnam. Cromer's experience in Egypt foreshadowed the American fate in another way, too. Like the modern missionaries, Cromer went to Egypt with "a sense of duty," to be a protector of "backward peoples," because he felt that he belonged to "a nation which had reached a comparatively high plane of civilization." Once there, however, he began to realize that the interests of the protector and the protected diverged far more than the Kiplingesque rhetoric of the era suggested. The primary reason was that the imperialist's motive in running the colonial country was often based on considerations having nothing to do with the country itself. Cromer saw Egypt as primarily a base to protect other interests. "The Englishman straining far over to hold his loved India," he wrote three years before taking over as consul-general, must "plant a firm foot on the banks of the

Nile."[78] The U.S. bureaucrats who followed in his tradition
saw Vietnam in exactly the same light. It was part of the
apparatus for containing China. It was not so surprising,
then, as it first appears, that the one country U.S. bureaucrats took over as conquerors and not as advisers, Japan,
became the most successful example of the American
presence. The United States military was able to build
effective institutions there and to reduce its own role
rather than increase it because Japan appeared important
in itself, not merely as a piece of strategically located real
estate.

In Vietnam the U.S. intervention steadily deepened in
the 1950's as U.S. officials tried to protect their earlier
investments. These investments included not only the vast
sums of prior years but also their personal reputations.
Men had begun to build careers on a series of claims.
Academic advisers had written in journals about the success of the Land Reform or the Education Projects. The
volunteer propagandists had gone far out on several limbs
in predicting the coming triumph of Diem's democracy.
The military had filled the pages of the military journals
with extravagant promises of the successes of "counterinsurgency." Thus they pressed continually for more effort,
more commitment, to make these promises come true.
They kept demanding just a few more men, just a few
more months, in order to postpone the accounting which
would measure performance against promise.

Seven

The U.S. intervention grew increasingly direct as
the political fabric of South Vietnam, fragile from the
first, began to unravel. Diem's dictatorship, supported with
a network of informers, military tribunals, and corrupt
functionaries, declared war not only on the communists,
who until 1957 were quiescent, but also against any group
whose personal loyalty was not assured. Indeed, more
noncommunists than communists ended up in Diem's jails.

"There are still people in our ranks who must be eliminated," the official journal *Cach Mang Quoc Gie* wrote in 1959. "Their crimes equal in gravity those of the communists and the nation must consider them as traitors. . . . We now have all the means necessary to exterminate the criminals."[79]

Diem's despotism, his shameless favoring of Catholic refugees from the North over the rest of the population, and his persecution of all political dissidents produced the coalition against him that he dreaded. A core of Vietminh members had remained behind in the South after the Geneva partition, who became principal activators of the new insurgency, which was also made up of army officers and dissidents of varied political views. In 1957 the Dai Viet and the National Salvation Movement, both as anti-communist as they were anti-Diem, organized guerrilla units and a clandestine radio to oppose the government. In 1958 a radio station calling itself the South Vietnam Liberation Front began to broadcast. The anthropologist Gerald Hickey reports that by 1958 the National Liberation Front, already called Vietcong by the South Vietnamese government, was operating in the villages.[80] Although in 1958 Radio Hanoi attacked the Front in a number of broadcasts for losing patience in the Geneva settlement and for advocating a prematurely radical program, it appears that the guerrilla activities, which in most cases started because of local political conditions in South Vietnam, came increasingly under the direction and coordination of Hanoi. U.S. intelligence reported at the time that Ho Chi Minh was initiating acts of terrorism in the South to put pressure on Diem to keep his agreements but that he did not contemplate a violent overthrow of the Diem regime.

In mid-1957 terrorist attacks broke out in South Vietnam. In July, seventeen customers at a bar were machine-gunned to death. The district chief of My Tho was killed with his whole family on a highway. Bombs were thrown at U.S. inst llations in Saigon and American servicemen were injured. Many of the early terrorist attacks were clearly aimed at men who were or were thought to be Diem police agents or their American helpers. As the attacks mounted in intensity, they became less discriminating. By mid-1961 President Kennedy was reporting to Congress that minor officials were being murdered at the rate of four thousand a year. In March, 1960, the secret coalition of anti-Diem forces published a letter calling for drastic reforms and a new government in Saigon. While the organization and initiative of the movement was communist, and the National Liberation Front and the Lao Dong (North Vietnamese Communist party) were intimately connected, most guerrillas joined the movement because they could no longer survive politically, psychologically, and physically in Vietnamese society. Ho's agents no doubt stirred up the rebellion once this policy was decided upon. But, as Philippe Devillers has pointed out, the rebels' state of mind had far less to do with "international communism," of which most were ignorant, than with the simple fact that Diem, contrary to the express prohibitions of the Geneva agreements, was hunting down all former Vietminh members.[81] In March, 1960, the Front issued a Declaration of Former Resistance Fighters, written in strongly nationalist, anti-American, but not particularly Marxist terms. Jean La Couture reports that Hanoi agents sent to the early meetings of the National Liberation Front were greeted with scorn: "What are you waiting for to help us? If you don't do anything, you communists, we will rise up against you too."[82]

Six months after the embryonic insurgent organization issued its declaration, the North Vietnamese Communist party voted at its Third Congress, held on September 5, 1960, to support the "southern people's revolutionary struggle." They helped the southern insurgent politicians set up the National Liberation Front two months later. There is little doubt that in the preceding three years the rebels were in touch with North Vietnamese intelligence agents, since the areas with the greatest insurgent activity also provided the most precise information on the operations of the Diem government, which Hanoi used to charge violations of the Geneva agreement before the International Control Commission.[83] It was also not entirely coincidental that the terrorist campaign was launched only after it became clear that the elections Ho had expected to win in July, 1956, would not be held.[84] But while northerners and others subject to the discipline of Ho's party supplied organizational initiative from the start, material aid from the North was nominal until the major U.S. intervention had begun. It increased in stages matching the stepped-up U.S. intervention. Neither Ho's weapons nor his efforts to control and direct the NLF was the cause of the insurgency in the South, any more than Yugoslav and Bulgarian aid had been the cause of the Greek civil war.

Eight

When John F. Kennedy came to the White House, he was the first American President to have visited Vietnam and to have acquired some firsthand impressions. In 1951 he made a congressman's junket to Indochina, became acquainted with Edmund Gullion, a foreign-service officer critical of the Acheson policy of supporting the French, and came away convinced that the United States must find a new way to relate to the revolutionary developments of Southeast Asia. Some of these ideas he expressed in a speech to the Senate three years later, during the critical week in which Dulles and Admiral Radford were trying to enlist support for an air strike against Dien Bien Phu:

> I am frankly of the belief that no amount of American military assistance in Indo-China can conquer . . . "an enemy of the people" which has the sympathy and covert support of the people. . . . For the United States to intervene unilaterally and to send troops into the most difficult terrain in the world, with the Chinese able to pour in unlimited manpower, would mean that we would face a situation which would be far more difficult than even that we encountered in Korea.[85]

In a meeting with outgoing President Eisenhower the day before taking office, the President-elect listened to his predecessor describe the mounting guerrilla activity in Laos, which, he said, was the key to all Southeast Asia. If the United States could not get its allies to act with

her—and once again Britain and France were against a
SEATO intervention in Indochina—the United States, Eisenhower urged, "as a last desperate hope" should "intervene
unilaterally." Recalling the Marshall mission to China,
Eisenhower warned against a settlement that would permit
communists a role in the Laotian government. The outgoing secretary of defense observed that the United States
could move a division into Laos in twelve to seventeen
days.

The Eisenhower policy since Geneva had been to build
Laos into another "bastion of freedom" with an aid program of three hundred million dollars, two hundred and
ninety-three million of which went to build a twenty-five-
thousand-man army. The policy was also to frustrate the
coalition agreements which Prince Souvanna Phouma had
worked out in 1957 with his half-brother Souphanouvong,
the head of the Communist Pathet Lao. The U.S. ambassador, as he himself later boasted, "struggled for sixteen
months to prevent a coalition."[86] The CIA set up a Committee for the Defense of the National Interest and
brought back a right-wing army officer from France,
Phoumi Nosavan, to head it. In 1959 they succeeded in
unseating the State Department's candidate, Phoui Sanani-
koune, and replacing him with their man. The result was a
coup engineered by Laotian army officers to restore
Prince Souvanna Phouma and to bring about a neutralist
coalition.

The United States now backed Phoumi's march on the
capital to oust the neutralists, and the coup was converted
into a civil war. What had been a minor bureaucratic
contest in exotic politics now suddenly emerged as a
first-class crisis when Souvanna appealed to the Soviets for
arms. Deputy Foreign Minister Pushkin told Ambassador
Harriman that the Kremlin considered supplying the Pathet Lao as vital to Soviet interests as fighting World War II
and the October Revolution. Kennedy's policy was to get
a settlement in Laos if at all possible. The country was too
small, its people too easygoing and pacific, U.S. involvement to date too clumsy, to make this tiny land the place
to stem the communist tide in Asia. Indeed, neutralization
of Laos was virtually a precondition to the successful
defense of Vietnam. Accordingly, Kennedy pressed the
Soviets for a meeting to discuss neutralization, backing up
the initiative with a tough warning at a press conference—

the United States would have to respond if the "present armed attacks by externally supported Communists did not cease"[87]—and a show of strength. Marines with helicopters arrived in Thailand. The Seventh Fleet sailed into the South China Sea. (The President's new guerrilla-warfare expert, Walt Rostow, had wanted to send in a few U.S. troops to fight the Pathet Lao, but the joint chiefs of staff opposed it on the ground that it might provoke China.) The effect of all this activity was to persuade the Soviets to meet in Geneva and to arrange neutralization and an uneasy truce.

The settlement in Laos cleared the way for more serious consideration of Vietnam. A few days after inauguration, Rostow had given the President Colonel Lansdale's still-celebrated report on his campaign against the Huks. Kennedy began to devour counterinsurgency literature. Increasingly he looked for advice to such guerrilla-warfare enthusiasts as Maxwell Taylor, who had resigned as Eisenhower's army chief of staff because he thought the new doctrines of counterinsurgency were being slighted; Roger Hilsman, a former oss officer now in charge of the State Department's intelligence operations; and Professor Rostow, who himself had been directing cia-supported research at the Massachusetts Institute of Technology. A "Special Group, Counterinsurgency," headed by the President's brother Robert, was set up. In the Pentagon, directly responsible to the joint chiefs of staff, was established a new Office on Counterinsurgency and Special Activities under a major general. "To fight guerrillas," so went a fashionable aphorism from this new learning, "you must adopt the tactics of the guerrilla himself."[88]

While the new administration was trying to figure out how it would apply to Vietnam the lessons its highest officers were learning from the works of Mao Tse-tung ("Guerrillas must move among the people as fish swim in the sea"), the situation in South Vietnam was collapsing. In May, 1961, the U.S. ambassador in Saigon thought "it would be a miracle if South Vietnam lasted three months longer."[89] That month Vice-President Johnson traveled to Saigon on an inspection mission for the President. Hailing Diem as the Winston Churchill of Asia (as years later as President he would refer to General Cao Ky, one of Diem's successors, as the Rex Tugwell of Asia), he reported that it was still possible to "build a sound structure capable of withstanding and turning the Communist surge."[90] He favored a Mekong Delta development plan suggested by an old friend, Arthur Goldschmidt, then working with the United Nations. He also made the customary demands on Diem for reforms and received the customary garrulous but evasive replies.

After an effort by Chester Bowles, under secretary of state, to develop a proposal for a neutral belt in Asia, including Burma, Thailand, and the three states of Indochina, was summarily rejected, Kennedy and Rusk, in Arthur Schlesinger's words, made "a conscious decision . . . to turn the Viet Nam problem over to the Secretary of Defense."[91] (Indeed, Rusk, according to his former Assistant Secretary Roger Hilsman, had always regarded Vietnam as "essentially a military problem."[92]) The President dispatched General Taylor and Walt Rostow, the leading guerrilla-warfare advocates of the administration, to Vietnam on a fact-finding mission. Kennedy had been disturbed by a speech of Khrushchev's delivered two weeks before his own inaugural in which the Soviet leader declared "a most favorable attitude" toward wars of national liberation, mentioning in particular the one in Vietnam. Kennedy saw Vietnam as a test case for Khrushchev's theories as well as for American doctrines of counterinsurgency. He was thus psychologically prepared for the advice Taylor and Rostow brought back: The United States should take over certain tasks of the war, including airlifting and reconnaissance. A force of about ten thousand combat troops should be sent. Rostow proposed a policy of "graduated retaliation" against North Vietnam—in plainer words, the United States should bomb them to force them to stop giving military aid to the Vietcong. (The increasing emphasis on North Vietnam continued throughout 1961-62 despite a series of Department of Defense studies and CIA reports that the "vast majority of Viet Cong troops are of local origin," and that there was "little evidence of major supplies from outside sources.") The report mentioned some political reforms, too, but concealed that Diem would not make them voluntarily. The only hope was that an increased U.S. presence could work "de facto changes in Diem's method of government."

Some suggested that perhaps Diem ought to be replaced. "Our trouble," J. K. Galbraith, then ambassador to India, remarked prophetically, "is that we make revolu-

tions so badly."[93] The United States was now "married to
a failure" and must "see it through." Kennedy resisted the
recommendation to send troops: "The troops will march
in; the bands will play; the crowds will cheer; and in four
days everyone will have forgotten. Then we will be told
we have to send in more troops. It's like taking a drink.
The effect wears off and you have to take another."[94] But
by the end of the year the President had authorized a new
U.S. military command in Vietnam under a four-star
general. In early 1962 two air-support companies of three
hundred men arrived in Saigon, the first of a steady
succession of small increments that would bring the level
up to about twenty-five thousand by the summer of 1964.
The President had rejected major military intervention as
a conscious policy but he had set in force the bureaucratic
momentum that would make it a certainty.

Nine

"When the right cause is identified and used correctly," General Lansdale continued to argue, "the *anti*-
Communist fight becomes a *pro*-people fight."[95] These sensible maxims for manipulating the politics of divided countries seemed more and more irrelevant as the Diem regime played out its final tragic moments. On May 8, 1963,
Buddha's birthday, Diem, now under increasing influence
of the Nhus, banned the display of religious flags, thus
provoking riots, to which he responded with a bloody
repression. The wave of suicides by self-immolation of
Buddhist monks aroused horror and sympathy in the
United States and mobilized internal opposition in Vietnam. Madame Nhu's offhand remark to a U.S. TV man
that "all the Buddhists have done for this country is to
barbecue a monk" revealed more about the state of the
Diem government than official handouts could overcome.
While Kennedy was assuring the country that "we are
going to stay there" because withdrawal would mean the

collapse of all Southeast Asia, Diem was preparing a war on pagodas and bonzes that would totally expose the demented fury of his regime.

Now Kennedy moved against him. He told a television interview that the chances of winning the war were "not very good" unless the Vietnamese government took steps to win back popular support. This meant "changes in policy and perhaps . . . personnel."[96] The U.S. officials in Saigon were divided on whether to withdraw support from Diem. General Harkins, the military commander, and Ambassador Nolting, as well as Richardson, the CIA chief, had staked a great deal on making the relationship with Diem work. The new ambassador, Henry Cabot Lodge, who arrived in late August, joined what was now the consensus of the foreign service and other non-military officials. Diem could not be saved. In October the White House reported the judgment of General Taylor and Secretary McNamara that "the major part of the United States military task can be completed by the end of 1965" and that one thousand U.S. troops would be withdrawn by the end of 1963. They also announced the suspension of the Commercial Import Program, a one-hundred-million-dollar-a-year expenditure designed to subsidize purchases by the South Vietnamese government. The effect of suspension was to turn the businessmen, who lived on these subsidies, against the regime. Payments to the Vietnamese Special Forces were also cut off, thus encouraging the army to move against Diem. The increasingly Kafka-like atmosphere of Saigon was now in the thrall of rumor. Nhu was reportedly negotiating with the Vietcong, Hanoi, and Paris. According to Roger Hilsman, there were repeated intelligence reports that Nhu "had been attempting to set up a secret channel of communications with Hanoi." The Americans, allegedly, were directing a coup to bring Diem down.

On November 2 Diem and Nhu were murdered. The coup, according to Arthur Schlesinger, Jr., was "entirely planned and carried out by the Vietnamese."[97] Lodge stated that although "there were opportunities to participate in the planning and give advice," Americans did not do so. But as John Mecklin, chief of the United States Information Service in Saigon at the time, has put it, "to assert that the U.S. was 'not involved' in the coup was a bit like claiming innocence for a nightwatchman at a bank who tells a known safecracker that he is going out for a

beer."[98] In fact, the U.S. Embassy in Saigon was in touch
with several groups of officers who were planning a coup
against Diem.[99] One was a group of younger officers,
including Tran Kim Tuyen, who had begun a serious plot
as early as June, 1963. Another included some of the
senior generals of the army such as Tran Van Don, the
acting chief of the joint chiefs of staff, and Duong Van
Minh, who later became premier. It was with this latter
group that Ambassador Lodge decided to cooperate. Although the exact hour when Diem's palace was surround-
ed by the conspirators was unknown to the United States,
American officials stayed in contact with them and, as it
appears, kept urging haste in consummating the coup.[100]
Kennedy did not want Diem killed but authorized Lodge
to encourage the conspirators. Lodge's handling of Diem
is preserved in his own account which became available
with the publication of the Pentagon Papers:

Diem: Some units have made a rebellion and I want
       to know what is the attitude of the U.S.?
Lodge: I do not feel well enough informed to be able
       to tell you. I have heard the shooting, but am
       not acquainted with all the facts. Also it is
       4:30 A.M. in Washington and the U.S. Gov-
       ernment cannot possibly have a view.
Diem: But you must have some general ideas. After
       all, I am a Chief of State, I have tried to do
       my duty. I want to do now what duty and
       good sense require. I believe in duty above all.
Lodge: You have certainly done your duty. As I told
       you only this morning, I admire your cour-
       age and your great contributions to your
       country. No one can take away from you the
       credit for all you have done. Now I am wor-
       ried about your physical safety. I have a
       report that those in charge of the current
       activity offer you and your brother safe con-
       duct out of the country if you resign. Have
       you heard this?
Diem: No. (And then after a pause.) You have my
       telephone number.
Lodge: Yes. If I can do anything for your physical
       safety, please call me.
Diem: I am trying to re-establish order.

Just as the Americans had been responsible for raising him up nine years before, they were now the agents of his destruction.

Diem's assassination let loose a flood of events that swiftly transformed the character of the American crusade. The first military junta, under General Duong Van Minh, fell after two months before the pressures of more enterprising generals, led by General Nguyen Khanh. "A necessary move to prevent neutralists from taking over the government,"[101] the new military leader explained to Ambassador Lodge, who promptly pledged full American support to the junta. There were now sixteen thousand U.S. military advisers and thirty-five hundred civilians attempting to spur on a South Vietnamese army of four hundred thousand men against a force which the U.S. military spokesmen at the time described as a "hard core" of twenty-five thousand guerrillas, supported by eighty thousand "irregulars" and perhaps three hundred thousand "sympathizers" (civilians who sheltered or fed the Vietcong). The guerrillas brought more and more territory under their control and grew increasingly bold. Just before the fall of Diem the Vietcong had blocked the highway from Saigon to Hue and forced all the vehicles off the road into a clearing, where their occupants were subjected to a lecture before being allowed to proceed. Vietcong attacks on strategic hamlets, still a major project of the regime, mounted. So also did the rate of assassination of local leaders. General Harkins continued to talk of "victory" being only "months away," but the eight-year experiment to create a separate South Vietnamese national identity was crumbling fast. "The old regime has destroyed all political life,"[102] General Minh explained to a French newspaperman a few days before his own removal by General Khanh.

Ten

On November 22 President Kennedy was assassinated. The new American President had little time for the grotesque little war he had inherited. During most of 1964 the management of the operation was left to the experienced, frustrated hands of the Kennedy national-security advisers. On November 26 the new President signed NSAM 273 which provided:

> that planning should include different levels of possible increased activity, and in each instance there should be estimates of such factors as (a) Resulting damage to NVN, (b) The plausibility of denial; (c) Possible NVN retaliation; (d) Other international reaction.[103]

Ralph Stavins summarizes the planning and objectives in the early months of the Johnson administration:

> NSAM 273 authorized General Victor Krulak to form a committee and develop a coherent program of covert activities to be conducted during 1964, while the rest of the national security apparatus explored the feasibility of initiating a wider war against the North . . . In a report issued by Krulak on January 2, 1964, a twelve-month program of covert activities to be performed in three phases was recommended to Johnson. The operational control of the program was assigned to MACV. The CAS (a code name for the CIA's operational work) and CINCPAC were to train and equip the ARVN. Phase one of the program, scheduled for the months of February to May, was to consist of intelligence collection and twenty destructive acts against the North. The second and third phases were to increase the tempo and magnitude of the first phase, and extend the destructive operations

to targets identified with North Vietnam's economic
and industrial well-being. President Johnson approved
the entire package on January 16 . . . Covert operations began on February 1, 1964. Six months later
they were to play a dramatic role in the Gulf of Tonkin incident and the subsequent escalation of the
war.[104]

After a trip to Vietnam in December, 1963, Secretary
McNamara recommended, according to Hilsman, "that a
committee of specialists be designated to develop a list of
targets and lay the groundwork for a future decision to
bomb the north."[105] The secretary of defense now lavished
praise on General Khanh, using the same terms he and his
predecessors had applied to Diem. Here once more was a
selfless patriot with the political and psychological skill to
save the country, a man in whom one could have "high
hopes."[106] While President Johnson concentrated his energies on building the political consensus that would make
possible the greatest whirlwind of legislative reform in
thirty years and the most overwhelming electoral victory
in over a century, the men in charge of the war continued
to run it according to the familiar pattern. As late as
March, 1964, the secretary of defense still characterized
the conflict as essentially an internal war. While North
Vietnamese support was a "critical factor," the fact that
the Vietcong receives "large indigenous support" means
that "solutions must be as political and economic as military," McNamara observed in language reminiscent of the
"hearts-and-minds" rhetoric of the Diem era. Indeed,
there was "no such thing as a purely 'military' solution to
the war in South Vietnam."[107] The President expressed the
same view of the war frequently during the 1964 campaign. "We are not about to send American boys nine or
ten thousand miles away from home to do what Asian
boys ought to be doing to protect themselves."[108] Taunting
Goldwater and his supporters in the military for their
seemingly endless supply of suggestions for military experimentation—bombing, mining, sending in an American
army—Johnson told the American Bar Association on
August 12, 1964, that all such actions "would offer no
solution at all to the real problem of Vietnam."[109]
Pressures were mounting in Washington and Saigon,
however, for a radical reassessment of the American commitment. In Saigon the Khanh regime was proving itself

incapable of either organizing an effective government or prosecuting the war. General Maxwell Taylor, who replaced Lodge as American ambassador in June, 1964, later told a Senate committee that "almost anything would be an improvement"[110] over the tiny Vietnamese general, who had to be rescued from periodic coups. As Khanh inflamed old passions by issuing a "constitution" giving himself dictatorial powers, thus provoking a resurgence of Buddhist riots, the Vietcong steadily extended their grip on the country. In February, 1965, the sixth coup since November, 1963, finally brought the end of the Khanh regime.

In Washington those who had long advocated tougher military measures were raising their voices. The deterioration of the South Vietnamese political structures and the consequent shift in loyalties to the Vietcong seemingly called for a drastic military response. Each of the military services had its own "school solution." Staff papers outlining a succession of recommendations for precision bombing of the "Ho Chi Minh Trail" in North Vietnam by the air force, a blockage of Haiphong by the navy, and a massive "search-and-kill" operation by the army in South Vietnam were forwarded up the bureaucratic ladder, waiting for the President's eye. "We are swatting flies when we should be going after the manure pile,"[111] Chief of Staff of the air force Curtis LeMay declared. "We could pulverize North Vietnam," General Powers, the chief of the Strategic Air Command, agreed. Political leaders and columnists also spoke out. Governor Nelson Rockefeller urged that the South Vietnamese forces, which were then being overrun in their own country in battalion-size attacks by the Vietcong, should now take the initiative and invade North Vietnam, Laos, and Cambodia.[112]

Notably absent in the months of feverish contingency planning in the summer and fall of 1964 were systematic considerations of negotiating positions or the uses of diplomacy. In July, 1964, De Gaulle, U Thant, and the Soviet government made various proposals for negotiations, including a suggestion for the reconvening of the Geneva conference. President Johnson's response was swift and categorical. "We do not believe in conferences called to ratify terror, so our policy is unchanged."[113] At about the same time, the North Vietnamese government made overtures through the secretary-general for a meeting with the United States in Rangoon. These too were rebuffed. The

Johnson administration refused to consider negotiations while the political life of the Saigon government was ebbing away. In the view of the National-Security Managers, what was needed was not disengagement, as Kennedy had hinted in the last days of the Diem regime, but rather a dramatic show of increased commitment.

By early summer, 1964, Secretary Rusk was instructing newsmen "to report that the U.S. commitment to Viet Nam was unlimited, comparable with West Berlin."[114] This meant, as President Johnson made explicit, that the United States was prepared to risk war.

The occasion for a spectacular show of commitment materialized shortly before ten P.M. on the night of August 4. The destroyer *Maddox* and her sister ship *Turner Joy* radioed that they were under attack from North Vietnamese torpedo boats. (For the *Maddox,* which had been serving as protection for South Vietnamese vessels carrying out raids in the Tonkin Gulf, this was the second encounter with enemy PT boats in two days.) There is considerable question as to the location of the encounter and its exact character. (The destroyers were undamaged.) There is also question, in view of the swiftness and scale of the retaliatory air raids on North Vietnam that followed less than twelve hours after the radio message was received, whether the incident in the Gulf of Tonkin was the inspiration or merely the pretext for a show of force desired for quite other reasons. Whatever the motivation, the attack provided a brief political stimulant for the Khanh government. The general publicly exulted in the raids, which demolished three naval bases, oil depots, and twenty-five boats; attempted to tighten his control over Saigon by outlawing strikes, imposing censorship, and increasing police intimidation; and boasted that he now had support for a march to the North. Polls in the United States showed eighty-five-percent approval for what the President called a "limited" response. In the first flush of shock and relief that greeted the Tonkin incident, the President secured a joint resolution from Congress empowering him to "take all measures . . . to repulse aggression and prevent further aggression."

Eleven

The long period of creeping escalation was now at an end. The U.S. commitment was about to take a series of quantum jumps. This escalation of force, as Theodore Draper has put it, required an escalation of theory. As the U.S. investment in the war, measured in billions per month and casualties per week, climbed sharply, so also did the promises of a high return on the investment. By the time the war was costing two billion dollars per month for the maintenance of a fighting force of over five hundred thousand American men, South Vietnam by itself was too small an object on which to focus so huge a commitment. As the advocates of stepped-up military action within the U.S. government pressed their arguments in the final months of 1964 and the early days of 1965, they declared that South Vietnam was not in itself the justification for the mammoth frustrating efforts. The war in Vietnam had to be fought to some sort of "victory," not to buy democracy for Vietnam, for there were few who still held that tattered illusion, but because it was a "test case," a symbolic engagement in a much larger and vaguer struggle. Here was the battlefield "International Communism" had chosen on which to test the strategy of "wars of national liberation." Here also was the place to "contain" China.

The National Security Council Working Group reported in November, 1964: "Essentially, the loss of South Vietnam to communist control, in any form, would be a major blow to our basic policies. U.S. prestige is heavily committed to the maintenance of a noncommunist South Vietnam, and only less heavily so to a neutralized Laos." America might not win, McGeorge Bundy concluded, but it must avert defeat. According to the NSC paper, the U.S. "must take forceful enough measures in the situation so that we emerge from it, even in the worst case, with our standing as the principal helper against communist expansion as little impaired as possible." Thus it no longer mattered that the political chaos in South Vietnam made it impossible for the Vietnamese to fight successfully or that neutralist sentiment in the country was growing at a rapid rate. Vietnam was merely an incidental scene in what U.S. spokesmen now characterized as a global campaign of international communism. The war in Vietnam was no longer "their war," as President Kennedy had called it—meaning the Vietnamese—it was, as his successor now called it, "part of a wider pattern of aggressive purposes."[115]

Prior commitments of men and money made originally for more modest reasons thus gave rise to a succession of grandiose intellectual distortions. For the truth was that the war in Vietnam was still essentially a civil war. When the decisions were being considered in late 1964 to send in a major American combat force, according to figures confirmed by the Pentagon, there were only four hundred North Vietnamese soldiers south of the 17th parallel.[116] There were no Chinese troops at all.[117] The charge of "aggression from the North" was based on several thousand guerrillas who had been infiltrated into the south and on Hanoi's alleged direction of the war. "International Communism" was quite divided on the issue, as it was on many others. The Soviets took cautious initiatives to bring about negotiations. The East European countries, eagerly but powerlessly, pressed for peace. China expressed its sympathy for the Vietcong and encouraged them to go on fighting. But if the threat truly justified the commitment, then American policy makers had to assume that communism was monolithic and infinitely expansive, despite the evidence that the reality was quite different.

More and more the war in Vietnam began to be characterized as an international war against North Vietnam and China. Curtis LeMay, just before retiring, urged that Chinese nuclear installations be bombed, and this possibility was "war-gamed" by the President and his top advisers in the Cabinet Room of the White House before being rejected.[118] The State Department prepared a White Paper which now characterized the conflict primarily as "aggression from the North." (A year and a half later, after a steady stream of infiltration of North Vietnamese regulars, these "foreign troops" accounted for fifty thousand out of a total enemy force of two hundred and eighty-six thousand.[119])

The attempt to hold Hanoi responsible for the activities of the National Liberation Front was politically self-defeating, for it helped consolidate North Vietnamese power over the insurgent movement and weakened the moderates who had joined it. But at the same time it was politically necessary to charge Hanoi with "intervention" in order to justify U.S. military operations as "counterintervention" and to focus attention on Hanoi's role as the instigator of the war. Thus, to explain to the world why U.S. escalation was not aggressive, the President painted a picture of the war that was reminiscent of the battle against Hitler but bore little resemblance to what was actually happening in Southeast Asia.

The final plan for escalation of the war was approved by President Johnson on December 1, 1964. The plan embodied the recommendations of the National Security Council Working Group, headed by Assistant Secretary of State William P. Bundy, known as "Option C." These recommendations were designed to avoid or at least to postpone the imminent defeat of the U.S. in South Vietnam without incurring a major risk of war with the Soviet Union or China. It was because of fear of these possibilities that the recommendations of the Joint Chiefs of Staff for more rapid escalation were rejected. Option C was put into effect in February 1965 after the NLF attacked the U.S. base at Pleiku. Option C called for

> additional graduated military moves against infiltration targets, first in Laos and then in the DRV, and then against other targets in North Vietnam. The military scenario should give the U.S. the option at any time to proceed or not, to escalate or not, and to quicken the pace or not.[120]

These planning documents also made it clear that the U.S. would not negotiate a political settlement unless it guaranteed "an independent noncommunist South Vietnam" (NSAM 288). In the minds of the National-Security Managers in independent South Vietnam could not be a neutral South Vietnam. It had to have a strongly pro-U.S.

orientation. The U.S. war planners were critically concerned that the South Vietnamese leadership under increasing military pressure would seek a political accommodation and order the United States out. (Indeed some
contingency planning was prepared on how to continue
the American war in Vietnam over the opposition of a
neutralist South Vietnamese government.) "Your mission," President Johnson had cabled Ambassador Lodge a
year before the major escalation began, "is precisely for
the purpose of knocking down the idea of neutralization
wherever it rears its ugly head . . ."[121] An essential aspect
of Option C was to prevent "premature pressure" for
political negotiations. As General Maxwell Taylor put it, it
was important to keep the bombing in North Vietnam
within certain limits "in order to avoid a build-up of
international pressures to negotiate."[122]

It was soon clear that the sytematic bombing of North
Vietnam would not stop pressure on the South. "Early in
1965 we knew that the enemy hoped to deliver the *coup
de grace* by launching a major summer offensive to cut the
Republic of Vietnam in two with a drive across the
central highlands to the sea. I had to make a decision and
did. I chose a rapid build-up of combat forces."[123]

Within one hundred twenty days more than one hundred thousand combat troops were landed in Vietnam. By
1967 it was largely an American war fought with a rain of
bombs that exceeded the monthly tonnage dropped on
Nazi Germany at the height of World War II. The number of American troops exceeded 500,000. Despite the
bombing, the North Vietnamese were able to step up their
infiltration into the South, and despite heavy air and
ground fighting below the nineteenth parallel the NLF
recruitment was higher than its casualty rate. U.S. "search-
and-destroy" operations exacted a heavy toll in American
casualties, which at the height of the war exceeded 1,000 a
week. By late 1967 the Joint Chiefs of Staff were pressing
for further ground forces, for elimination of the political
restrictions which exempted the "doughnut" (the central
portion of Hanoi) and Haiphong Harbor from aerial
attack, and for an invasion of Cambodia to attack the
"sanctuaries" which served as NLF staging areas and bases.
In late January the NFL and the North Vietnamese
launched their Tet offensive. The effect was stunning, for it

offered a dramatic demonstration to the world that despite the massive U.S. militray campaign the Vietnamese were not defeated and showed no signs of giving up. It was now clear to the Johnson administration that the costs of maintaining and escalating the war outweighed the risks of deescalation. A little more than a month later Lyndon Johnson at the urging of Secretary of Defense Clark Clifford and with the strong support of representatives of the business community turned down the requests of the military for the 206,000 additional troops and announced he would not seek reelection. The deescalation process began with a partial bombing halt and a call for negotiations which the North Vietnamese and the NFL accepted. Within the Pentagon plans for what in the next administration would be called "vietnamization" were developed.

A few days before the November, 1968, election President Johnson halted all bombing of North Vietnam, but the South Vietnamese, encouraged by prominent Republicans, delayed responding to the administration's bid for deescalation, which by now had become a popular policy. Nixon, who had campaigned on the strength of an unrevealed "plan" to end the war, was narrowly elected.

The plan turned out to be "vietnamization": a staged series of highly publicized withdrawals of ground troops, intensification of the air war in Laos and parts of South Vietnam, resumption of so-called "protective reaction" air strikes against North Vietnam, and the expansion of the battlefield through invasions of Cambodia and Laos. By the end of Nixon's fourth year in office the number of U.S. ground troops in Indochina had fallen below 100,000. At least one third of the population of Indochina were refugees in their own land. The war was disappearing from the headlines, but the United States could not bring itself to stop it.

NOTES—CHAPTER NINE

1. This incident was recently discovered by Bernard Fall in the U.S. Naval Archives. This indefatigable and brilliant scholar had promised to send me the exact reference, but he met a sudden, tragic death in Vietnam in early 1967.

2. Cordell Hull, *Memoirs* (New York, 1948), p. 1014.

3. *Ibid.*, p. 1595.

4. Franklin D. Roosevelt, quoted in *ibid.*, p. 1597.

5. Chiang Kai-shek, quoted in Ellen E. Hammer, *The Struggle for Indochina* (Stanford, Calif., 1966), p. 44.

6. Frank D. Roosevelt, quoted in *ibid.*

7. Franklin D. Roosevelt, quoted in Hull, *Memoirs*, p. 1598.

8. Letter from Brigadier General Philip Gallagher to Major General R. B. McClure, Chinese Combat Command, September 20, 1945, U.S. Army Archives.

9. Quoted in Hammer, *The Struggle*, p. 130n.

10. Ho Chi Minh, quoted in *ibid.*, p. 155.

11. *Ibid.*, p. 183. It now appears that the local military command may have acted contrary to the orders of the Paris government.

12. *Ibid.*, p. 201.

13. Quoted in *ibid.*, p. 190.

14. George Marshall, quoted in *The New York Times*, February 8, 1947.

15. Quoted in Hammer, *The Struggle*, p. 235.

16. *The New York Times*, editorial, quoted in Earl Latham, *The Communist Controversy in Washington* (Cambridge, 1960), p. 220.

17. Dean Acheson, quoted in U.S. Department of State, *United States Relations with China* (Washington, 1949), p. xvii.

18. Quoted in Hammer, *The Struggle*, p. 267.

19. Dean Acheson, quoted in U.S. Congress, Senate, *Nomination of Philip C. Jessup, Hearings*, before the Senate Committee on Foreign Relations, 82nd Congress, 1st session, 1951, p. 603.

20. Dean Acheson, quoted in *Department of State Bulletin*, May 22, 1950, p. 821.

21. Quoted in Hammer, *The Struggle*, p. 271.

22. Dean Acheson, quoted in *ibid.*, p. 315.

23. Quoted in *ibid.*, p. 278.

24. David C. Bruce, quoted in U.S. Congress, Senate, *United States Foreign Aid Program in Europe, Hearings*, before the Senate Committee on Foreign Relations, 82nd Congress, 1st session, 1951, p. 207. I am grateful to Professor Gabriel Kolko for calling this reference to my attention.

25. Dwight D. Eisenhower, *Mandate for Change*, vol. I of *Memoirs* (New York, 1963), p. 341.

26. *Ibid.*, p. 340.

27. *Ibid.*

28. *Ibid.*, p. 341.

29. *Ibid.*, p. 343.

30. *Ibid.*

31. Dwight D. Eisenhower, quoted in Sherman Adams, *Firsthand Report: The Story of the Eisenhower Administration* (New York, 1961), p. 128.

32. Eisenhower, *Memoirs*, vol. I, p. 345.

33. *Ibid.*

34. Walter B. Smith, quoted in *ibid.*, p. 346.

35. Bidault told Roscoe Drummond and Gaston Coblentz that there was "no doubt in my mind" that Dulles had offered the "use of . . . one or more [nuclear weapons] near the Chinese border against supply lines" and "two" to be used against the Vietminh at Dien Bien Phu. See Roscoe Drummond and Gaston Coblentz, *Duel at the Brink* (New York, 1960), p. 26.

36. Arthur F. Radford, quoted in C. Roberts, "The Day We Didn't Go to War," in M. Gettleman, ed., *Viet Nam: Documents & Opinions on a Major World Crisis* (New York, 1965), p. 98.

37. Adams, *Firsthand Report*, p. 126.

38. Eisenhower, *Memoirs*, vol. I, p. 346.

39. *Ibid.*, p. 347.

40. Richard Nixon, quoted in *The New York Times*, April 17, 1954.

41. Quoted in Adams, *Firsthand Report*, p. 125.

42. Richard Rovere, *Affairs of State* (New York, 1956), p. 193.

43. *Ibid.*

44. Eisenhower, *Memoirs*, vol. I, p. 340.

45. Anthony Eden, *Memoirs: Full Circle* (London, 1960), p. 83.

46. John Foster Dulles, Speech to the Overseas Press Club, March 29, 1957, *Department of State Bulletin*, April 12, 1954, pp. 539–540.

47. Walter B. Smith, quoted in Eden, *Memoirs*, p. 90.

48. *Ibid.*, p. 92.

49. *Ibid.*, p. 101.

50. *Ibid.*, p. 104.

51. Arthur F. Radford, quoted in Eden, *Memoirs*, p. 104.

52. *Ibid.*

53. John Foster Dulles, quoted in Eisenhower, *Memoirs*, vol. I, p. 350.

54. Dwight D. Eisenhower, quoted in Adams, *Firsthand Report*, p. 126.

55. Dwight D. Eisenhower, quoted in Eden, *Memoirs*, p. 128.

56. Quoted in *ibid.*, p. 132.

57. Walter B. Smith, quoted in Eisenhower, *Memoirs*, vol. I, p. 371.

58. Douglas Pike, *Viet Cong* (Cambridge, Mass., 1966), p. 52.

59. John Foster Dulles, quoted in *The Washington Post*, March 26, 1967.

60. John Foster Dulles, quoted in Adams, *Firsthand Report*, p. 128.

61. William O. Douglas, quoted in Robert Sheer, "How the United States Got Involved in Viet Nam," reprinted in Gettleman, *Viet Nam*, p. 237.

62. Cardinal Spellman, quoted in *The New York Times*, September 1, 1954.

63. Quoted in John J. Mecklin, *Mission in Torment* (New York, 1965), p. 4.

64. Leo Cherne, quoted in Gettleman, *Viet Nam*, p. 245.

65. Graham Greene, quoted in Hammer, *The Struggle*, p. 350.

66. Bernard Fall, *Viet Nam Witness* (New York, 1966), p. 180.

67. Tran Van Don, quoted in *ibid.*, p. 62.

68. Victor Bator, *Vietnam—A Diplomatic Tragedy* (New York, 1965), p. 140.

69. Quoted in John J. Montgomery, *The Politics of Foreign Aid* (New York, 1960), p. 66.

70. Quoted in *ibid.*

71. Quoted in Gettleman, *Viet Nam*, p. 223.

72. Mecklin, *Mission in Torment*, p. 61.

73. *Ibid.*, p. 46.

74. Henry Cabot Lodge, quoted in Gareth Porter, "Globalism—The Ideology of Total World Involvement," in Marcus G. Raskin and Bernard B. Fall, eds., *The Viet-Nam Reader* (New York, 1965), p. 325.

75. Mecklin, *Mission in Torment*, p. 20.

76. Quoted in *ibid.*, p. 21.

77. Lord Cromer, quoted in Hannah Arendt, *The Origins of Totalitarianism* (Cleveland, 1958), p. 213.

78. Lord Cromer, quoted in *ibid.*, p. 211.

79. Quoted in Jean La Couture, *Vietnam: Between Two Truces* (New York, 1966), p. 31.

80. John W. Lewis and George McT. Kahin, *The United States and Vietnam* (New York, 1966), p. 110.

81. See Philippe Devillers, *The Nation*, December 5, 1966, p. 599.

82. Quoted in Lewis and Kahin, *The United States*, p. 114.

83. Fall, *Viet Nam Witness*, p. 237.

84. *Ibid.*, p. 131.

85. John F. Kennedy, quoted in Arthur Schlesinger, Jr., *A Thousand Days: John F. Kennedy in the White House* (Boston, 1965), p. 322.

86. Quoted in *ibid.*, p. 325.

87. John F. Kennedy, quoted in Mecklin, *Mission in Torment*, p. 25.

88. Quoted in *ibid.*, p. 17.

89. Quoted in Theodore Draper, "The American Crisis," in *Commentary*, January 1967, p. 32.

90. Lyndon B. Johnson, quoted in Schlesinger, *A Thousand Days*, p. 542.

91. *Ibid.*, p. 545.

92. Roger Hilsman, *To Move a Nation* (New York, 1967), p. 42.

93. J. K. Galbraith, quoted in Schlesinger, *A Thousand Days*, p. 547.

94. John F. Kennedy, quoted in *ibid.*

95. Edward Lansdale, quoted in *ibid.*, p. 986.

96. John F. Kennedy, quoted in Mecklin, *Mission in Torment*, p. 182.

97. Schlesinger, *A Thousand Days*, p. 997.

98. Mecklin, *Mission in Torment*, p. 278.

99. Personal communication with members of the United States mission in Saigon. See also Hilsman, *To Move a Nation*, p. 518, for an account of private contacts between a Vietnamese general and "an American official."

100. A former United States official in Saigon informed me that he had personally seen a cable from Washington urging the Embassy to get the coup over with. I have seen a letter from Ambassador Henry C. Lodge directly denying the existence of such a cable.

101. Nguyen Khanh, quoted in La Couture, *Viet Nam*, p. 133.

102. Duong Van Minh, quoted in *ibid.*, p. 36.

103. "Pentagon Papers" as quoted in *Washington Plans an Aggressive War* (New York, 1971), pp. 93–94.

104. *Ibid.*, p. 94.

105. Robert McNamara, quoted in Hilsman, *To Move a Nation*, p. 534.

106. Draper, "The American Crisis," p. 35.

107. Robert McNamara, quoted in *ibid.*, p. 36.

108. Lyndon B. Johnson, quoted in Rowland Evans and Robert Novak, *Lyndon B. Johnson: The Exercise of Power* (New York, 1966), p. 532.

109. Lyndon B. Johnson, quoted in *ibid.*

110. Maxwell Taylor, quoted in Draper, "The American Crisis," p. 37.

111. Curtis LeMay, quoted in Mecklin, *Mission in Torment*, p. 301.

112. *Ibid.*

113. Lyndon B. Johnson, quoted in Franz Schurmann *et al.*, *The Politics of Escalation* (Boston, 1966), p. 37.

114. Dean Rusk, quoted in Mecklin, *Mission in Torment*, p. 287.

115. Lyndon B. Johnson, quoted in Evans and Novak, *Lyndon B. Johnson*, p. 540.

116. Draper, "The American Crisis," p. 36.

117. See U.S. Department of State, *Aggression from the North: The Record of Vietnam's Campaign to Conquer South Vietnam*, February 1965.

118. Evans and Novak, *Lyndon B. Johnson*, p. 538.

119. U.S. Department of Defense, Office of Public Affairs.

120. "Pentagon Papers," quoted in *Washington Plans an Aggressive War*, p. 141.

121. *Ibid.*, p. 112.

122. *Ibid.*, p. 163.

123. William Westmoreland, quoted in Draper, *The American Crisis*, p. 36.

CHAPTER **10**

The Subversion
of Undesirable Governments

One

"WE WOULD BE FOOLISH," Allen Dulles once answered an interviewer who asked whether his function as
director of the Central Intelligence Agency was "to stir up
revolutions," "if we did not cooperate with our friends
abroad to help them do everything they can to explore
and counter the Communist subversive movement."[1] With
a budget in excess of three billion dollars and a staff in
excess of twenty thousand, the Central Intelligence Agency
has conducted operations against legitimate governments
on three continents. In a few cases, such as the Trujillo
assassination of 1961, U.S. intelligence operations have
worked against traditional right-wing dictatorships.[2] Most
of their activities, however, have been directed against
regimes which have tried to take a radical or nationalist
position on questions of development and foreign policy.
Such regimes have attempted to nationalize foreign enter-
prises, have flirted with Marxist rhetoric, or have invited
persons with real or suspected communist associations into
the government. Any of these deviations from the standard which the United States has set for judging whether

a foreign government is a responsible member of the Free World has been sufficient to convince the State Department that the government in question is "subverted" and that it is fair game for "countersubversive" operations from our side. While on occasion CIA agents may act prematurely and display too much zeal, and even sometimes, as in Laos in 1960, may act counter to official State Department policy at the moment, in most cases the agency is carrying out official policy that has been approved by the President. Subversion is simply another facet of the campaign against revolution. It is a technique which is cheaper and politically less embarrassing than open support of one side in a protracted civil war or landing American troops.

The intervention in Iran in 1953 to unseat Premier Mohammed Mossadeq was America's first successful attempt in the postwar period to subvert a nationalist government. Mossadeq came to power on May 1, 1951, and three days later seized the British-owned Anglo-Iranian Oil Company. In a fiery speech the wispy premier announced that Iran was taking rightful possession of "a hidden treasure upon which lies a dragon."[3] Oil companies in the West boycotted the nationalized oil company and Iran lost the major source of its foreign exchange. Much to the annoyance of the British, the United States did not totally cut off aid to the Mossadeq government. In 1951 and 1952 it gave sixteen and a half million dollars for a small agricultural-assistance program and to make up foreign-exchange deficits. "It seemed to the United States," Eden writes in his memoirs, "a reckless policy to allow the situation to deteriorate, as they considered it would if Mossadeq were left without any help." Eden's own reading of the situation was different. He believed that if Mossadeq fell, "his place might well be taken by a more reasonable Government with which it would be possible to conclude a satisfactory agreement."[4]

A year later the newly elected Eisenhower administration had come to the British view. Mossadeq must go. Although the State Department continued to hint that there was a link between Mossadeq and communism, the political reality in Iran was quite different.[5] Mossadeq had come to power as the head of the National Front, a nationalist coalition that had been energized chiefly by the oil issue. The Tudeh party, as the local communist organization was called, attacked the Front and on July 15, 1951, Mossadeq suppressed a communist-sponsored demonstration of the National Association for Struggle Against the Imperialist Oil Companies in Iran, killing one hundred and injuring five hundred demonstrators. In mid-1952 the Tudeh reversed its position, began to shift its attacks from the premier to the shah, and asked for a united front. But Mossadeq resisted the communists' call for a coalition, restated his refusal to legalize the Tudeh, and imposed martial law in Tehran. Less than a month before the coup that finally overthrew him, he received another open appeal to join forces with the communists, but despite the now transparent efforts of the United States and its allies to get rid of him and the mounting opposition of the shah, the army, the landowners, and the middle classes, Mossadeq refused to accept their help. Two days before he fell, his troops turned on communist demonstrators in Tehran. Nine years after these events Soviet analysts ascribed the failure of the Tudeh, which sharply declined in strength after Iran became a U.S. ally, to the fact that the party "was in fact fighting on two fronts—against imperialism and against Mossadeq."[6]

The Eisenhower administration began its campaign against Mossadeq with economic pressure. "There is a strong feeling in the United States," the President wrote the Iranian, ". . . that it would not be fair to the American taxpayer for the United States Government to extend any considerable amount of economic aid to Iran so long as Iran could have access to funds derived from the sale of its oil products if a reasonable agreement were reached."[7]

Exactly five weeks later, Mossadeq having rejected this offer, Kermit Roosevelt, a grandson of President Theodore Roosevelt, formerly a history professor and oss agent and at the time CIA's principal covert operative in the Middle East, arrived in Iran to direct a coup against Mossadeq. His mission was to replace him with General Fazollah Zahedi, who, despite his suspected Nazi sympathies during the war, was considered far more willing to cooperate with the oil companies and the State Department. Assisting in the operation was Brigadier General H. Norman Schwartzkopf, famous twenty years earlier as the New Jersey State Police officer who investigated the Lindbergh-baby kidnapping and later as the weekly narrator of the radio program "Gangbusters." With the help of five U.S. agents and seven Iranian intelligence operatives, Roosevelt plotted the coup from a Tehran basement. An admiring CIA colleague called it "a real James Bond operation."[8]

Shortly after the U.S. agent's arrival, the shah dismissed Mossadeq, but Mossadeq's supporters rioted and forced the shah to flee the country. On August 19, 1953, while his chief, Allen Dulles, was conferring with the shah in Rome, Roosevelt was recruiting street mobs to oppose the Mossadeq supporters and the Tudeh, which was also demonstrating against the impending coup. With the help of substantial sums, which Roosevelt used for hired demonstrators to whip up the growing anti-Mossadeq mobs, and the support of the Iranian army, heavily dependent on U.S. equipment, the insurgents were able to turn the tide against the intractable premier and to drive him from office. The U.S. Military Assistance Mission in Iran took an active part in the operation. Major General George C. Stewart, director of military assistance, later told the House Foreign Affairs Committee:

> When this crisis came on and the thing was about to collapse, we violated our normal criteria and among other things we did, we provided the army immediately on an emergency basis, blankets, boots, uniforms, electric generators, and medical supplies that permitted and created an atmosphere in which they could support the Shah. . . . The guns that they had in their hands, the trucks that they rode in, the armored cars that they drove through the streets, and the radio communications that permitted their control, were all furnished through the military defense assistance program . . . had it not been for this program, a government unfriendly to the United States probably would now be in power.[9]

Once installed as premier, Zahedi concluded an agreement for an oil consortium which was highly favorable to United States companies. The details of the consortium agreement are still classified by the National Security Council. ("Making them public," Secretary Dulles explained to Congress, "would adversely affect the foreign

relations of the United States."[10]) But the basic nature of
the agreement is known. The British lost their former
monopoly on Iranian oil. U.S. companies, including Gulf
and Standard Oil of New Jersey, received a forty-percent
interest in the consortium, which was negotiated for the
United States by such oil-company executives on loan as
Herbert Hoover, Jr., of Union Oil, and Howard W. Page,
vice-president of Jersey Standard.

U.S. aid began to pour in. In 1954, 85 million dollars was
sent, of which 1.7 million dollars was earmarked as
"bonuses" for the Iranian army and police.[11] In the twelve
years which followed, the United States spent 1.3 billion
dollars on aid, about 500,000 dollars of which went to
support the twenty-thousand-man army. "Do you know
what the head of the Iranian army told one of our
people?" Senator Hubert Humphrey demanded in the
course of an investigation of the aid program. "He said
the army was in good shape, thanks to U.S. aid—it was
now capable of coping with the civilian population."[12]

In 1955 the shah joined the Bagdad Pact. While in
recent years he has attempted some land reform, the
country continues to fit the familiar pattern of mass misery—in 1957 a congressional committee estimated illiteracy as high as ninety-three percent—coexisting with
fabulous privilege. The events of the last several years
have not overtaken the tempered judgment which Professor T. Cuyler Young, director of Near Eastern Studies at
Princeton, pronounced in the January, 1962, issue of Foreign Affairs: "They [Iranian patriots and nationalists]
believe that the United States is interested primarily in the
status quo and fearful of permitting any change that could
mean social revolution. That may seem unfair to Americans, but we need to realize that this is our dominant
image in Iran today." There is little in the recent history
of U.S.-Iranian relations to suggest that the image is
false.[13]

Two

Almost exactly nine years after the event, President Eisenhower reminisced before the American Booksellers' Association about the successful subversion of the government of Guatemala in 1954:

> There was a time when we had a very desperate situation, or we thought it was at least, in Central America, and we had to get rid of a Communist government that had taken over. . . .[14]

The "desperate situation" had its origins in the revolution of 1944, which overthrew General Jorge Ubico, a brutal police figure who alternately compared his brand of justice to God's and Hitler's. Proudly noting his similarity to the German dictator, he liked to warn those he called his domesticated enemies, "I execute first and give trial afterward." Because the people of Guatemala "are not prepared for democracy and need a strong hand," Ubico not only banned labor unions but also declared the word "worker" subversive.[15] After a military junta overthrew the dictator in 1944, Juan Arevalo was elected president by a wide margin. The new president abolished forced labor on the banana plantations, raised the minimum wage (to twenty-six cents a day), permitted unions, and began to pry the economy from its near-total dependence upon the United Fruit Company and other foreign corporations. (In 1948 the export of bananas accounted for forty-one percent of the country's foreign exchange.) Such efforts to shake up the economic and political stagnation of the country provoked violent reactions.[16] His program, which Ronald Schneider in his book *Communism in Guatemala* found to be "essentially moderate,"[17] was attacked as "communistic," and more than two dozen attempts were made to overthrow him in his first four years in office. By 1950 the attempts to oust President Arevalo, who showed a willingness to use local communists in the bureaucracy, were growing more serious. He asked Ambassador Richard C. Patterson to leave the country because he sympathized openly with the conspirators and publicly attacked Arevalo for his "persecution of American business." The ambassador "represented Boston" (home of United Fruit), Arevalo charged in an interview with *The New York Times*.[18]

U.S. firms cut down their operations in Guatemala in retaliation against such Arevalo reforms as the social-security provision, which cost United Fruit about two hundred thousand dollars annually. W. R. Grace and Pan American Airlines stopped promoting tourism. Banana exports plummeted eighty percent between 1948 and 1952. According to a United Nations report, "several companies which were engaged in prospecting discontinued their activities subsequent to the passage in 1949 of a petroleum law which they considered unfavorable."[19] The World Bank withheld loans and the United States cut off military assistance.

In 1951 Jacobo Arbenz Guzmán, a member of the military junta that had overthrown Ubico, was elected president, receiving 267,000 votes, almost twice as much as all the other candidates combined. Javier Araña, probably the most popular member of the junta, had been assassinated two years earlier under circumstances that appeared to implicate Arbenz. The new president's principal interest was land reform. About two percent of the population owned seventy percent of the land. By far the greatest landowner was United Fruit, and much of the land was uncultivated. In March, 1953, Arbenz expropriated 234,000 uncultivated acres, offering as compensation six hundred thousand dollars' worth of twenty-five-year bonds. (This was the value the company had declared for tax purposes.) United Fruit protested and demanded compensation in the amount of 15,854,849 dollars. The State Department, now headed by John Foster Dulles, intervened to suggest that this was exactly the amount of compensation required under international law.[20]

A mammoth public-relations campaign was launched by United Fruit. Articles appeared in *The New York Times Magazine* and in other leading periodicals celebrating the company's beneficial impact on the Guatemalan economy, with special emphasis on the schools and hospitals it had built there. But the major thrust of the campaign was that communism was taking over in the Western Hemisphere. Spruille Braden, a former assistant secretary of state for Latin-American affairs turned unofficial adviser for United Fruit, told the Great Issues Seminar at Dartmouth College in a discussion of recent events in Guatemala:

> Communism is so blatantly an international and not an internal affair, its suppression, even by force, in an American country by one or more of the other republics would not constitute an intervention in the internal affairs of the former.[21]

In March, 1954, Dulles persuaded the Organization of American States to pass a resolution declaring that "the domination or control of the political institutions of any American State by the international communist movement, extending to the Hemisphere the political system of an extra-continental power, would constitute a threat to the sovereignty and political independence of the American States. . . ."[22]

What was the role of the communists in Guatemala? What sort of a threat did they pose? There were perhaps as many as three thousand Communist-party members or active sympathizers in a country of three million. The Communists had no position in the cabinet but they held four key seats in Congress. Although José Manuel Fortuny, the party secretary-general, had lost his seat to an anticommunist in 1953, persons who called themselves "communists" held important positions in the labor movement and the official bureaucracies. Most of them, however, were scarcely under the discipline of Moscow. Indeed, the communist leadership itself was split between Moscow-oriented and nationalist factions. The U.S. White Paper charged Arbenz with implicitly accepting the communists as "an authentic domestic political party and not as part of the worldwide Soviet Communist conspiracy,"[23] and the charge is essentially correct. Arbenz, according to Ronald Schneider's study, *Communism in Guatemala*, had a confused relationship with communists, but there is no doubt that he numbered some of the communist leaders among his close friends and that he turned to them to help outline and administer some of his programs in education, agrarian reform, and social security. Arbenz' principal support, however, came from other leftist parties. The communists, who had previously disparaged land reform as a reformist trick, switched their position and lined up behind Arbenz. Communists took over key positions in the ministry of education, and some Marxist-leaning texts were distributed. They were also a leading influence in the labor unions. To put the communist issue in its darkest light, as Schneider does ("The author knows of no government, short of an openly Communist one, in which the Communists were so influential as they were in the Guatemalan government during the last two years of the Arbenz regime"[24]), local communists were the leading source of ideas and political energy in the country. It also appears true that a few top Guatemalan communists took continuing direction from Moscow, but while they sought to deal with genuine local concerns, they had neither a revolutionary program nor a broad local constituency.

What did all this mean? Guatemala was far from adopting a communist economy or social system. She was receiving no aid from the Soviet Union or indeed had any relationship with the communist bloc. Arbenz was actually using the communists to help administer a continuation of the moderate reformist program of Arevalo, who was a rather strong anticommunist. Arbenz's program of nationalization was neither more rapid nor more onerous than those of other noncommunist countries of Latin America and Asia. The cry of communism had been the traditional pretext for opposing reformers in Guatemala. Now that both the pace of reform and the participation of communists had been stepped up, anticommunism reached hysterical proportions.

In late 1953 the Eisenhower administration decided to arrange a coup to rid the hemisphere of the Arbenz regime. Miguel Ydigoras Fuentes, the conservative who later became president of Guatemala, has given us an account of what the Eisenhower administration proposed to him in order to accomplish this:

A former executive of the United Fruit Company, now retired, Mr. Walter Turnbull, came to see me with two gentlemen whom he introduced as agents of the CIA. They said that I was a popular figure in Guatemala and that they wanted to lend their assist-

ance to overthrow Arbenz. When I asked their conditions for the assistance I found them unacceptable.
Among other things, I was to promise to favor the
United Fruit Company and the International Railways of Central America; to destroy the railroad
workers labor union; . . . to establish a strong-arm
government, on the style of Ubico. Further, I was
to pay back every cent that was invested in the undertaking.[25]

The CIA succeeded, however, in locating Colonel Castillo
Armas, who had been involved in earlier coups against
Arevalo and was quite prepared to become the American
candidate for president. John Peurifoy, a veteran diplomat
who had been active in dealing with the Greek insurgency,
was suggested to the President by Allen Dulles as an
experienced man to lead the operation. Details of "Operation el Diablo," most of which turned out to be accurate,
were discovered by Arbenz and published along with intercepted correspondence of Armas. In early 1954 the CIA
set up a headquarters for Armas's forces in Honduras and
later a training center on Momotobito, a volcanic island
off Nicaragua supplied by Nicaragua's President Somoza,
who was delighted to help overthrow the leftist Guatemalan
government. Arbenz appealed to the Soviet Union for aid,
offering to buy ten million dollars' worth of weapons. In
mid-May the Swedish ship *Alfhem,* with an estimated two
thousand tons of small arms, set sail for Guatemala. The
daily progress of the *Alfhem* was plotted in newspapers
throughout Central America, and despite the blockade
which the United States had imposed on arms shipments,
the vessel was allowed to land. The rifles and machine
guns, which Dulles suggested might be used against the
Panama Canal one thousand miles away, provided a new
pretext for tightening the pressure on Arbenz. U.S. arms
were now sent openly to Nicaragua and secretly dropped
inside Guatemala at the United Fruit Company headquarters at Tiquisate.

On June 18 Armas, who had been trained at the Army
Command and General Staff School at Fort Leavenworth
shortly after World War II, led his band of one hundred
and fifty exile mercenaries across the border. U.S. pilots
flying four P-47 Thunderbolts were bombing Guatemala
City. (On June 20 Guatemala's charge that U.S. fliers

were involved was denied by U.S. ambassador to the
United Nations, Henry Cabot Lodge, but William A.
Beall, a Texas pilot, publicly admitted that he and two
other U.S. fliers had crashed off Guatemala since the
beginning of the invasion.[26]) Allen Dulles urged the President to send reinforcements to save the operation. Henry
F. Holland, the assistant secretary of state for Latin-
American affairs, thought, however, that such action
would amount to "intervention" under international law.
Since the United States had already spent on the order of
five million dollars on the invasion, the legal arguments
did not sit well. President Eisenhower recalls the scene:

> Now different people, including Mr. Dulles and a
> member of the State Department and so on, came into
> my office to give their differing views. . . .
>   And the man who opposed going any further was
> very vehement in his representation and he wanted
> no part. He thought we should stop right there, wash
> our hands of the thing and let it stand right there.
> Well, Mr. Dulles was on the other side. And when all
> of the views were presented, I decided we would go
> ahead and the orders went out [to send more planes].
>   . . . I said to Mr. Dulles . . . before I made this
> decision I said "What are the chances that this will
> succeed?" Well, he said he thought about twenty
> percent. I told him later, "If you'd have said ninety
> percent, I'd have said no, but you seemed to be
> honest."
>   He told me later, "Well, you know, I knew that my
> opponent had lost the argument because he came
> in your office with three law books under his arm."[27]

On June 27 Arbenz capitulated. Colonel Carlos Enrique
Díaz took over briefly but broadcast indiscreet remarks
about "the mercenary invaders" and promised to fight.
Ambassador Peurifoy strapped a .45 to his belt and began
to lead the operation against Díaz. The next day a U.S.
pilot bombed the radio station and the army headquarters
in Guatemala City. Díaz was arrested by fellow officers
and Armas arrived in Peurifoy's embassy plane to take
charge of the government. In this way, as John Foster
Dulles reported in a TV address to the American people

the next day, was the situation "being cured by the Guatemalans themselves."[28]

Arbenz had known about the impending invasion for a long time. On June 2 his minister of the interior had publicly announced the plot, and throughout the months Arbenz' police were arresting suspects from the opposition. According to Schneider's book, which is based on affidavits collected by the Guatemalan Secretaría de Propaganda y Divulgación, Arbenz made widespread use of terror, torture, and murder to discourage the plotters. The crucial factor in his downfall was the refusal of the army to fight for him and to distribute arms to the peasants. They refused to supply units of the people's militia as Arbenz urged, because they feared that this would strengthen the communists and destroy their own power. The army turned on Arbenz because of their concern with the growing influence of the communists and their disillusionment with the government's program, which was causing dislocation but had yet to show impressive results. Perhaps the most important consideration was their altogether realistic fear that the United States would not permit Guatemala to chart so independent a course as Arbenz was attempting. The commitment of U.S. power, through the bombing of Guatemala City, was looked upon by the officer corps as an invitation to prudence. Arbenz's general popularity was probably down from his peak strength in the last election, but there is no evidence that popular feeling had turned decisively against him. His downfall was the direct result of the defection of the army under the stimulus of a foreign invasion financed and directed by the United States.

In the next two years ninety million dollars poured into Guatemala to shore up the Armas government. (In the previous ten years Guatemala had received about six hundred thousand dollars, exclusive of road subsidies.) Armas promptly returned United Fruit's expropriated lands and abolished the tax on interest and dividends to foreign investors, a reform which saved United Fruit about eleven million dollars. His National Committee for Defense Against Communism launched a campaign which resulted in the jailing of between five thousand and eight thousand persons.[29] Armas also reformed the election law to eliminate the secret ballot and to disenfranchise the "illiterate masses" (about seventy percent of the country), enabling him to win what President Eisenhower in his memoirs calls a "thundering majority" in a one-candidate election.[30]

In the United States the Subcommittee on Latin America of the House Select Subcommittee on Communist Aggression conducted an investigation of the history of communist penetration in Guatemala.[31] Congressman Thomas G. Dodd and subcommittee adviser Patrick McMahon, who played active roles in the investigation, were also at the time registered agents for the Armas government. Three years later, Armas himself was assassinated. In the next decade the tiny country would undergo other coups. But U.S. influence in Guatemala remained secure. In 1961 Guatemala was used as a training base for an operation against Cuba modeled on the success in Guatemala. Again a group of exiles was organized and trained by U.S. agencies. U.S. planes were provided. The story of the ill-fated operation is too well etched in the American consciousness to require repeating here.

Three

In 1957-58 the United States tried unsuccessfully to support the subversion of the Sukarno government in Indonesia. For a year the Indonesian leader had been moving leftward. After a visit to Moscow he began to expropriate remaining Dutch property and launched a drive against west Irian (New Guinea). He suspended the old parliamentary system, substituting for it a "guided democracy," a coalition government run by himself, in which the one-million-member Communist party had an important role.

On February 15, 1958, a Revolutionary Council was set up in Sumatra under Sjafruddin Prawiranegara, Sukarno's former minister of finance, who had been head of the Bank of Indonesia. The Council accused the government of corruption and inefficiency and of permitting the communists too great an influence. But the major sentiment behind the revolt was Sumatran separatism. In his autobiography Sukarno recounts how his cabinet analyzed the revolt:

> A few discontented regional leaders claim three-fourths of all revenue comes from Sumatra, but only a fraction returns there because most of the money stays in Java. They complain the country suffers from Djakartism [Djakarta is the capital city]. They demand a greater division economically.[32]

In 1957 Allen L. Pope, a former air-force pilot in the Korean War who for three years had been flying for the Civil Air Transport, a CIA airline that had helped drop supplies to the French at Dien Bien Phu, was asked by the agency to fly missions in support of the rebels. A small number of B-26 bombers were to be flown to a rebel airstrip from the U.S. Air Force Base at Clark Field, Manila. Sukarno charges in his autobiography that "tens of thousands of light, American-made weapons were dropped by air. Non-Indonesian pilots were smuggled in."[33]

As the rebellion gathered momentum, the United States professed neutrality. "The United States views this trouble in Sumatra as an internal matter," John Foster Dulles declared. "We intend to conform scrupulously to the principles of international law that apply to such a situation."[34] At a news conference President Eisenhower denied that the United States was helping the rebels but observed that he could not control the activities of private "soldiers of fortune."[35] A few days later, on May 18, Allen Pope's B-26 was shot down. The ambassador continued to insist that Pope was a "private American citizen involved as a paid soldier of fortune,"[36] but the Indonesians held a press conference in which they displayed the evidence of Pope's official status—his past association with the air force and the CIA; the possession of substantial foreign currency, including scrip good only in U.S. military installations; and, above all, his use of the air-force landing strip at Clark Field. At his trial two years later Pope admitted that he received two hundred dollars a bombing mission.

As a result of the exposure of its modest effort to overthrow a government with which it had diplomatic relations, the United States found it expedient to shift course and to support Sukarno. Within five days of Pope's capture, the State Department had sold rice and one million dollars in small arms to the Djakarta government. Shortly thereafter the United States made available to Sukarno twelve Globemaster aircraft, with which the Indonesian leader stamped out the last traces of the rebellion. When Kennedy came in, he recognized that Sukarno's distrust of America was compounded, as Schlesinger puts it, by "his knowledge that in 1958 the CIA had participated in an effort to overthrow him."[37] Relations with Indonesia did not substantially improve, however, until Sukarno was finally overthrown in 1966 in an army coup with which the State Department openly sympathized but in which, so far as can be determined, U.S. agents did not play a significant role.

Four

British Guiana, a British colony bordering Venezuela, composed of about three hundred thousand East Indians and a slightly smaller number of Negroes, had been the scene of anticolonial agitation for many years. The key political figure was Dr. Cheddi Jagan, an Indian dentist, trained at Howard University, a man who sometimes spoke like a Marxist and whose American wife had once been a member of the Young Communist League. For many years he had tangled with the British authorities. In 1953 the British had suspended the constitution and sent in troops after Jagan's Progressive People's party had won the election and had begun some legislative reforms, including repeal of the Undesirable Publications Law and the passage of a labor-relations bill to strengthen unions. "It has been evident," the Colonial Office stated, "that the intrigues of Communists and their associates, some in Ministerial posts, threaten the welfare and good administration of the colony. . . . The faction in power have shown by their acts and their speeches that they are prepared to go to any lengths, including violence, to turn British Guiana into a Communist state."[38] Jagan spent some time in jail after being turned out of office, but in 1957 was returned again to the colonial government and in 1961 was reelected premier by a substantial vote. (Jagan's party won twenty out of thirty-five seats in Parliament.) The premier now began to press for immediate independence for the colony.

In October, 1961, he came to the United States to meet President Kennedy and to seek economic assistance. "We are not engaged in a crusade to force private enterprise on parts of the world where it is not relevant," Kennedy told Jagan. "If we are engaged in a crusade for anything, it is national independence. That is the primary purpose of our aid."[39] The President and his aides then began to examine Jagan on his political beliefs. Arthur Schlesinger, Jr., describes the scene:

> Jagan, after avowing his commitment to parliamentary government, went on to say that he also admired the *Monthly Review* and the rather pro-communist writings of Paul Sweezy, Leo Huberman and Paul Baran. George Ball and I pressed him on this point, declaring there was a large difference between Bevan and the Sweezy group. [Jagan had said that he was a "Bevanite" and the President had "responded agreeably" to this.] Jagan finally said, "Well, Bevanism, Sweezyism, Hubermanism, Baranism—I really don't get those ideological subtleties." Kennedy observed later that this was the one time when his exposition rang false.[40]

Jagan failed to pass ideological muster. The conversation gave the President the "feeling that in a couple of years he will find ways to suspend his constitutional provisions and will cut his opposition off at the knees. ... With all the political jockeying and all the racial tensions, it's going to be almost impossible for Jagan to concentrate the energies of his country on development through a parliamentary system."[41] It was decided to give him no commitments for aid but to consider support for such individual projects as Guiana might submit. The State Department thought that there was at least a fifty-percent chance that Jagan would "go communist" and that therefore the risk of congressional criticism made it unwise to give him any aid. The British, anxious to cut loose their colonial responsibilities in the Western Hemisphere, insisted that there was no alternative to independence under a Jagan government. The Colonial Office, as Schlesinger reports, responded somewhat sarcastically to U.S. suggestions for a delay in the timetable of independence, since the State Department had been prodding them for years to give up their colonies in the rest of the world.

The British government had told the Kennedy administration that Jagan was "possible to work with." Although a Marxist in outlook, he had made no move to become part of the Soviet orbit. Indeed, he had in seven years succeeded in doing virtually no socialist planning and had continually applied to the United States for aid. Despite the visits of trade missions from the U.S.S.R., Cuba, and Hungary, a contract with Cuba for rice at an advantageous price and Castro's offer of thirty-five million dollars in loans (which the British refused to let Jagan accept), the Kennedy administration itself had no hard evidence that Jagan was about to make a "Cuba" of his country. When the premier had asked the President in 1961 whether the United States would object to a trading agreement with the Soviet Union, Kennedy replied that he would not, provided it did not involve a "condition of economic dependence."[42] But as the early months of the new administration passed, the Latin-American specialists in the State Department and the White House became convinced that Jagan, "though perhaps not a disciplined communist, had the kind of deep pro-communist emotion which only sustained experience with communism could cure."[43] Hence, he had to go. The British, bowing to U.S. pressure on a matter in its own hemisphere, acquiesced in the developing campaign to oust Jagan.

The United States had for some time been conducting political activities in British Guiana. During the 1961 election the U.S. Information Service, departing from its usual practice, had taken its films depicting the evils of Castroism from its own building and had shown them on street corners. Fred Schwartz' Christian Anti-Communist Crusade admitted spending seventy-six thousand dollars in the election, a questionable activity for a private organization, which the State Department did nothing to discourage.[44] Jagan wrote Kennedy that the opposition candidates claimed they had commitments from the United States for "half a billion dollars as loans to the Government for 'infra-structure' development and half a billion for industrial development by private U.S. investors." The prime minister noted that, "these statements met with no denial from your Consulate-General, or any other U.S. official."[45]

Now U.S. activities in British Guiana were intensified. The major U.S.-sponsored anti-Jagan campaign in Guiana was conducted through labor unions.[46] A CIA agent, Gerald O'Keefe, posing as an official of the Retail Clerks International Association; William McCabe, inter-American representative of the AFL-CIO; and a host of other U.S. labor officials flocked to the British colony in 1962 and 1963. (There were more visits by trade-union representatives from the United States in eighteen months than in the previous eighteen years, Jagan observes.) They established close contact with the Trade Union Council (TUC), an anti-Jagan union, headed by Richard Ishmael, who had been trained in the United States at the American Institute of Free Labor Development. The institute, an organization set up by the AFL-CIO, with a board made up of business and labor leaders, is designed, according to its charter, to assist "in the development of free democratic trade union structures in Latin America."[47] Although officially described as a partnership between labor, business, and government, it receives about ninety-five percent of its annual six-million-dollar budget from the U.S. Treasury. When Jagan was reelected in 1961, the institute began a major campaign against him. "It appeared to me," Serafino Romualdi, the AIFLD director, later declared, "that young democratic trade union leaders would need intensive training to combat Dr. Jagan's efforts."[48] Several Guianan labor leaders were brought to Washington for training and upon returning to their unions continued to receive a monthly stipend of two hundred and fifty dollars from the institute. According to the London *Times*, which in 1967 conducted an investigation of happenings in British Guiana four years earlier, the account that Jagan gives in his book *The West on Trial* is essentially correct.[49] The British government agreed to a campaign of subversion to unseat Jagan.

In 1962 Jagan presented his budget, but Ishmael's union called a six-day general strike and the premier was forced to withdraw it. The AFL-CIO; ORIT, a Latin-American AFL-

CIO affiliate; and the Retail Clerks International sent large amounts of food to the strikers. The following March, Jagan introduced his labor-relations bill, which provided for a commissioner of labor, a civil-service official, to be in charge of determining proper bargaining units and arranging representational elections. The Trade Union Council demanded that the board administering the law have a majority of TUC members and business leaders. Although Jagan accepted a few amendments to his bill, which was modeled on the Wagner Act, he refused to compromise on the major objective of the bill, the elimination of company unions and the strengthening of trade unionism.

The TUC declared a general strike, which this time lasted eighty days. The strikers were supported from the U.S. Treasury in the amount of approximately one million dollars. Jagan puts the figure at 1.2 million dollars. Polidor, a TUC official, estimates that U.S. sources paid each of twenty thousand strikers three dollars a week for about twelve weeks. One official of the Public Service International personally paid out about one hundred thousand dollars in strike benefits.[50] Much of the money was paid through the International Affairs Department of the American Federation of State, County, and Municipal Employees, which, according to *The New York Times*, was "actually run by two [CIA] aides who operated out of the union's former headquarters in Washington with the knowledge of the union leadership."[51] Funds were transferred to the union from the CIA through a paper organization known as the Gotham Foundation. The activities of the CIA and the U.S. unions in their service in British Guiana have been well publicized. None of it has been denied by the government or the unions involved, and some—such as the role of the American Federation of State, County, and Municipal Employees—has been specifically admitted. In the October 3, 1963, issue of *Machinist*, George Meany noted with pride that "in British Guiana other Institute graduates are participating in the fight against the Cuba-oriented government of Prime Minister Cheddi Jagan."

In June, 1963, rioting broke out in Georgetown, and in the space of a week dynamite attempts were made on the principal public buildings, including the ministries of home affairs, labor, health, and housing. Rocks were thrown at

Jagan and other government leaders while they were attending a funeral. Mobs roamed the streets of Georgetown, attacking people of Indian ancestry. At least fifty were injured. According to a secret report of the British police superintendent in British Guiana to the British commissioner, written on September 11, 1963, which came to light in a debate in the House of Commons in 1966, the violence was instigated by a terrorist group which included British agents. The document states that O'Keefe, the CIA agent, financed these operations through "monetary transactions" with Ishmael. The report also included a letter of Jagan to the British governor charging that the Americans "by lockouts and blockade ... hope to strangle my government financially and economically." U.S. agents cooperated with Jagan's opponents to exploit the delicate racial situation in Guiana by inciting feelings against the Indians, who comprised an important element of Jagan's support. The anti-Jagan union, TUC, began to distribute handbills urging violence ("Let us not be afraid to SHOOT"; "We must be as RUTHLESS AND MORE DESTRUCTIVE than CHEDDI's Armed Forces").[52]

The effect of all this subversive activity was to weaken seriously Jagan's political position and to provide a justification for securing British agreement to the future delay of Guianan independence. When U.S. oil companies cooperated with the strikers in refusing to unload petroleum, Jagan appealed to Cuba, which sent oil. Just as Arbenz nine years earlier had under pressure turned increasingly to the Soviet bloc, so Jagan now tried to get assistance from the only governments willing to defy the United States.

While Jagan's rule was being undermined through these illegal means, the United States was working to change the election law so as to make possible the defeat of Jagan by the constitutional process. Having concluded that Forbes Burnham, a former Jagan associate and now his arch political rival, "would cause us many fewer problems than an independent British Guiana under Jagan," Schlesinger reported to the President that the "way was open to bring it about" by persuading the British to adopt an election law based on proportional representation.[53] (In 1961 Jagan's party had won a plurality of 42.6 percent of the popular vote and under the existing law a substantial majority of parliamentary seats.) In October, 1963, as a result of Kennedy's conversations with Prime Minister Macmillan a few weeks earlier, the British changed the law. In the elections the following year, Jagan, despite the increase in his popular vote, giving him almost six percent more than any other party, lost to Burnham, now backed by a coalition of the other two parties. The terrorism that had continued throughout 1964 came to an end. The Burnham government quickly made it clear that despite election slogans advocating nationalization, it did not intend to disturb the investments of the Aluminum Company of America in bauxite, the Texas Oil Company's oil field, or the manganese industry, also under U.S. control.

A few months after leaving the White House, where by his own account he played an important role in the Jagan episode, Arthur Schlesinger summed up these events in an olympian postscript so apolitical in tone that he might have been describing a phenomenon of nature rather than a clash of men: "With much unhappiness and turbulence, British Guiana seemed to have passed safely out of the communist orbit."[54]

Five

U.S. intervention in the Congo does not fit easily into the familiar patterns that emerge from the cases of subversion discussed in this chapter. In the typical situations a constitutionally elected regime had demonstrated sympathy for communist ideology or dependence on communist governments or had taken or threatened some action inimical to U.S. business interests in the country (including the foreclosing of future opportunities). Small-scale clandestine operations conducted in collaboration with local politicians and military men who opposed their own legally constituted regimes were sufficient (except in Indonesia in 1958, Cuba in 1961, and other failures that may not yet have come to light) to bring down regimes which the United States did not like. The situation in the

Congo was considerably more complex than this simple model.

The Congo became a world problem on June 30, 1960, when the Belgians granted the colony independence. As recently as 1955 the Belgians had been thinking in terms of a thirty-year program leading to independence, but riots in 1959 and mounting world pressure convinced them that they could preserve their economic interests, which were considerable, only by giving up political control. At the independence ceremonies Patrice Lumumba, the prime minister, revealed how deep ran the anticolonialist sentiment in the Congo by lashing out at the assembled dignitaries, including the Belgian king, for the fifty years of "humiliating bondage" and "colonial oppression" they had brought to the Congo. Although it is common to call these bitterly anticolonial feelings "nationalist," it is important to keep in mind that tribal and regional allegiances were much stronger than any sense of national identity.

Step by step the major powers were sucked into the Congo vortex. In early July Congolese army units mutinied against their white Belgian officers. Belgian civilians were attacked. Some women were raped. A few days later Katanga province, the home of Union Minière du Haut-Katanga, a huge Belgian enterprise and the source of over sixty percent of the wealth of the whole country, declared its independence from the central Congolese goverment in Leopoldville. Moise Tshombe, the Katangan prime minister, had tried unsuccessfully to arrange for a separate province before the grant of independence, for neither he nor the Belgians wished to have their mines taxed to support the rest of the Congo. On the night of July 9 the Belgians decided upon military intervention to rescue their technicians and their families and to subdue the mutineers. Tshombe invited the Belgians in and later police forces from Britain and Rhodesia as well, wishing, as he later explained it, "to profit from the occasion to proclaim independence for Katanga"[55] under Belgian protection.

The Eisenhower administration, which wanted to avoid "bringing the Cold War into Africa," supported Lumumba's urgent request for UN military intervention to keep out the Belgians and to end the secession of Katanga. Lumumba had also cabled Khrushchev "to watch hourly

over the situation," but the Soviets at first were reluctant
to act independently in a traditional Western preserve and
supported the creation of a UN force. The Eisenhower
administration was split between those who felt that the
United States must support the nationalist element in
Africa, represented by Lumumba and Joseph Kasavubu,
the Congolese president, and those who could not bring
themselves to oppose a NATO ally. But the State Department decided to give wholehearted support to the UN
operation, and the UN force that was supposed to restore
peace in the Congo was transported in U.S. planes.

The Soviets, meanwhile, contrary to this agreement in
the United Nations, had decided to send trucks and planes
outside of the UN framework to strengthen Lumumba.
The Congolese prime minister, as Roger Hilsman has
characterized him, was a man who "played with Marxist
verbiage"[56] but above all was an African nationalist. In
response to growing Soviet influence, President Kasavubu
dismissed Lumumba, who was later kidnapped to Katanga
and murdered, and closed the Soviet and Czech embassies.
The United States and the Soviet Union were now in open
diplomatic warfare over the Congo as the Kennedy administration took office.

Lumumba had turned on the UN because the force was
not aggressive enough in his opinion in ending the Katangan secession. But the new moderate premier, Cyrille
Adoula, elected in the summer of 1961, also insisted on
vigorous UN action to end the Katangan revolt which
Tshombe was maintaining, with the help of about five
hundred white mercenary officers recruited from South
Africa, Belgium, Rhodesia, and France. Arrayed against
the pressure of the Congolese government and African
nationalists and their sympathizers in Asia and Latin
America was a powerful U.S. lobby, "The American
Committee for Aid to Katanga Freedom Fighters," organized by Michel Struelens, a Belgian public-relations man.
It included Senator Thomas Dodd, who thundered that the
suppression of the Katangan secession was "the Hungary
of 1961" and continually pressed the State Department to
restrain the UN force. The Kennedy administration became increasingly split under the mounting pressure between the Bureau of African Affairs and the American
ambassador, Edmund Gullion, who thought that the
United States would lose all influence in Africa if it did

not identify with the nationalists by backing strong UN action, and those in the White House, who, in Arthur Schlesinger's words, "had become openly critical of deeper American involvement in the Congo." The latter group, who "regarded the conflict as essentially an internal matter,"[57] had become convinced that the communist danger had receded.

Around Christmas, 1962, political negotiations which Kennedy had been promoting for a Congolese settlement broke down. The British refused to support sanctions against Katanga, which did not appear to be effective in any event, and Tshombe talked confidently of a "scorched-earth" campaign against the central government and the UN.

In Washington the Kennedy administration surveyed the alternatives; there turned out to be only two because of the failure of political negotiations and economic sanctions. One was disengagement, which was rejected because of the fear, as Hilsman puts it, "that the Communists would parlay our disengagement into a position of considerable influence, through a military aid program. ..."[58] The remaining choice was to use U.S. military power, either directly or through the UN. Thus the State Department, in conjunction with the UN secretariat, began to develop a plan to crush the Katanga revolt. The day after Tshombe made a speech threatening to "destroy everything," the United States sent a military mission to the Congo under Lieutenant General Louis Truman, a move which the Soviet ambassador to the United Nations, Valerian Zorin, denounced as "direct subversion," despite the Soviets' own unilateral activities in the Congo. A few days later the UN began an offensive which pushed into Katanga, and by the first of the year the force had occupied approximately three-quarters of the productive facilities of Union Minière. When Tshombe threatened to make a stand at Kolwezi and destroy all remaining facilities in his hands, the State Department announced that the United States was about to send trucks, armored personnel carriers, mine-clearing equipment, transport craft, and aircraft within the week. President Kennedy had also decided to send fighter aircraft upon request of the UN command.[59] Under the threat of the mounting advance and a stronger U.S. military commitment, and the promise of an important political role for himself in the reunified

Congo, Tshombe ended the secession on January 16, 1963. Willing to face the opposition of every other major power involved in order to block possible Soviet initiatives in the area, the United States had lent the crucial power to make the shaky international peacekeeping operation a success.

It was, however, only a momentary success. The major U.S. intervention in the Congo was still ahead. Tshombe was the principal rival to the authority of the central government, but he was not the only one. By the end of 1960 Lumumba and his associate Antoine Gizenga had set up a government in Stanleyville, in the northern province of Kivu, and had claimed to be the legitimate government of the entire Congo. The Stanleyville regime was nationalist, anti-Western, and sympathetic to Marxist rhetoric, and it looked to the African neutralists such as Nkrumah and Sekou Touré as well as to the communist countries as its natural friends. When Lumumba was murdered in February, 1961, while in Tshombe's custody, the more radical nationalist African states, including Guinea, Ghana, Mali, and the United Arab Republic, as well as the communist countries, including East Germany and Yugoslavia, promptly recognized Gizenga's regime in Stanleyville as a legitimate government. The Soviets also announced that Stanleyville was the "lawful government" and that they were considering giving it aid. The Kennedy administration favored a negotiated settlement of the Congolese situation, and in the summer of 1961 an agreement was reached with representatives from Stanleyville, which resulted in Gizenga being named vice-premier in the central Congolese government in Leopoldville. Gizenga's joining the government did not end the rebel movement. Gizenga's party (Parti Solidaire Africaine) sent representatives to Egypt, Ghana, and Nigeria to enlist support. The Chinese sent small quantities of weapons. (In late 1960, while he was deputy premier to Lumumba, Gizenga had written Peking "to learn to what extent your government would be in a position to support us in personnel ... arms ... and finances."[60])

On January 14, 1962, the United Nations force, with strong U.S. encouragement, defeated the three-hundred-man Stanleyville gendarmerie and arrested Gizenga, who was deposed as vice-premier. Meanwhile, Pierre Mulele and Christopher Gbenye, two radical members of the

Gizenga group, enlisted the help of Nasser and other governments in setting up a Council of National Liberation, the purpose of which was intended to restore the Stanleyville government and eventually to provide the basis for extending a radical nationalist regime over the entire Congo. During 1963 they attempted to carry out a coup d'état against the Leopoldville government. At the end of the Katangan secession, political opposition to the central government mounted furiously in Kivu province. Gbenye returned to lead the rebellion, which controlled a large area in the northeast of the country. The Soviet Union agreed to replace any weapons which African governments such as Guinea, the United Arab Republic, or Ghana might care to give the Congolese rebels. The Chinese supplied some arms directly through their embassy in Burundi. Most important, units of the central Congolese army were defecting to the Stanleyville government.

On June 30, 1964, the last units of the United Nations force were withdrawn, having turned over many of their installations and some of their equipment to the Leopoldville government. Beginning in October, 1962, the United States began a program of direct military aid to the Congolesse government without going through the UN. By mid-1964 this amounted to over six million dollars. Almost one hundred military personnel had been sent to train Congolese troops, and a dozen Congolese officers were receiving training at Fort Knox, Kentucky, in what the Defense Department called techniques for protecting "legally constituted governments against subversion and domestic disorder."[61] According to a report of the Brookings Institution, "two or three Americans recruited by the Central Intelligence Agency (CIA) reportedly flew combat missions in Kivu Province until they were grounded by the State Department. Under contract with the Congo Government, they had flown American-built T-28 fighters and attacked rebel positions near Bukavu."[62] When the Soviets objected to the use of American citizens for what they called "punitive operations against Congolese patriots," Cuban exiles were used instead.

In the spring of 1964 there broke out in the Congo three separate revolts. These were apparently coordinated by Gbenye but sparked mostly by three local organizers, each with a base of rural support: Pierre Mulele, Gaston Soumialot, and Nicolas Olenga. A Popular Liberation army was formed, and on August 4 rebel forces again captured Stanleyville.

With that victory behind them the rebels were able to recruit thousands of partisans, who were called *simbas* (lions). The rebel force was soon strong enough to confiscate UN trucks, together with considerable stocks of weapons and ammunition left by the retreating Congolese army. The rebel army spread out in many directions and succeeded in ending the central government's administration of Orientale province. The rebels were divided along factional and tribal lines. The earliest group to seize power in Stanleyville were extremists, and a wave of assassinations followed.

President Kasavubu decided that only Tshombe and the five hundred South African, Belgian, and other foreign mercenaries he controlled could save his government. The regular Congolese army was both inefficient and politically unreliable. So, although he was the symbol of treason for most black Africans, Tshombe was invited out of exile to become premier. He lost no time in launching an offensive into Kivu province.

As the mercenaries advanced on Stanleyville, the United States sought to use this new pressure on Gbenye to force him to negotiate an acceptable settlement with the Tshombe government. The rebels let it be known that they had over thirteen hundred foreigners in Stanleyville whom they intended to use as hostages. In Kenya Ambassador William Attwood tried to persuade President Kenyatta to intercede or mediate between the rebels and Tshombe. He also sought intervention on behalf of the Congolese government by the Organization of African Unity. Finally, he negotiated directly with Thomas Kanza, a representative of the Congolese rebels. "If you persist in helping Tshombe," the Congolese told Attwood, "the Algerians, the Egyptians and others will soon be in the Congo and you will regret it."[63] Gbenye agreed, however, to release the hostages if Tshombe agreed to stop bombing Stanleyville, but neither was willing to make the first move.

Early in November Gbenye arrested two hundred and eighty Belgians and sixteen U.S. citizens as "prisoners of war"[64] and declared war on the United States. Having earlier announced that Congo-Stanleyville was a "people's republic," he appealed for more help from the communist countries.

In his study of the rebellion, Professor M. Crawford Young, chairman of African studies at the University of Wisconsin, concludes that the "communist role in the Stanleyville rebellion was very small." Mulele had spent time in China and had studied guerrilla tactics and Maoist ideology, but there is no evidence, Young concludes, that he became a communist. Other rebel leaders had contact with Chinese representatives in their embassy in Burundi, but the Chinese, though they gave some aid, neither instigated nor controlled the events. Indeed the rebels, despite their radical rhetoric, had no revolutionary program whatever.

The United States had quite accurate information about the extent of Chinese and communist influence in the rebellion. What really alarmed them was the mounting wave of executions which the rebels conducted throughout their territory. In all, Professor Young estimates, as many as twenty thousand may have been killed in a few weeks, many of them after being publicly tortured. The State Department's humanitarian concerns were aroused only when it appeared that Americans and Europeans might be the next victims. But the earlier assassinations worried them for other reasons. It looked like the entire country was out of control and that the resulting chaos might be exploited by a communist power.

When Gbenye refused to release the American and Belgian hostages, the United States prepared to execute Operation Dragon Rouge, a drop from U.S. transport planes of five hundred and forty-five Belgian paratroopers to rescue the white civilians. The paratroopers were moved to Ascension Island and put on alert status. A few days later Stanleyville radio announced that a U.S. medical missionary, Paul Carlson, was in reality a spy and had been sentenced to death. On November 24, 1964, the paratroopers landed. They not only rescued the hostages (not including Carlson, who had been killed), but they seized the strategic points of the city and coordinated their operation with the advancing columns of Tshombe's mercenary army that was moving swiftly toward the city. The combination of the two Western forces armed with advanced weapons brought the downfall of the rebel government. It is likely that had Gbenye not taken U.S. hostages, the operation would not have been mounted. Once the humanitarian basis was laid, however, the para-

troopers' mission was to destroy the Stanleyville regime.
Ambassador Attwood has given a good account of the
African reaction to the stunning act of unilateral interven-
tion:

> We saw the Stanleyville rescue operation as a dra-
> matic effort to save hundreds of helpless, innocent
> people. It was humanitarian, and it was necessary,
> since all other attempts to release them had failed.
> And the operation had to take place before the ANC
> column entered the city, for the panicky Simbas would
> probably have mowed down the hostages before flee-
> ing from the mercenaries.

> But if you could put yourself in the shoes of an
> average educated African, you got a quite different
> picture. When he looked at the Congo, he saw a black
> government in Stanleyville being attacked by a gang
> of hired South African thugs, and black people being
> killed by rockets fired from American planes. He did
> not know about the thousands of blacks who were
> tortured and murdered by the Simbas, but he did know
> that the mercenaries and their Katangan auxiliaries
> left a trail of African corpses in their wake. (The
> orgy of looting and killing that followed the capture
> of Stanleyville by the ANC was so bad that the Belgian
> paratroop commander was glad to pull his men out
> of the city for fear they'd start fighting the mercen-
> aries.)

> Even more galling to the educated African was the
> shattering of so many of his illusions—that Africans
> were now masters of their own continent, that the
> OAU was a force to be reckoned with, that a black
> man with a gun was the equal of a white man with a
> gun. For in a matter of weeks, two hundred swag-
> gering white mercenaries had driven through an area
> the size of France, scattered the Belgians in American
> planes, had defied the OAU, jumped into the heart of
> Africa and taken out nearly two thousand people—
> with the loss of one trooper.

> The weakness and impotence of newly independent
> Africa had been harshly and dramatically revealed to
> the whole world and the educated African felt deeply

humiliated: the white man with a gun, the old plunderer who had enslaved his ancestors, was back again, doing what he pleased, when he pleased, where he pleased. And there wasn't a damn thing Africa could do about it, except yell rape.[65]

There is little doubt from Attwood's own account that had the United States ordered Tshombe to stop bombing Stanleyville, the U.S. and Belgian hostages would have been released. It is equally clear that the prime objective of U.S. policy in the Congo in 1964 was to bring down the Gbenye regime because of its reckless character and radical orientation. Unlike the other cases discussed in this chapter, Congo-Stanleyville, although it had earlier been recognized by a number of African and communist states, had an ambiguous status. It was not clearly a legitimate government that had come to power according to constitutional processes, as had Mossadeq, Arbenz, and Jagan. However, Kivu province had never been brought under the administration of the central government in Leopoldville. In fact, Gizenga and Gbenye had carried on administrative and governmental operations in Stanleyville and the surrounding area since 1960, an accomplishment which the Kasavubu government had never been able to equal. Although U.S. officials sought to justify the operation not only on the grounds of humanitarian necessity but also on the UN mandate, the overwhelming majority of black Africans who had approved of the suppression of Katanga were outraged at Operation Dragon Rouge.

The Congo was a unique experience because of the role of the United Nations force in the Katanga war and the use of a variety of non-American troops in the Stanleyville operation. But once again the criterion for intervention was traditional American fear of communism, for the Congo was another case, along with the Dominican Republic and British Guiana, of preemptive intervention to forestall the possibility of a local communist government.

As Attwood's account makes clear, United States officials were vigorous in lobbying the African states for support, but the State Department showed very little willingness to be guided by their wishes.

NOTES—CHAPTER TEN

1. Allen Dulles, quoted in Sanche de Gramont, *The Secret War* (New York, 1962), p. 24.

2. The involvement with the conspirators against Trujillo is discussed in Norman Gall, "How Trujillo Died," in *The New Republic*, April 13, 1961. Gall states that the CIA supplied arms to the Dominican assassins.

3. Mohammed Mossadeq, quoted in Anthony Eden, *Memoirs: Full Circle* (London, 1960), p. 194.

4. *Ibid.*, p. 202.

5. The hostility of Mossadeq to the communists is discussed in Manfred Halpern, "The Middle East and North Africa," in C. E. Black and T. P. Thornton, eds., *Communism and Revolution* (Princeton, 1964), pp. 316–319.

6. Quoted in Halpern, "The Middle East," p. 318.

7. Dwight D. Eisenhower, quoted in Robert Engler, *The Politics of Oil* (New York, 1957), p. 205.

8. Quoted in David Wise and Thomas B. Ross, *The Invisible Government* (New York, 1964), p. 110.

9. George C. Steward, quoted in Engler, *The Politics of Oil*, p. 206.

10. John Foster Dulles, quoted in *ibid.*, p. 209.

11. The bonuses to the Iranian police are discussed in Engler, *The Politics of Oil*, p. 206.

12. Hubert Humphrey, quoted in David Horowitz, *The Free World Colossus* (New York, 1965), p. 190.

13. The Shah of Iran has recently received considerable publicity for initiating reforms in his country. Undoubtedly some progress in land reform and illiteracy has been made. But for the view of one who participated in Iran's 1962–1967 Development Plan, see George B. Baldwin, *Planning and Development in Iran* (Baltimore, 1967), which describes "the unhappy condition of Iranian politics and administration."

14. Dwight D. Eisenhower, quoted in Wise and Ross, *The Invisible Government*, p. 166.

15. The account of the Ubico regime is based on Ronald Schneider, *Communism in Guatemala, 1944–1954* (New York, 1958), pp. 6–12.

16. Arevalo's attempts at reform and the reaction to it are discussed in *ibid.*, p. 21. See also C. Wright Mills, *Listen Yankee* (New York, 1960), p. 69.

17. Schneider's judgment of the Arevalo program is found in *Communism in Guatemala*, p. 21.

18. Arevalo's attack on Ambassador Patterson is reported in *The New York Times*, June 27, 1950.

19. UN Department of Economic and Social Affairs, *Foreign Capital in Latin America* (New York, 1955), p. 97.

20. For a discussion of expropriation and the U.S. State

Department reaction, see Philip B. Taylor, Jr., "The Guatemala Affair: A Critique of United States Foreign Policy," in *American Political Science Review*, September 1956, pp. 788, 791.

21. Spruille Braden, quoted in William Sloat, an unpublished manuscript "The Wind Must Blow Only in Our Sails," p. 10. See also John Gerassi, *The Great Fear in Latin America* (New York, 1965), p. 241.

22. U.S. Department of State, *Intervention of International Communism in Guatemala* (Washington, D.C., 1954), p. 69.

23. *Ibid.*, pp. 8–9.

24. See Schneider, *Communism in Guatemala*.

25. Miguel Ydigoras Fuentes, *My War with Communism* (New York, 1963), pp. 49, 50.

26. The admission of the U.S. fliers is discussed in Wise and Ross, *The Invisible Government*, p. 177n.

27. Dwight D. Eisenhower, quoted in *ibid.*, p. 167.

28. John Foster Dulles, quoted in the *New York Herald-Tribune*, July 1, 1954.

29. For accounts of policies of the Armas regime, see David Graham, "Liberated Guatemala," in *The Nation*, July 17, 1956.

30. Dwight D. Eisenhower, *Mandate for Change*, vol. I of *Memoirs* (New York, 1965), p. 426.

31. The official position on the Armas regime was summarized in the testimony of Ambassador John E. Peurifoy before the Subcommittee on Latin America, of the House Select Committee on Communist Aggression:

> In a six hour conversation he listened while I counted off the leading Communists in his regime, but he gave no ground; many notorious Reds he denied to be Communists; if they were, they were not dangerous; if dangerous, he could control them; if not controllable, he would round them up. He said, in any case, all our difficulties were due to the malpractices of American business. The trips of Communists to Russia were not to get training and instructions, he said, but merely to study Marxism, just in the same way as other Guatemalans may come to the United States to study economics. Meanwhile, they would continue to enjoy the full advantages accorded all Guatemalans, as they were valuable allies to him in the fight for social reform. . . . It seemed to me that the man thought like a Communist and talked like a Communist, and if not actually one, would do until one came along. I so reported to Secretary Dulles, who informed the President; and I expressed to them the view that unless the Communist influences in Guatemala were counteracted, Guatemala would within six months fall completely under Communist control.

This testimony is quoted in Eisenhower, *Memoirs*, vol. I, p. 422.

32. Quoted in Sukarno, *Autobiography* (as told to Cindy

Adams) (New York, 1965), p. 268. As the rebellion mounted the theme switched from separatism to anticommunism.

33. *Ibid.*

34. John Foster Dulles, quoted in *The New York Times*, April 2, 1958.

35. Dwight D. Eisenhower, quoted in *The New York Times*, May 1, 1958.

36. Allen Pope, quoted in Wise and Ross, *The Invisible Government*, p. 136. The account of the capture of Pope is found on pp. 136–146. For a discussion of the Indonesian civil war of 1958, see William Stevenson, *Birds' Nests in their Beards* (Boston, 1964).

37. Arthur Schlesinger, Jr., *A Thousand Days: John F. Kennedy in the White House* (Boston, 1965), p. 522.

38. Quoted in Cheddi Jagan, *The West on Trial* (London, 1966), p. 146.

39. John F. Kennedy, quoted in Schlesinger, *A Thousand Days*, p. 775.

40. *Ibid.*, p. 776.

41. John F. Kennedy, quoted in *ibid.*, p. 777.

42. John F. Kennedy, quoted in *ibid.*, p. 777.

43. Quoted in *ibid.*, p. 778.

44. The activities of the United States Information Service and the Christian Anti-Communist Crusade are described in Jagan, *The West on Trial*, p. 307.

45. Letter of Cheddi Jagan to President Kennedy, June 12, 1963, quoted in a report of the British police superintendent in British Guiana to the British Commissioner as revealed by members of Parliament in a parliamentary debate. See *Hansard*, May 4, 1966, col. 1767.

46. The activities of union officials in British Guiana are described in many sources. The identification of O'Keefe is made in Paul Jacobs, "American Unions and the CIA," in *Memorandum*, from the Center for the Study of Democratic Institutions, August 2, 1967, p. 22. See also Stanley Meisler, "Meddling in Latin America: The Dubious Role of the AFL-CIO," in *The Nation*, February 10, 1964, p. 134; Philip Reno, *The Ordeal of British Guiana* (New York, 1964); Sidney Lens, "Labor and the CIA," in *Progressive*, April 1967.

47. The account of the purposes and funding of the American Institute of Free Labor Development is based on Jacobs, "American Unions," p. 28.

48. Serafino Romualdi, quoted in Meisler, "Meddling in Latin America," p. 134.

49. The *Times*'s investigation is reported in Jacobs, "American Unions," p. 22.

50. Payments of strike benefits are discussed in Lens, "Labor and the CIA." See also Jagan, *The West on Trial;* Jacobs, "American Unions," p. 23.

51. *The New York Times*, February 22, 1967.

52. The inflammatory handbills are described in Jagan, *The West on Trial*, p. 281.

53. Report of Arthur Schlesinger, Jr., to President Kennedy, quoted in Schlesinger, *A Thousand Days*, p. 779.

54. *Ibid.*

55. Moise Tshombe, quoted in Jules Gerard-Libois, *Katanga Secession* (Madison, Wisc., 1966), p. 98.

56. Roger Hilsman, *To Move a Nation* (New York, 1967), p. 240.

57. Schlesinger, *A Thousand Days*, p. 577.

58. Hilsman, *To Move a Nation*, p. 266.

59. The Katanga war is described in Ernest LeFevre, *Crisis in the Congo: A United Nations Force in Action* (Washington, 1965); Jules Gerard-Libois, *Katanga Secession* (Madison, Wisc., 1966); Conor Cruise O'Brien, *To Katanga and Back: A United Nations Case History* (New York, 1962).

60. Antoine Gizenga, quoted in Fritz Schatten, *Communism in Africa* (New York, 1966), p. 211.

61. Quoted in LeFevre, *Crisis in the Congo*, p. 131.

62. Quoted in *ibid.*

63. Quoted in William Attwood, *The Reds and the Blacks: A Personal Adventure* (New York, 1967), p. 205.

64. For an account of the ordeal of the hostages, see David Reed, *111 Days in Stanleyville* (New York, 1965). Also see Crawford Young, "Significance of the 1964 Rebellion," in *Africa Report*, April 1965.

65. Attwood, *The Reds and the Blacks*, p. 218.

Part
THREE

CHAPTER **11**

Patterns of Intervention

One

AS THE CONFRONTATION between the United States and revolutionary movements has come into sharper focus, the euphemistic rhetoric of American Responsibility (defending freedom, self-determination, etc.) has yielded to the starker idiom of *realpolitik*. We are readier than we were a few years ago to concede that the far-flung bureaucracies we dispatch to Asia, Africa, and Latin America are less concerned with bringing the town meeting and the ballot box to their backward inhabitants than in making sure that they do not confiscate, collectivize, or chant communist slogans. The presence of a communist threat, even the *possibility* of a communist threat (as in the Dominican Republic), has supplied adequate justification for a variety of interventions. To identify the threat has been enough to preclude any further challenge to the necessity or morality of its suppression. In such cases the only questions left open for debate have been the existence of the threat: Were the fifty-three Dominican communists on the State Department list really behind the revolution?—and the propriety of the means for dealing with it: Is military repression the best way to reach the hearts and minds of the people?

The United States has become increasingly outspoken in

claiming the unilateral right to make the determination whether a conflict anywhere in the world constitutes a threat to its national security or international order and what should be done about it. Only those states "with enough will and enough resources to see to it that others do not violate" the rules of international law, Secretary of State Rusk has declared, are the ones to be entrusted with enforcing the peace. When he was under secretary of state, George Ball suggested that such responsibility "may in today's world be possible . . . only for nations such as the United States which command resources on a scale adequate to the requirements of leadership in the twentieth century."[1] In other words, power is the basis of legitimacy. Conceding that the "world community" has not granted the United States the warrant to police the world in any legal sense—the United Nations Charter gives the Security Council the primary responsibility for dealing with threats to the peace—those in charge of United States national-security policy nonetheless assert that because of the deep divisions in the United Nations, which render that organization immobile, the United States must act alone. John Foster Dulles recognized that "most of the countries of the world" did not share his ideological view of international politics—"the view that communist control of any government anywhere is in itself a danger and a threat." Pointing out that it was not difficult "to marshal world opinion against aggression," he noted in the midst of the 1954 Indochina crisis that "it is quite another matter to fight against internal changes in one country. If we take a position against a communist faction within a foreign country we have to act alone." His brother, Allen, formerly director of the Central Intelligence Agency, candidly stated the unilateral criteria by which the United States decides whether or not to intervene in a civil war:

. . . we cannot safely limit our response to the Communist strategy of take-over solely to those cases where we are invited in by a government still in power, or even to instances where a threatened country has first exhausted its own, possibly meager, resources in the "good fight" against Communism. We ourselves must determine when and how to act, hopefully with the support of other leading Free World countries who may be in a position to help, keeping in mind the requirements of our own national security.[2]

There is nothing exceptional about powerful countries asserting the imperial prerogative of using force and coercion on the territory of another without its consent. The Athenian Empire minced no words about this. "The strong do what they can and the weak do what they must," the Athenian general reminded the Melians. Empire is its own justification, the fifteenth-century Italian humanist Lorenzo Valla advised his prince. The expansion of a nation's power comes through "mere violence," but this should not dismay a conscientious leader, his contemporary Poggio Bracciolini observed, for has it not always been "the most powerful empires, such as Athens, which promoted letters and learning?"[3] Most empires have claimed the right to control the politics of other peoples in the name of a great idea. Athens offered protection and civilization, Rome the blessings of the law, Britain enlightenment of savages, and so on. Once having assumed "responsibility" for other countries, imperial bureaucracies feel as Pericles did, that "it is not safe to let it go."

The United Nations Charter rests on the principle that the preservation of peace and the protection of national security is a matter for multilateral decision. The community of nations is supposed to decide what action to take to meet threats to the peace. In a bow to realism, the framers of the Charter vested the primary "community" responsibility in the hands of the Big Powers, who were given permanent seats on the Security Council. Adlai Stevenson remarked shortly before his death that it was time "to decide whether we're going to be international and multilateral or not."[4] He was alluding to the fact that despite the rhetorical commitment to multilateralism the United States was more and more making the great decisions alone. No other country or international organization was consulted over the Kennedy administration decision to force a nuclear confrontation over the Cuban missile crisis or the Johnson administration decision to send a huge expeditionary force to Vietnam and to subject that country to daily aerial bombardment. The State Department has been sensitive to the charges of unilateralism and has tried to deal with them in two ways. One is by asserting that since the criminal elements in world politics make the operation of a true multilateral structure impossible, the United States, by vigorously opposing them, is actually working to build a true "world of diversity." As Secretary of State Rusk put it, "Once we remove this kind of aggression, as we are trying to do in Vietnam, the human race can perhaps look forward to peace, to the solution of lesser problems, and to the benefits deriving from the conquest of science."[5] This is the image of a surgeon removing a cancer. The operation, President Johnson hinted in his more optimistic moments, can be completed "in this generation." Once the enemies of freedom are defeated, then the United States can perhaps share some of its police responsibilities with others.

The second way the United States has tried to deal with charges of unilateralism has been increased reliance on nominal or subservient multilateral organizations such as the Inter-American Force for the Dominican Republic, which was called into being at the initiative of the United States and was always under its operational direction. Where the United States is a member of a regional organization which excludes another Great Power, that organization, simply because of the overwhelming might of the United States, inevitably becomes its instrument. The essential difference between the Organization of American States and the United Nations is that the latter organization contains some nations that are economically and politically independent of the United States.

Behind the speeches and diplomatic maneuverings to soothe "world opinion," the architects of U.S. foreign policy have developed a rationale to justify global intervention which frankly recognizes that the American Responsibility to police the world is inconsistent with the multilateralism of the United Nations Charter and the dictates of traditional international law. Anthony Eden recalls that when John Foster Dulles warned the British foreign secretary in 1954 that he would stop British vessels on the high seas to prevent any arms shipments to Guatemala, he observed that the United States was prepared to take "whatever action was necessary, whatever the law might be,"[6] and went on to remark that "in the cold war conditions of today, the rules applicable in the past no longer seemed to him to meet the situation and required to be revised or flexibly applied." The Johnson

Doctrine, which denies the validity of the distinction between civil wars and international wars, and the State
Department's "modern" view of the doctrine of nonintervention are more recent additions to official legal revision-
ism.

Two

        The ideology of the American Responsibility rests
on a fundamental assumption concerning American self-
interest. The only alternative to a Pax Americana is a Pax
Sovietica or the Peace of Peking. The most powerful
nation in the world has always dominated the rest. The
only question is which one will emerge on top. Comforted
by Talleyrand's fashionable aphorism about nonintervention—"a metaphysical term which means about the same
as intervention"—the National-Security Manager concludes that the fate of the powerful is to dominate, whether they wish to do so or not. There is much to this
observation. If the United States never sent a soldier or an
aid dollar beyond her shores, it would still wield enormous
power over other nations, particularly in the Third World,
by virtue of the fact that it is the world's biggest custom-
er. The power to cut off imports from a one-crop country
is as effective an instrument of control as occupying its
capital. The United States has the dominant voice in the
World Bank and the International Monetary Fund, and
private United States financial interests control much of
the world money market. Countries struggling to indus-
trialize are heavily dependent upon U.S. machinery. Most
of the state-owned airlines of the world, to take one
example, fly American equipment and are dependent upon
U.S. corporations for servicing and replacement.
        But beyond the operation of what is still termed the
"private market," despite the considerable involvement of
the government in these activities, is the panoply of techniques available to the national-security bureaucracy to

influence the political behavior of other countries. In many countries of the world the United States is the sole supplier of the army, the primary source of training for its officers, and the educator and supplier of its police force. In addition, through its aid program the United States is likely to have conceived and staffed the educational system and to be the dominant voice in its agricultural development, the organizer of its labor movement, and the decisive influence in setting the national priorities for economic development. U.S. views, private and official, predominate as a consequence of Voice of America, the armed-forces radio and television stations, which are widely distributed, and the increasingly wide circulation of U.S. periodicals. Many of the individuals who provide these services do so with generous intentions, but the effect of their efforts is to give the United States a supreme voice in the internal affairs of many other countries. And that, as a succession of secretaries of state have promised Congress, is their primary purpose. Desmond Fitzgerald, formerly a high official of the International Cooperation Administration (predecessor of AID), who later directed covert operations for the CIA, put it this way:

> A lot of criticism of foreign aid is because the critic thought the objective was to get economic growth, and this wasn't the objective at all. . . . The objective may have been to buy a lease or to get a favorable vote in the UN, or to keep a nation from falling apart, or to keep some country from giving the Russians airbase rights or any one of many other reasons.[7]

In a small country like the Dominican Republic, or even a larger one with a fairly primitive political structure and a large contingent of American officials like Ethiopia, the U.S. Embassy is inevitably the center of power in the country, if only because its capacity to control communications and intelligence is so far superior to that of the native government. In Ethiopia, the United States dramatized this fact by returning the emperor to his kingdom (he had been deposed in a military coup while on a foreign visit) in a U.S. airforce plane. John Bartlow Martin's account of his activities in the Dominican Republic, on which I have leaned heavily in my discussion of the Dominican intervention, suggests that even before the arrival of Marines, the American ambassador was more a proconsul than an envoy.

These facts of international life are cited by the proponents of an interventionary foreign policy as proving the inevitability of the unilateral use of force for "peacekeeping," i.e., police purposes. The United States is so deeply involved anyway in the use of coercive techniques to influence political behavior that the overt use of force, regrettable as it is, is merely a difference in degree, not in kind. If the United States were not prepared to use violence to deal with internal political problems in other countries when it conceives that its own national interests warrant it, its chief rivals would sponsor violence to their own advantage. In short, the prevailing official view is that there is no way for a great country to relate to a small one other than as manipulator or exploiter.

History appears to support this view. All the pressures of contemporary politics seem to push great nations into familiar imperial patterns. Indeed, when the United States adopted the policy embodied in the Truman Doctrine, State Department officials quite consciously saw themselves as inheritors of Britain's imperial responsibilities, which, they assumed, they would exercise more wisely and more humanely. As a State Department publicity release would put it years later, "Strict adherence to our ideals requires us to face the challenge of reshaping the world in the image of human dignity, political freedom, and authority by consent, not decree."[8] Like their models in Whitehall, the National-Security Managers too assumed that if America could bring order to the world as a consequence of amassing an empire, that was not a bad bargain for the rest of mankind.

Thus, despite the rhetorical hopes for collective security and community responsibility which U.S. officials voice in speeches before the United Nations, back in their own offices they see no better alternative model for world order than the imperial model, to be constructed, hopefully, with as light a touch as possible. It is not surprising that they should come to this conclusion. The very nature of the nation-state, their oath of office, and their primary allegiance as well as the pressures of Congress and their superiors all require the National-Security Manager to serve the national interest, as the military, the corporations, the farmers, and the labor unions see it, rather than an abstract "world community" or so altruistic a goal as removing the grossest inequalities among the developed and undeveloped nations. He is quite free to think about a world-security system as long as he does not compromise the power of the joint chiefs of staff to decide where the forces should be deployed, what weapons should be used, and when. He is encouraged to develop an aid program, provided U.S. business benefits adequately and he can convince Congress that the United States has recieved sound value in influence, business concessions, or political support. Above all, he must not be so indiscreet as to sponsor a "giveaway." The pressures of various interest groups within the United States for an imperialist relationship are enormous, but one should not ignore the role of the bureaucracy itself. It is an exhilarating experience for a GS-14 to run the police force, lecture the minister of the interior, or reform the agriculture of a little country. Many Americans have found an outlet for social and political experimentation on new frontiers abroad that is denied them at home. Since the overseas bureaucracy totals some two to four million individuals, it constitutes in itself an impressive group with a vested interest in keeping the mechanics of foreign relations much as they are.[9] This means retaining control of vital decisions concerning a country's policies on defense and economic development in American hands.

Three

Unilateralism is a more polite and perhaps less image-rich term than imperialism, which not only evokes memories of Lord Clive, Cecil Rhodes, and the French Foreign Legion but also has become saddled with Lenin's particular theories of economic causation. But they mean essentially the same thing—"the extension of control" by a single nation. Unilateralism is so much taken for granted within the national-security bureaucracy that when critics point out the discrepancy between our professed political and legal ideals as embodied in the United Nations Charter and our actual behavior as a nation, it makes very little impression. What's wrong with imperialism or unilateralism? Is there anything better?

There are two ways of trying to answer the first question. One is to look at unilateralism from the point of view of U.S. national interests. The second is to consider it from what might be called a "world-order" perspective, looking specifically toward the development of a strong legal and constitutional structure for dealing with war, hunger, disease, and other overriding global problems. I recognize that the two categories are not wholly distinct, that there are few objective criteria for determining national interests, and that a sensible government in the nuclear age would have as a primary "national interest" the development of a good system for "world order." But the categories are useful for distinguishing the most short-range and parochial considerations from longer-range perspectives.

From the standpoint of a President of the United States, thinking about reelection, concerned with solving domestic problems, and assuring himself a decent place in history, unilateralism is proving to be a disastrous policy. C. E. Black in *The Dynamics of Modernization* estimates that we must anticipate "ten to fifteen revolutions a year for the foreseeable future in the less developed societies."[10] The suppression of a single revolutionary movement in Vietnam, admittedly a long-developing and powerful one, costs the U.S. Treasury almost forty billion dollars a year, results in almost ten thousand battle deaths annually, and has stirred up political dissension unprecedented in our history. The attempt of one nation to deal simultaneously with insurgent movements in a dozen other places and to forestall still others in a variety of backward countries on three continents would tax the intellectual and political energies of the government to the breaking point.

One of the problems with imperialism is that as decision-making authority becomes centralized, the burdens on the imperialist leaders become intolerable, for along with the trappings of added power come political headaches. The Founding Fathers wisely spared the President of the United States the burden of appointing state and local officials. I suspect that they would be appalled to discover that he must now regularly pass on the qualifications of provincial governors in South Vietnam and ministers of agriculture in the Dominican Republic. There is literally no country in which the foreign-policy bureaucracy cannot discover a "U.S. interest," and since the President has at his disposal an almost infinite variety of techniques for furthering those interests, he is constantly called upon to exercise his judgment. Having no firsthand knowledge of the politics of the countries he is asked to set on one course or another, this imposes something of a strain on him. As Telford Taylor puts it, "the road to everywhere leads nowhere." The President faces a familiar problem of empire. Having asserted an interest in a faraway land, he is expected to be able to control events there. In fact, as the biographies of the commitments examined in this book reveal, the events begin to control him. Once military forces are committed, for example, it is usually impossible to limit the objectives to those which originally impelled the intervention. The commitment of national power unleashes political forces both in the country concerned and in the United States which then severely limit future choices.

The essence of unilaterialism is that you recognize no limits except those of your own making. Such enlargement of the area of political discretion invites miscalculation and error. One of the functions of legal limits in a society is to provide external standards to relieve men of the responsibility to decide every issue anew. Sharing responsibility for decision with others who are also affected by it, the essence of democratic theory, is another old political device for rescuing human leaders from the dangers of distorted vision, a disability that always afflicts those who exercise power despotically. The possession of great power is not, as Secretary of State Rusk and others have suggested, a justification for using it unilaterally. It is, rather, a condition, as the framers of the U.S. Constitution recognized, which cries out for legal restraints to protect the community from tyranny and the possessor from his own hubris.

The assertion of a police responsibility to prevent violent revolution and insurgency inevitably requires a militarization of a nation's foreign policy. *Webster's International Dictionary* uses the terms "militarism" and "imperialism" interchangeably, and this makes good political as well as linguistic sense, since no nation, no matter how great its economic and political resources, can hope to maintain control of events in distant lands without eventually relying chiefly on force. We have seen how, in Greece, for example, and later in Vietnam, nonmilitary strategies of "counterinsurgency" were swallowed up in the military effort. If the United States sets as a goal the prevention of regimes in the Third World which call themselves communist or which seem to lean to communism, it must be prepared to fight for that goal with its military power.

The result of such a decision, and it is one that was made a long time ago, is to make the United States Number One Enemy of a great number of people. State Department officials are privately scornful about foreign-policy criticism based on the argument that "world opinion" is turning against us. They point out, rightly, that no one knows what that means or how to measure it. The United States, however, is very much interested in those leaders of the Third World who are convinced that only radical change can rescue their societies from political tyranny and economic stagnation. Such leaders, who are coming increasingly to see violence as the only avenue of change, are being drawn together only by their common fear and hatred of the United States. American foreign policy is providing what Marxism-Leninism has failed to offer revolutionary movements—an ideological bond to tie together nationalist revolutionary movements spread across three continents. These movements originate in the local political soil. They are primarily concerned with local issues and local enemies. But the leaders of insurgent movements are establishing international links and are attempting to help one another, despite their limited resources. They do this not because of shared ideological goals so much as because of the belief that they are partisans in the same war. What gives unity to the struggle in their analysis is "imperialism," which means chiefly the United States. To be able to characterize the enemy in an insurgent struggle as a giant White Imperialist Power helps to bring nationalists of all classes into the revolutionary coalition. Juan Bosch exaggerated only slightly when he declared that where there were fifty-three communists in the Dominican Republic before the intervention, there were now fifty-three thousand.

Nationalism and anti-imperialism are such strong forces

that only those politicians, businessmen, and generals who
benefit directly and personally from the American
presence in their country can be counted on to oppose
nationalist movements. Such movements may start, as we
have seen, with the efforts of a few energetic individuals.
A small minority always takes the lead. But the nationalist
impulse runs through the societies of the Third World. If
the United States continues to make it a policy to oppose
nationalism wherever it is entwined with a radical political
and economic program or with communist rhetoric, it
must count on being hated and feared by political leaders,
who will increasingly come to speak for a majority of the
world population. It must be prepared to pay heavily to
keep the loyalty of its clients. Pericles warned the people
of Athens that the fate of greatness was to be hated and
feared, and some of the same philosophy prevails today in
the corridors of the State Department. Yet even the most
powerful country in the world takes a reckless view of
national security if it ignores repeated historical patterns.
As Walter Lippmann has pointed out, where one nation
arrogates to itself the responsibility to shape a world
order, it invites others to combine against it. In a world
where nuclear weapons will, in all likelihood, be widely
distributed before the end of the century, this is not a
reassuring road to national security for the American
people.

Four

Now let us examine the policy of the American
Responsibility—suppressing revolution—from the point of
view of the world community. Assume that the two overriding minimum requirements of world order are, first, the
prevention of nuclear war and such lesser violence as
threatens to lead to nuclear war; and second, the creation
of economic and political conditions in the southern half
of the globe which can support human life there. The
portion of the earth where the per-capita income is less

than two hundred dollars a year is literally a giant death camp. It is possible to make reasonably accurate projections of the numbers of people within the Southern Hemisphere who are condemned to die from starvation and disease. If predictions of the growing disparity between population and resources are even substantially correct, the toll in lives that will be sacrificed by the end of the century must be reckoned in the tens of millions.

"I think what you are saying," Senator Vandenberg suggested to Secretary Acheson in an attempt to sum up the import of the Truman Doctrine, "is that whenever we find free peoples having difficulty in the maintenance of free institutions, and difficulty in defending against aggressive movements that seek to impose upon them totalitarian regimes, we do not necessarily react in the same way each time, but we propose to react." "That," Acheson replied, "I think is correct." The kind of reaction which the United States has contemplated has brought the world to the brink of nuclear war at least twice. (President Eisenhower reports that the use of nuclear weapons was seriously considered in Korea in 1953 and in Indochina in 1954.) The Marines who landed in Lebanon in 1958 brought atomic howitzers with them. Had they been faced by a hostile army rather than Coca-Cola salesmen, as happily turned out to be the case, the situation would have been incredibly dangerous. In the Vietnam war, W. W. Rostow has wondered out loud how to make nuclear weapons "relevant" to the conflict.[11] There is no doubt that the chief of staff of the air force thinks he has an answer. The only successful strategy for suppressing a "war of national liberation" so far discovered has been a military strategy. (This does not mean that, as in the Philippines, nonmilitary techniques such as pacification and reform are not also used, but that the crucial element in the victory was the application of overwhelming military power.) Nor, as Vietnam suggests, does it mean that the military strategy always works. The only decisive victories over insurgents have been in Greece, Malaya, and the Philippines, and these are attributable to a combination of internal political dissension in the ranks of the insurgents combined with a military superiority of at least ten to one in the antiguerrilla army. (In the Philippines, at least, the final chapter of the revolt has yet to be written. Guerrilla activity by the Huks has increased in recent years.)

The commitment to suppress an insurgency, particularly if it is a stubborn one, leads, as we have seen in Vietnam, to a rapid rise in the level of violence. It also exerts pressure on those powers who claim to support wars of national liberation to back their rhetoric with their guns and rockets. The most plausible spark for a nuclear war (outside of Germany) is some future Haiphong (or perhaps Haiphong itself), where the giants are led by their respective clients into a direct confrontation.

There is also a world-order interest in limiting violence short of nuclear war. One consequence of a massive military intervention by a great country in a small one is that it destroys the people it is claiming to liberate. The lethal technology of the United States is so advanced and the welfare of the client population so secondary a consideration compared with winning the war that the "defense of freedom" actually requires making a desert of a primitive society. Since many of the societies facing insurgencies are living just above the subsistence level anyway, the scorched-earth strategy for dealing with the problem—destroying villages, wholesale removel of populations, destruction of crops—is particularly cruel, for it pushes poor countries further down into the depths of misery.

Five

There are two principal arguments advanced in support of the policy of U.S. intervention in civil wars and insurgencies which purport to rest on broad world-community interests rather than narrow nationalistic considerations. One is that the United States is defending "freedom" against "totalitarianism." If this is the policy, it is applied with something less than consistency. Many of the free governments that have received either generous U.S. military aid, friendly nods from the U.S. Embassy, or direct military intervention in their behalf constitute a group that on the whole is rather careless about civil liberties—Formosa, Korea, South Vietnam, Iran, Brazil,

Paraguay, etc. Actually, a very substantial portion of U.S. aid has gone to a series of military dictatorships located at the periphery of Russia and China.[12]

Nor has the test of U.S. concern been the violent character of a government's accession to power. Military coups which seize power from constitutional regimes are consistently recognized and supported, and on occasion (Brazil in 1964, for example) encouraged. Here are a few examples of military takeovers which the United States did not oppose (and in most cases welcomed): Argentina (1955), Turkey (1960), South Korea (1961), Burma (1962), Indonesia (1966), Ghana (1966). In recent years the trend of military takeovers has continued. In Latin America some military regimes such as Peru are becoming nationalistic and seeking to restrict foreign investment; others, as in Brazil welcome it; U.S. policy is notably warmer to the latter. The degree of internal violence or repression of the regime makes no perceptible difference. Thus the legally elected leftist government of Salvador Allende Gossens in Chile has been subjected to economic pressure by the Nixon administration while the military government of Yahya Khan in Pakistan, responsible for murdering thousands of Bengali civilians and driving millions more from their homes, was supported in its effort to crush the Bangla Desh independence movement.

The defense of the "free world" has not even resulted in a consistent anticommunist policy. In the area under the direct control of the Soviet Union and China, United States involvement has been circumspect. After the State Department lost the diplomatic battle at the close of World War II to retain some Western influence in Eastern Europe, the United States did not take military measures to oppose the communist coup in Czechoslovakia in 1948 or to aid anti-Soviet insurgent movements, including the Berlin uprising of 1953, the Poznan riots, and the Hungarian Revolution. Low-level covert operations were conducted against the Eastern European regimes from 1946 into the 1960's, including espionage and U-2 overflights, as well as subversive propaganda over Radio Free Europe and Radio Liberation. But the rhetorical goal of "liberation" was proclaimed by Dulles only after the actual attempt to roll back Soviet power in Eastern Europe had been abandoned. With respect to China, the United States has given the Taiwan government two billion dollars with which to equip its six-hundred-thousand-man army and has put U-2 aircraft at its disposal for overflights of the mainland; but the United States since the failure of the intervention in Vietnam is now belatedly prepared to recognize the 1949 revolution in China (and even the 1917 revolution in Russia).

While most United States support has gone to right-wing dictatorships, the United States has since the late 1950's been attempting to modernize its strategy of intervention. The Truman administration and the Eisenhower administration in its first term had given wholehearted support to "legitimate" governments if they were noncommunist and friendly to the United States, no matter how oppressive or reactionary they might be. (In 1952 the United States did aid a leftist revolutionary regime in Bolivia which earned American support by lowering the price of tin and adopting a properly anti-Soviet foreign policy.) President Eisenhower symbolized U.S. willingness to support reaction in Latin America by inviting Perez Jiménez, the brutal dictator of Venezuela, to Washington and awarding him the Medal of Merit. But a few years later American intelligence agencies and private groups acting in their behalf began to support more liberal and even leftist elements in Latin America and Africa. The Central Intelligence Agency gave funds for the support of institutions like the Inter-American Center of Economic and Social Studies and the Institute for International Labor Research in the Dominican Republic and the Institute of Political Education in Costa Rica. These institutions train, finance, and encourage political groups which often oppose their own governments for being too conservative and are also critical of official U.S. policy in Latin America but are anticommunist. It appears that resistance leaders from Mozambique and South Africa have been offered covert assistance by the CIA and in certain cases have received it. In Algeria the AFL-CIO, acting for the CIA, gave direct financial assistance to the National Liberation Front from 1957 until the successful end of the War of Independence. The American labor organization sponsored the Algerian rebels in international labor circles and arranged for membership of the FLN union in the ICFTU, the U.S.-dominated world federation of trade unions. The National Student Association, an ostensibly private organization, distributed CIA funds to Algerian resistance leaders in the form of scholarships. The operation in Algeria in support of the rebels was designed to discourage them from turning to communist countries for help. At the same time, the U.S. State Department, still officially supporting France, continued to sanction military aid for use against the FLN.[13]

The shock of the Vietnam War has compelled changes in interventionist strategy. The official lessons of this searing national experience are embodied in the "Nixon Doctrine" around which a new foreign policy consensus seems to be forming. The Nixon Doctrine proclaims the end of the era of indiscriminate American "world responsibility." The United States will "lower its profile" by encouraging "indigenous" troops to fight each other with American weapons or, where possible, by resorting to automated war through the technology of the "electronic battlefield." The goal is to preserve American positions in the world through more judicious management of military power without involving the American people in an interminable, ambiguous war in which large numbers of Americans continue to get killed week after week.

The new strategy is the product of the belated recognition of the costs of empire. The United States has been seriously weakened in a number of ways by its national security policy. Money and energy diverted from the domestic economy to the arms race has made it impossible to confront crises of health, nutrition, housing, transportation, and the environment. The failure to solve pressing domestic problems that are tearing at American society has made Americans increasingly insecure at home without purchasing any added protection from abroad. The costs of empire include uncontrollable inflation, decline in real wages, deterioration of domestic industry, mounting unemployment, and, of course, the balance of payments crisis. America's heavy industry, mobilized for military production, is no longer able to compete with foreign nations for civilian markets, including the American market. Ironically, the quest for an empire which was supposed to expand American influence has left the American economy more and more vulnerable to the decisions of foreigners. Those who hold the American dollars and the American gold that have been poured out to support the empire are now in a position to exert control over jobs, prices, and interest rates in the United States or else force the United States into extreme economic isolation. By the standards of *realpolitik* America's imperial overreach has resulted in a real loss of power.

Because the managers of American foreign policy have been made aware of these realities, the rules of the game are indeed changing. The Nixon administration now appears to favor a neo-Metternichean vision of shared responsibility. The setting for the "era of negotiation," as Henry Kissinger sees it, is a world of multiple superpowers—at least three, the U.S., the U.S.S.R., and China. Formal and informal agreements to recognize "primary responsibility" for each in its own area of the world, i.e., spheres of influence, will now be negotiated regardless of the intensity of conflicts over ideology. Limited arms agreements will be sought. The Administration will follow its own advice and speak more softly in the world, all the while following "America first" economic policies. But the attempt to maintain control over the internal politics and economic development of weak countries will continue. The United States has not abandoned the efforts to maintain a global system of dependent states known as the "free world." But U.S. officials are now concerned that use of military and paramilitary power must be more sparing and more subtle.

Six

United States officials claim, and apparently believe, that the United States is somehow acting in the interest of the international community by undertaking a worldwide campaign against revolution. In the past the argument has been that by stamping out insurgent movements the United States is preventing World War III. With his eyes firmly fixed on the shore he has left, to quote De Tocqueville's phrase, the National-Security Manager is trying to squeeze the baffling chaos of postwar revolution into the familiar mold of Great Power politics as practiced in the 1930's. Ho Chi Minh becomes Hitler. Vietnam is the Rhineland. Negotiation is Munich. If the insurgents are not stopped in Vietnam, they will have to be stopped eventually in San Francisco.

President Kennedy's speech to the American people after his encounter with Khrushchev in Vienna is a good example of this official thought process:

[Khrushchev] was certain that the tide was moving his way, that the revolution of rising people would eventually be a communist revolution, and that the so-called wars of national liberation supported by the Kremlin would replace the old methods of direct aggression and invasion. In the 1940's and early 50's the great danger was from communist armies marching across free borders, which we saw in Korea . . . now we face a new and different threat. We no longer have a nuclear monopoly. Their missiles, they believe, will hold off our missiles, and their troops can match our troops should we intervene in the so-called wars of liberation. Thus, the local conflicts they support can turn in their favor through guerrillas, or insurgents, or subversion. . . .[14]

The essence of the argument is that guerrillas in Vietnam, Thailand, Peru, Guatemala, and Angola are all part of the same army. If the army can be defeated in Vietnam, it will not be necessary to fight it in Thailand or the Philippines. If the insurgencies are not opposed, that will demonstrate a lack of resolve, just as Munich did, and eventually the guerrillas will challenge the United States directly and then we will have to fight World War III to defend our homes and honor. The assumption that insurgencies are inspired by outside powers or that they are orchestrated by some central authority is, as I have tried to show in Part One, false. The defeat of the Vietcong will not mean that the insurgents in Thailand will surrender. Nor will a guerrilla victory in Vietnam insure a guerrilla victory in Thailand. True, revolutionary successes will encourage insurgents elsewhere. More important, it will demonstrate to governments whose survival depends upon U.S. military aid to rule their discontented populations that since the United States cannot keep its commitments to them, their days are numbered unless they can learn to govern.

Why, however, the overthrow of corrupt feudal regimes by local insurgents should pose a danger of world war or a direct military threat to the United States is hard to see. The danger of world war arises only if the United States is committed to resisting revolution by force and is prepared to "pay any price" to do it, and then only if another major power is prepared to stand in the way. Even if we assume a wave of successful revolutions throughout Asia, Africa, and Latin America, the notion that the Castros of the future will muster an army of millions, transport them by sampan and burro, and loose them on our cities is nothing less than a psychotic fantasy, so absurd in fact that it is never explicitly stated, only hinted at in vague anxiety-producing historical analogies. (What is so sad about being ruled by such fantasies is that the diversion of money and energy to the fight which is supposed to keep Asian communists from landing on our shores helps perpetuate the conditions which have created native insurgents and guerrilla warfare in American cities.)

Thus the means which the United States has chosen to deal with the phenomenon of revolution make war more likely rather than less. The idea of preventive war, that you fight a little one now to avoid a great one later, has some validity if you are facing a single adversary such as Hitler. Where there are many adversaries, each with its own local reasons for fighting, the idea can be understood only as an exercise in mysticism, not logic. In short, the arrogation by a single power of the policeman's warrant is not a solution to the problem of war.

Nor is the suppression of revolution an answer to the problem of development, the second overriding concern of the world community. The official State Department conception of driving out "bad" communist development with "good" democratic capitalist development is revealed as allegory rather than history in most of the world by a mountain of UN and world bank documents, which shows that there is no development in much of the world. By all standard tests—capital, literacy, rise in productive capacity—things are getting worse. Even in countries such as Brazil, which manifests an extraordinary growth rate, the benefits are felt only by a few. Most of the population is rural and effectively out of the money economy. "It must be said aloud," Robert Heilbroner has written, "that our present policy prefers the absence of development to the chance for Communism—which is to say that we prefer hunger and want and the existing inadequate assaults against the causes of hunger and want to any regime that declares its hostility to capitalism."[15]

Development, as C. E. Black has argued, requires the

modernization of economic, political, and social structure. A facade of modernization that creates a small middle class, an enclave of a consumer economy in the midst of peasant backwardness, or a few examples of imported technology such as jet aircraft, will not bring about the pervasive change that is needed. "When we speak of the revolutionary nature of economic development," Heilbronner writes, "it is this kind of deeply penetrative change that we mean—change that reorganizes 'normal' ways of thought, established patterns of family life, and structures of village authority as well as class and caste privilege."[16] Communist revolutions in China, Cuba, Vietnam, and Russia have, on the other hand, succeeded in mobilizing and transforming peasant masses who elsewhere in backward societies have been immovable. That the methods used have been brutal, that injustice has resulted, that, in Stalinist Russia, but apparently nowhere else, the official repression of the peasantry reached genocidal proportions, is undeniable. Nor is the economic balance sheet for the communist countries yet complete. It appears that starvation in China, which was very widespread, has been largely eliminated—even in the agricultural crisis of the late 1950's. During the first decade of the Chinese revolution, Mao's regime succeeded in creating the image, in Alexander Eckstein's words, "of a vigorous, dynamic and rapidly growing economy with some singular accomplishments to its credit,"[17] including the restoration of the war-damaged economy, control of inflation, land redistribution, and rapid industrial growth. Since 1958 the problems of the communist regime in China have been revealed to be serious. Nonetheless, it is a fact that communism has produced profound change in a decade, whereas the process of modernization in a noncommunist country like India is mired in obsolete institutions, crippling traditions, and political malaise. In Cuba, too, for all of its problems, the government has succeeded in communicating a sense of urgency to the people as well as the feeling that the sacrifices demanded are for their own benefit, not for foreigners or their own upper classes.[18] Heilbroner has summarized the positive impact of communism as an agent of modernization in these words:

Hundreds of millions who would have been confined to narrow cells of changeless lives have been liberated from prisons they did not even know existed.

Class structures that elevated the flighty or irresponsible have been supplanted by others that have promoted the ambitious and dedicated. Economic systems that gave rise to luxury and poverty have given way to systems that provide a rough distributional justice. Above all, the prospect of a new future has been opened. It is this that lifts the current ordeal in China above the level of pure horror.[19]

Barrington Moore's study of peasant revolutions reaches the conclusion that "the costs of moderation [i.e., gradual and piecemeal reform] have been at least as atrocious as those of revolution, perhaps a great deal more." The consequences of modernization without a social revolution, as in Germany, he contends, have been fascism and aggressive war. If he is right, this is a cost of suppressing revolution which must be reckoned in the millions. Moore points out, however, that these conclusions do not point to the moral superiority of revolution. "Communism as a set of ideas and institutions cannot escape responsibility for Stalinism. In general, one of the most revolting features of revolutionary dictatorships has been their use of terror against little people who were as much victims of the old order as were the revolutionaries themselves, often more so."[20]

So the making of a moral calculus of the costs and benefits of alternative paths to development turns out to be a far more complicated task than one gathers from State Department White Papers and speeches to the American Legion—or from the *Peking Review*. Revolutions kill the innocent (along with the not so innocent), but "the prevailing order of society always grinds out its tragic toll of unnecessary death year after year." And in all probability it is a far larger toll.

The point of these reflections is not that Americans must "stand up and be counted," as Dulles used to say, as either revolutionaries or counterrevolutionaries. It is, rather, that the processes of change in the Third World have so far escaped our present modes of analysis, much less our techniques of control. It is not only that the national-security bureaucracy lacks the power to make revolutionary developments around the world conform to an American model, although this is true, but that it lacks the wisdom to play God to other societies. Communism, it may well turn out, does not have an answer to the problems of development, but it is clear that America has neither the incentives nor the capacity to solve them for the benefit of the other countries. Communist approaches to development have at times been dogmatic, wildly impractical, and capriciously punitive. But, in the final analysis, the failure of communism in other countries is their problem. The failure of American intervention is ours. It is cruel and arrogant to attempt to block desperate social remedies to desperate social problems that local leaders elect to try when you have nothing better to offer. Perhaps revolution in the end will turn out to be worse than starvation bred of economic and social stagnation. Perhaps revolution in some places will mean repression *and* starvation. But these are judgments which U.S. officials sitting in Washington have neither the capacity nor the right to make for others.

The preceding discussion has assumed that the primary motivation behind America's crusade against revolution is an altruistic desire to save the people of Asia, Africa, and Latin America from the terrors of Stalinism. No doubt a few members of the national-security bureaucracy have been passionately concerned about this. But the primary allegiance of national officials in any country is to their own populations. Such considerations as the feared loss of billions in corporate assets invested in Asia, Latin America, and the Near East as a result of expropriation by radical regimes influence policymakers at least as much as the urge to rescue undeveloped countries from one particular form of totalitarianism. Further, the National-Security Manager, who takes it as an article of faith that this is to be the American Century, is haunted by the fear that a towering event of the century, the rise of the Third World to international visibility, will not take place under United States control, that the models and the inspiration will be found somewhere else, and that, indeed, hatred of the United States and the civilization it represents may be one of the Third World's peculiar dynamics.

The best indication that the American Responsibility is designed more to ensure a sense of economic and political well-being at home than to achieve any particular lasting results abroad can be found by looking at the great Cold War successes. For years the model of a successful counterinsurgency was Greece. It was more than politeness to an old man when President Johnson called Harry Truman for his birthday and exclaimed, "We've had thirteen years to see the wisdom of your policies. There's not a right-thinking person in the free world today who would want to go back and change one of them."[21] Greece was considered a success for many years because it ended in the surrender and disappearance of the rebels. It required no negotiation or compromise. But in the process, the political structure of the country was undermined. In the atmosphere of suppression, the extreme-right wing flourished. Twenty years after the Truman Doctrine was announced, the most reactionary military dictatorship in Europe or the Near East came to power and at present writing still rules. In the Dominican Republic, order has been purchased at the price of democratic progress. The Balaguer government suppresses and harasses political opposition and has relied on the same elements of the society Trujillo marshaled for his purposes—foreign-owned business and the military.[22] In Lebanon, where the political structure was relatively strong at the time of the U.S. intervention, progress has been made in the ten years since the Marines left. In Guatemala, Iran, Indonesia, and the Congo, on the other hand, all of which have been the scene of major U.S. interventions to change the politics of the country, it is highly debatable how much progress has been made. To say with absolute certainty whether things would have been worse or better had not the United States intervened is impossible. One thing is certain, however. Significant progress toward the goals of stability, democracy, and substantial economic progress, for which the effort was ostensibly made, has not been achieved in any of them.

Seven

The United States has sought to apply the imperial model to the postimperial world. If the earth were still a place where a relatively few governments could speak for the billions of inhabitants, and the business of international politics were limited to a competition among them for the right to exploit the rest of mankind, one would have to predict a glorious history for the American Empire. One could even dare to hope that American rule would be relatively benign and that her colonized populations would receive some material, and perhaps even spiritual, benefits from the relationship. But all this is an anachronistic dream. An empire can work only if the subject populations are submissive. Otherwise, the attempt to impose colonial administration leads to a permanent, debilitating war. A glance at the rising tide of revolutions, coups, secessions, assassinations, and insurgencies in the Third World since 1945 gives an indication of the vanity of one nation's hope to bring order to mankind in what is probably its most volatile moment in all history.

Is there, then, an alternative to the imperial posture for a great nation? No nation that has achieved first-class power has yet found one. What are the possibilities now?

Another way of asking the question is to speculate on the possibility of substituting multilateral action for the achievement of order in place of unilateral action. By multilateral action I have in mind a political framework in which decisions on intervention are truly arrived at by common deliberation, not by the dictate of a single power and not by a "multilateral" organization which leaves out major powers who have asserted an interest in the issue at hand. This is essentially the framework of the United Nations Charter.

Articles 39–44 contemplate United Nations authorization for the use of military force to restore order, and Article 51 permits a single nation to resort to self-defense under the narrow circumstances of "armed attack," which, the history of the charter negotiations at San Francisco makes clear, means an invasion across national frontiers. The United States acknowledged the relevance of these provisions when it requested United Nations authorization for the intervention in Korea. Giving practical effect to what seems the clear intent of the words of the United Nations Charter both reduces the dangers of escalating war and also enhances the chances of a satisfactory settlement. Unlike an armed attack, which materializes suddenly and requires an immediate large-scale military response if it is to be repelled, an insurgency grows relatively slowly. It starts usually with random acts of terrorism and small raids and slowly gathers strength as the government fails to respond effectively. There is ordinarily time for the United Nations, either the Security

Council, the General Assembly, or the Secretary-General, where appropriate, to investigate and to make recommendations and take action with respect to the specific breaches of the peace. Observation teams are among the techniques available to an international organization to help limit and to settle an internal conflict. The Vietnam experience shows that a large-scale military effort by a Great Power acting alone or with a few allies has the effect not only of escalating the scale of violence but also of stimulating greater insurgency and greater aid to the insurgents.

A rehabilitation of the rule in the United Nations Charter prohibiting foreign intervention in a civil war, as opposed to collective defense against a foreign invasion, would mean that a government would have to handle its own insurgency problems unless it could get assistance, including the help of an international police force, from either the Security Council or the General Assembly.

The two major arguments against a policy of literal application of the UN Charter highlight the problems involved and in so doing help make the case against unilateralism. The first objection to a real peacekeeping role for the United Nations is immobilism. The Soviet Union and the United States will always have opposing interests in the outcome of an insurgency, and therefore United Nations military action will be blocked. The second objection is that multilateral processes are too slow. In President Johnson's words, "The moment of decision must become the moment of action."[23]

Both objections reveal the frustration of living in a community. Any sort of democratic procedure inevitably involves a sacrifice by the powerful of discretionary power and speed of decision. A meeting does not offer as expeditious a procedure for doing business as the command of the powerful. Some provision for compromise or vote is, however, the only alternative to anarchy or *dictat*. If the powerful nations of the world cannot agree on the desirability of a military intervention to deal with a problem of internal disorder or civil war, then it is in the interests of world peace that no nation intervene. But, some will no doubt ask, is this not a one-sided rule despite its guise of reciprocity? In other words, doesn't this mean that communist insurgents will always win?

If one believes that a handful of foreign revolutionaries who slip across a border can topple governments at will unless they are buttressed by a U.S. military effort, such a prohibition on unilateral intervention as I have suggested will appear to favor revolution. But the facts seem to be quite different. In fact, the constituted goverment enjoys enormous advantages. It has money to spend. It has an army and a police force. Isolated acts of terrorism by revolutionaries will not prevail against such power unless the authorities have lost the capacity to govern. If, as has often happened, they attempt to maintain themselves in power through corruption, terrorism, and persecution, they are vulnerable to insurgency. They can lose only if those elements of society which represent their main support "change hats" and turn against them. As all the standard textbooks on counterinsurgency insist, guerrillas cannot grow in numbers or strength unless the surrounding population is willing to protect them. If the guerrillas do not have this vote of confidence from the people of the village, they cannot hope to elude the police for long. Indeed, the guerrilla movement in Bolivia that Che Guevara tried to promote in 1967 failed because the peasants, who were either apathetic or suspicious of the foreigners who came to liberate them, reported them to the police.[24] The failures confirm the lesson of the successes. If local political conditions are not ripe for revolution, terrorist activities, particularly if committed by foreigners, can be easily suppressed. If the conditions are ripe, no amount of repressive force short of wholesale murder and resettlement of the population has a chance of achieving lasting success. When foreign powers do not intervene militarily, the internal dynamics of revolution itself provide an important measure of the popularity of the contending forces. If self-determination is more than a rhetorical goal— and it should be in the interests of long-range stability— then outside powers should not interfere with the expression of a popular demand for change through revolution where all other means are denied.

Eight

Not only is it not possible in the long run for another nation to maintain governments in power in the face of revolution, it is not desirable from the standpoint of world peace or world development. If the United States were to announce that it was no longer in the business of suppressing revolution, it would confront the Third World governments with the choice it now helps them to avoid: Learn to govern effectively and justly or face mounting insurgency. Prepare to transform traditional societies into nations or give way to revolutionaries who can convince the people that they can do it better. The third option, which is now the basic policy of both the United States and our Third World clients—make those changes necessary to maintain stability and we will help you put down challenges from those of your own people who demand more radical action—would no longer be available.

To adopt such a policy would go a long way toward breaking the new revolutionary international whose principal bond is a common enemy. The policy should be implemented by a flat ban on military assistance. The United States should challenge the other great powers to competitive non-intervention and press the Soviet Union and China in embargoing shipment of arms to particular areas of the world. The Soviets have not had such spectacular success with their military-assistance programs that they could afford to ignore such an offer. In the countries that have been the chief recipients of their overage military equipment, local communists have been jailed, the party outlawed, and in Indonesia, thousands of communists and suspected communists massacred. In the Middle East the obligation to supply the Arab armies has turned out to be more of an embarrassment than a political weapon for the Soviets. The Chinese have had little military aid to spare for other countries. Their economic situation underscores what their doctrine proclaims: sympathetic rhetoric, agents, small amounts of money, a few arms, advice they have for export, but not the skill, the commitment, or the quantity of weapons needed to make a revolution. No one can say for certain that the communist powers would reduce their material support for wars of liberation if the United States stopped helping local governments to suppress revolution. All we know from experience is that the more engaged the United States has become in aiding governments threatened with insurgency, the more Russia and China have aided the revolutionaries and the more weak independence movements have fallen under their sway.

If it appears unlikely that the United States and the communist powers can reach an explicit agreement on limiting arms shipments and military assistance to opposing political forces in the Third World, then the United States might try to reach such agreement indirectly. The State Department could announce that it was phasing out its military-assistance program and that henceforth it would send training missions and arms shipments only to match arms sent by other foreign powers. The disengagement of the great powers from internal political crises in other countries is a necessary first step to the development of multilateral machinery for dealing with problems of security and development in the Third World. The issue is not isolationism versus interventionism, for the developed world and the underdeveloped world are fated by geography and economics to be involved with one another. The question is rather the legitimacy of the forms and the purposes of intervention. The old imperial relationship, even in modern dress, is unequal to the needs of the modern world because the basic premise on which it rested is now revealed as an illusion. The security problem is not the balance of power. The danger is not aggression and conquest by a single state or group of states. Mass acquiescence in a world order guaranteed by an imperial policeman, which is required if such a model is to work, is a thing of the past. The assumption of basic social stability, on which any system of policing rests, is not warranted in a world that has been in the throes of a giant civil war since the beginning of World War II.

In 1918 Joseph Schumpeter painted a haunting picture of imperial Rome caught up in the terrors of an aging civilization:

Here is the classic example of that kind of insincerity in both foreign and domestic affairs which permeates not only avowed motives but also probably the unconscious motives of the actors themselves—of that policy which pretends to aspire to peace but unerringly generates war, the policy of continual preparation for war, the policy of meddlesome interventionism. There was no corner of the known world where some interest was not alleged to be in danger or under actual attack. If the interests were not Roman, they were those of Rome's allies; and if Rome had no allies, then allies would be invented. When it was utterly impossible to contrive such an interest— why, then it was the national honor that had been insulted. The fight was always invested with an aura of legality. Rome was always being attacked by evil-minded neighbors, always fighting for a breathing space. The whole world was pervaded by a host of enemies, and it was manifestly Rome's duty to guard against their indubitably aggressive designs. They were enemies who only waited to fall on the Roman people. . . .[25]

Schumpeter goes on to argue that Rome's wars of conquest made no sense "from the point of view of concrete objectives." Rome continued to relate to the rest of the world in an increasingly self-destructive way because imperial institutions, gathering their own momentum, could not be stopped. It is worth remembering that in the end the empire succumbed to the barbarians from sheer exhaustion.

What is now needed are new institutions for assisting the modernization of poor countries without making them the vassals of the rich ones. Such institutions cannot spring forth full-blown. While the United Nations may already offer an appropriate structure for shifting the responsibility for security and development from the hands of a single nation into community hands, the structures cannot function unless the United States, from its commanding height of power, makes the fundamental decision to renounce its claim to "organize the peace."

The seeds of revolution now sprouting on three continents confront humanity with two seemingly contradictory imperatives. To the United States, as the richest and most

powerful human organization on the planet, they represent
a continuing crisis. The first imperative is that the world
must be made safe for revolution. If, as appears in many
parts of the world, ruling elites are unwilling or unable to
exercise power effectively over large political organizations
for the benefit of the members but refuse to give up the
personal rewards of power, then, sooner or later, revolutions against them will be attempted. It is critical that
these essentially local political phenomena not become the
occasions for power plays among the Great Powers for all
the reasons we have mentioned: the danger of nuclear
war, the destruction of the countries themselves, and the
diversion of energies from the incredibly difficult tasks of
political reconstruction. We now have more than enough
evidence that if a government is unwilling to deal seriously
with the economic and political conditions from which
rebellion springs, the United States cannot successfully
suppress their discontented populations for them. Moreover, it has never been satisfactorily explained why such a
counterrevolutionary posture advances American national
interests or democratic ideals. Once having decided to
suppress a revolution, American leaders have been forced
to justify the commitment to themselves and to the rest of
the world by a series of bizarre interpretations of the
contemporary political environment. Thus, almost ten
years after the Greek civil war, Harry S. Truman could
still write in his memoirs that the Greek rebels were
"masterminded" from outside, despite impressive evidence
to the contrary.[26] The danger in treating local revolutions
as part of a worldwide conspiracy and not as expressions
of nationalist feeling and indigenous political sentiment is
that so faulty an analysis cannot be the basis of a practical strategy. That lesson became clear in Vietnam and, I
fear, will be taught to us again. Where the greatest power
in the world scares itself with a set of beliefs that have at
best only a tangential connection with the reality of revolution, that nation becomes a menace to itself and to
others.

The second imperative for the community of nations
and for the United States is to attempt the creation of a
world environment in which revolution will be unnecessary. Revolution is a wasteful, destructive, and inhuman
engine of political change. It must be allowed to happen if
there is nothing better, but the great challenge to human
ingenuity is to find alternative paths to economic and

political reconstruction, which can bring basic changes without the massive use of violence. The societies of the Third World can ill afford the economic and human costs of prolonged civil war. But virtually all of the thinking to date about revolutionizing underdeveloped societies through technology rather than through violence has been designed to serve the political interests of the powerful countries at the expense of the weak. The avoidance of revolution has been an end in itself, and very little commitment has been made to the achievement of radical political change through nonviolent means in societies needing revolution. For this reason the United States can use its still great power to help create a world environment in which poor nations can pursue their own paths to development. But until Americans give up the pretense that we have a right or a duty to manage social and political changes around the globe, there will be no peace for Americans.

NOTES—CHAPTER ELEVEN

1. George Ball, quoted in Gareth Porter, "Globalism: The Ideology of Total World Involvement," in Marcus G. Raskin and Benard B. Fall, eds., *The Viet-Nam Reader* (New York, 1965), p. 324.

2. Allen Dulles, *The Craft of Intelligence* (New York, 1963), pp. 235–236.

3. A discussion of the views of Valla and Bracciolini may be found in Richard Koebner, *Empire* (Cambridge, England, 1961), pp. 48–49.

4. Adlai Stevenson, quoted in John Bartlow Martin, *Overtaken by Events: The Dominican Crisis from the Fall of Trujillo to Civil War* (New York, 1966), p. 733.

5. Dean Rusk, quoted in Porter, "Globalism," p. 324.

6. Anthony Eden, *Memoirs: Full Circle* (London, 1960), p. 134.

7. Interview, in *United States News and World Report*, January 24, 1961, quoted in Carl Oglesby and Richard Shaull, *Containment and Change: Two Dissenting Views of American Society and Foreign Policy in the New Revolutionary Age* (New York, 1967), p. 81n.

8. U.S. Department of State, *Foreign Policy Briefs*, June 24, 1960.

9. At the end of 1965, before the major troop increases in Vietnam, the total military personnel overseas was about 800,-000. The number of federal civilian employees totaled about 40,000, and the number of individuals working overseas for corporations, foundations, and other private U.S. organizations was about 100,000. See Ernest Rubin, "A Statistical Overview

of Americans Abroad," in *Annals of the American Academy of Political and Social Science*, November 1966, pp. 1–10. The number of military personnel has of course grown substantially in the intervening years, as has private U.S. corporate activity, thus the number of Americans employed overseas now approaches 2,000,000. While many of the GI's do not constitute a vested interest for anything except their own desire to go home as soon as possible, the professional soldier finds great career advantages in overseas assignments, as does his counterpart in civilian agencies and corporations. But most of the members of what I call the "overseas bureaucracy" administer far-flung military, foreign-assistance, education, and private-corporate activities from the United States. Bureaucrats in the Pentagon and the State Department, executives and workers in defense industries, and managers of the mushrooming "multinational corporation" centered in the United States depend on far-flung foreign activities for their livelihood and sense of purpose.

10. C. E. Black, *The Dynamics of Modernization* (New York, 1966), p. 166.

11. The Rostow paper, which circulated within the government, is only one of several "think pieces" reflecting the frustration of the world's greatest military power in its inability to bring its most lethal weapons to bear on limited wars. During the last five years, several papers have been circulated through the bureaucracy proposing the use of nuclear weapons for "demonstration effect." A leading academic analyst, Professor Thomas Schelling, was awarded a contract by the United States Arms Control and Disarmament Agency for a paper in which he discussed "the diffident use" of nuclear weapons.

12. Of a total of 24,972.3 million dollars in foreign aid, including military aid, given from the years 1946–1967, outside of Marshall Plan aid to Europe, 22,597.1 million of it has gone to Taiwan, Korea, Vietnam, Turkey, Iran, Thailand, and Pakistan. (The figure for total foreign aid does not include aid to India, Nepal, or Laos, as this information is classified.) Source: Agency for International Development, Special Report for the House Foreign Affairs Committee: *U.S. Overseas Loans and Grants, July 1, 1945–June 30, 1966* (Washington, D.C., 1967).

13. The discussion of CIA support for liberal or radical groups is based on personal interviews with U.S. union officials, African nationalist leaders, and a leading member of the Algerian resistance movement. The CIA funding of the Latin American institutes mentioned in the text was widely reported during the CIA disclosures of 1967.

14. John F. Kennedy, Report to the American People on the Vienna Meetings, June 6, 1961.

15. Robert Heilbroner, "Counterrevolutionary America," in *Commentary*, April 1967, p. 38.

16. *Ibid.*

17. Alexander Eckstein, "Economic Growth and Foreign Trade," in Franz Schurmann and Orville Schell, *Communist China*, vol. III in *The China Reader*, (New York, 1957), p. 426.

18. In the case of Cuba, it should be pointed out that despite the great changes Castro has brought, the regime, largely as a consequence of the economic isolation which the United States has attempted to impose, continues to depend upon Soviet aid of about a million dollars a day to maintain itself.

19. Heilbroner, "Counterrevolutionary America," p. 34.

20. Moore, *Social Origins*, p. 507.

21. Lyndon B. Johnson, quoted in *The New York Times*, May 14, 1967.

22. For an account of the Balaguer regime, see S. Rodman, "The First Nine Months," in *The New Republic*, March 23, 1967.

23. Lyndon B. Johnson, address at Baylor University, May 28, 1965.

24. Guevara's last diary entry describes a frustrating encounter with a peasant woman: "The woman would not give any reliable information about the soldiers. To every question, she replies that she does not know. . . ," quoted in Norman Gall, "The Legacy of Che Guevara," in *Commentary*, December 1967, p. 34.

25. Joseph Schumpeter, *Imperialism* (Cleveland, 1951), p. 51.

26. Harry S. Truman, *Years of Trial and Hope*, vol. II of *Memoirs* (New York, 1955), p. 131. President Truman cites "intelligence reports" (p. 121) to the effect that the Greek rebels were "under Soviet direction." Such reports have been a recurring phenomenon of the Cold War, suggesting that fact gathering, which is always difficult, is heavily influenced by an ideological view of the world which minimizes spontaneous or indigenous politics.

Index

About the Author

IN ADDITION TO his distinguished academic career, RICHARD J. BARNET has served with the U.S. State Department, the Arms Control and Disarmament Agency, and the Department of Defense. In 1963, he helped found the Institute for Policy Studies, and has served as its Co-Director for many years. He is now Senior Fellow at the Institute. Mr. Barnet is recognized as one of the foremost historians and political scientists writing today. He is co-author of *Global Reach: The Power of the Multinational Corporation* (Simon & Schuster, 1975) and, more recently, *The Lean Years: Politics in the Age of Scarcity* (Simon & Schuster, 1980).